The Illicit Global Economy and State Power

Sponsored by the Social Science Research Council–MacArthur Foundation Program on International Peace and Security.

The Illicit Global Economy and State Power

Edited by H. Richard Friman
and Peter Andreas

ROWMAN & LITTLEFIELD PUBLISHERS, INC.
Lanham • Boulder • New York • Oxford

ROWMAN & LITTLEFIELD PUBLISHERS, INC.

Published in the United States of America
by Rowman & Littlefield Publishers, Inc.
4720 Boston Way, Lanham, Maryland 20706

12 Hid's Copse Road
Cumnor Hill, Oxford OX2 9JJ, England

British Library Cataloguing in Publication Information Available

Library of Congress Cataloging-in-Publication Data

The illicit global economy and state power / edited by H. Richard
  Friman and Peter Andreas.
      p.   cm.
   Includes bibliographical references and index.
   ISBN 0-8476-9303-1 (cloth : alk. paper). — ISBN 0-8476-9304-X
(pbk. : alk. paper)
    1. Transnational crime.   2. Organized crime.   3. International
economic relations.   I. Friman, H. Richard.   II. Andreas, Peter,
1922–   .
HV6252.I45   1999
364.1'06—dc21   98-48274
                                                           CIP

Printed in the United States of America

∞ ™ The paper used in this publication meets the minimum requirements of
American National Standard for Information Sciences—Permanence of Paper
for Printed Library Materials, ANSI Z39.48–1984.

Contents

Preface   vii

1   Introduction: International Relations and the Illicit
Global Economy   1
H. Richard Friman and Peter Andreas

2   Transnational Organized Crime: The New Authoritarianism   25
Louise I. Shelley

3   State Power and the Regulation of Illicit Activity in
Global Finance   53
Eric Helleiner

4   The Illicit Trade in Hazardous Wastes and CFCs:
International Responses to Environmental "Bads"   91
Jennifer Clapp

5   When Policies Collide: Market Reform, Market Prohibition,
and the Narcotization of the Mexican Economy   125
Peter Andreas

6   The Limits of Coercive Diplomacy: U.S. Drug Policy and
Colombian State Stability, 1978–1997   143
William O. Walker III

7   Obstructing Markets: Organized Crime Networks and
Drug Control in Japan   173
H. Richard Friman

Index   199

About the Contributors   209

Preface

Illicit cross-border flows, such as the smuggling of drugs, migrants, weapons, toxic waste, and dirty money, have emerged as an increasingly important source of conflict and cooperation among states and nonstate actors. Yet the illicit global economy remains noticeably underexplored in the international political economy literature. With few exceptions, edited volumes, readers, texts, and leading journals in the field fail to discuss or even acknowledge the clandestine side of globalization.

Contrary to scholars and policymakers who claim a generalized erosion of state power in the face of globalization, this volume explores the selective nature of the state's retreat, persistence, and reassertion in relation to the illicit global economy. Our intent is to begin to fill an important gap in the literature and to offer a new and powerful lens through which to examine core issues of concern to international relations scholars. These issues include the changing nature of states and markets, the impact of globalization across place and issue areas, and the sources of cooperation and conflict between and among states and nonstate actors.

The origins of this volume lie in a series of informal discussions between the editors over the past five years on how best to promote scholarship on the illicit global economy. In 1995, these discussions led to an American Political Science Association panel and, with the assistance of Jennifer Clapp and Eric Helleiner, the subsequent drafting of a proposal for a Social Science Research Council (SSRC)–MacArthur Foundation Workshop Grant. Hosted by the Peace Studies Program at Cornell University the following year, the workshop brought together scholars from the United States, Canada, and Europe to explore the interaction between states and illicit markets in the age of globalization. This volume draws on a significantly revised selection of workshop papers.

We have benefitted from the suggestions and criticisms of numerous colleagues and friends. We especially thank Peter Katzenstein and Janice Thomson for helping us to clarify the reasons for exploring the illicit economy and for challenging us to develop a broad conceptual framework for doing so. A special debt of gratitude goes to the participants in the November 1996 SSRC–MacArthur workshop. Rawi Abdelal, Susan Buck-Morss, Jennifer Clapp, Albrecht Funk, Derek Hall, Eric Helleiner, Peter Katzenstein, Jonathan Kirshner, Melanie Orhant, Thomas Princen, Hector Schamis, Louise Shelley, Janice Thomson, and William Walker sparked a lively dialogue beyond our expectations. We are also grateful to Philip Cerny, Louis Pauly, James Rosenau, and Susan Strange for their valuable input during the early stages of this project.

This volume would not have been possible without the generous support of the SSRC–MacArthur Foundation's Program on International Peace and Security, the Peace Studies Program at Cornell University, and Marquette University. We also greatly appreciate Jennifer Knerr, Brenda Hadenfeldt, Scott Horst, and Dorothy Bradley of Rowman & Littlefield for their efforts in guiding the manuscript to publication. Finally, our special thanks go to Julie Friman and Jasmina Burdzovic for their support, patience, and understanding.

H. Richard Friman   Peter Andreas

1

Introduction: International Relations and the Illicit Global Economy

H. Richard Friman and Peter Andreas

This volume focuses on the illicit global economy and its ramifications for international relations. The illicit global economy consists of the system of transnational economic activities that are criminalized by states in importing or exporting countries. As in the licit global economy, state and nonstate entities participate in the production, trade, and marketing of goods and services as well as in an array of financial practices. However, the wide variety of goods, services, and practices that distinguish the illicit global economy includes psychoactive substances (such as cocaine, cannabis, and heroin), the trafficking in endangered species, migrant smuggling, toxic waste dumping, prostitution, weapons trafficking, and money laundering. The nonstate actors that distinguish the illicit economy, although increasingly active in the licit economy as well, include mafias, drug cartels, and other transnational criminal groups. In some form or another, the illicit global economy has existed as long as the licit global economy has. What has changed over time are the particular illicit cross-border economic activities; the method and speed of transport; the size, structure, and location of the trafficking organizations; the content of state laws and the intensity and form of their enforcement; and the nature and level of consumer demand.

Why study the illicit global economy? Estimates of the economy's sheer magnitude increasingly capture the interest of scholars, policy practitioners, journalists, and the broader public alike. While obviously impossible to measure with any degree of precision, official estimates

1

suggest that illicit cross-border transactions are proliferating on a global scale.[1] It is estimated that the trafficking in illegal drugs generates as much as $500 billion in annual retail sales, a dramatic jump from just a decade ago.[2] The smuggling of illegal immigrants into advanced industrial countries has developed into a multibillion-dollar business with smugglers charging up to $50,000 per head.[3] Dumping and illicit trafficking comprise a growing portion of the cross-border trade in toxic waste, a trade conservatively estimated at 30–45 million tons and $15 billion annually.[4] The clandestine global trade in endangered species is estimated at $10 billion annually.[5] Illicit arms sales are fueled by the potential for a "nuclear 'yard sale' in the former Soviet Union" and the black market component of the annual $40–$50 billion conventional arms trade.[6] There is even a growing illicit transnational trade in human body parts, thanks to modern technologies that make it possible to store and ship high-demand organs such as kidneys, livers, and bone cartilage.[7] Finally, the "financial reflection" of these and other illicit transactions contribute to wide-scale money laundering, tax evasion, and capital flight.[8] According to the International Monetary Fund (IMF), an estimated $500 billion is laundered through the global financial system every year.[9]

This book, however, does not examine the illicit global economy simply because it exists, but rather because it powerfully affects international relations. The following chapters suggest that the illicit global economy has emerged as an important source of conflict and cooperation between nation-states, state agents, nonstate entities, and international organizations. As the magnitude of the illicit global economy has expanded, so too have domestic and international control efforts. This has often meant more punitive laws, an enhanced criminal justice apparatus, expanded cross-border police collaboration, and a growing fusion between law enforcement and security missions.[10]

The repercussions for international politics are significant. With the end of the Cold War, many states have refocused their energies from fighting communism to fighting transnational crime. In the new security environment, cross-border law evasions rather than military invasions increasingly dominate state concerns. Indeed, in search of new missions, some security agencies built up during the Cold War are being retooled and redeployed for law enforcement tasks.[11] As control efforts have intensified, so too have tensions between exporting and importing countries of prohibited commodities. These conflicts are exacerbated further as some debt-strapped developing nations have become dependent on the illicit global economy.[12]

Despite these trends, the illicit global economy has been curiously overlooked by most of the international relations literature. The gap is all the more noticeable in light of the extensive scholarship on the international political economy that fails to discuss or even acknowledge its illicit side. This neglect is mirrored in the main international political economy texts, edited readers, and leading international relations journals.[13] In short, economic activity that takes place outside of the parameters of licit trade, finance, production, and development also lies outside the parameters of mainstream international relations scholarship. The intent of this volume is to begin to redress this gap in our understanding of international relations by exploring the state in relation to the illicit global economy.

Debating the Retreat of the State

As recently noted by Susan Strange, the prominent theoretical debates in international relations at century's end need to explore the retreat of the state in the face of increasingly global markets and pervasive transnational actors.[14] This volume's contribution to the debate lies in exploring the selective nature of the state's retreat, persistence, and reassertion in relation to the illicit global economy and how such patterns complement and challenge those found in the more mainstream literature. Before considering the ramifications of the illicit global economy, however, it is useful to briefly review the evolution of the broader scholarly debate.

Deliberations over the retreat of the state are clearly not a new phenomenon. During the early 1970s, scholars argued that the economic and political linkages stemming from deepening interdependence and intensifying transnational interactions were challenging the ability of states, including those in more advanced industrial countries, to meet the rising demands for relief raised by their citizenry.[15] The primary counterargument noted the pivotal role of dominant political and economic powers in facilitating the rise of interdependence in the first place. By extension, dominant powers were inherently capable of constraining the rise of interdependence if it became in their interest to do so.[16]

During the late 1970s and 1980s, the debate became more nuanced. Robert Keohane and Joseph Nye introduced the concept of "complex interdependence" to suggest that the relative influence of interdependence and transnational processes varied by issue area.[17] Scholars of international institutions emphasized the mitigating effects of international regimes and other international linkages on state responses.[18] Others suggested that the impact of interdependence and transnational processes was mitigated further by cross-national variation in state capacity and other elements of domestic structure.[19]

At century's end, the debates over the retreat of the state remain far from settled and continue to occupy a prominent place in the international relations literature. Questions concerning the fate of the state in the face of globalization currently dominate. Often characterized as an intensification of interdependence and transnationalism, globalization's dynamics operate on economic as well as political and sociocultural dimensions.[20] Economic linkages, however, remain at the core of the globalization process. The global division of labor and expanding power of global production and finance have increased the accountability of states to global markets and pressures from nonstate entities.[21] The triumph of the market and the retreat of the state are themes emphasized by both advocates and critics of globalization.

More nuanced perspectives on globalization stop short of contending that the state is in full retreat. Recent scholarship on the dynamic nature of state sovereignty raises questions as to the baseline against which the erosion of state power should be judged. For example, Janice Thomson suggests that since state capacity to control cross-border flows has historically never been "assured or secure," scholars should explore changes in the political authority over such flows held by state versus nonstate actors.[22] For Hans-Henrik Holm and Georg Sorensen, the impact of globalization varies as it is filtered through different regions and societal structures. States also seek to "push, resist, attempt to circumscribe or twist this [the globalization] process to their own advantage."[23] James Mittelman offers a useful typology of activist state responses to globalization. These include efforts to mitigate its effects through multilateral institutions or accommodation with nonstate actors, as well as efforts at outright resistance through new regulatory measures on cross-border flows or, more broadly, authoritarian repression.[24]

Despite comprising a significant dimension of (and in some ways a most dramatic and even violent expression of) the transnational challenge to the state, the illicit global economy has been missing in large part from the past and present debates over transnational relations, interdependence, international institutions, domestic structure, and globalization. With few exceptions, even the most recent scholarship includes only passing references to the illicit economic practices of clandestine transnational actors.[25] This volume turns to the illicit global economy to cast new light on the contemporary debate over the nature and scope of the transnational challenges to state power.

Defining the Illicit Global Economy

The illicit global economy consists of the system of transnational economic activities that are criminalized by states in importing or exporting countries. This definition reflects a focus that differs from the contending concepts of black, underground, or informal economies, concepts distinguished by the absence of consensus on their precise definition and scope. What distinguishes our definition of the illicit global economy is an emphasis on the transnational nature of the illicit activity and its global scope.

Webster's defines a black market as a "place or system for selling goods illegally, especially in violation of rationing."[26] Thomas Schelling notes that black markets sell "commodities and services contrary to the law." They also can include commodities that are "not illegal per se" but are "handled outside of legitimate markets."[27] For R.T. Naylor, the concept of black market is more nuanced, distinguished by five main characteristics emphasizing its clandestine, high-cost, and restricted nature.[28]

Others define the black or underground economy more broadly as "economic activity which goes unrecorded in official statistics." Such activity can range from unregistered employment to the "underrecording" of economic activities often with the intent of tax evasion. As such, the concept of the black economy is slightly narrower than the informal economy, which is shaped extensively by employment that is not legal, stable, regulated, or registered in official statistics.[29] Scholars of the "underground economy" adopt an even broader focus encompassing illegal, unreported, unrecorded, and informal activities. Each set of activities violates institutional rules but the rules in question differ, ranging from legal and fiscal statutes to "macroeconomic accounting conventions."[30]

As defined in this volume, the activities that comprise the illicit global economy are narrower than implied by the concepts of underground and informal economies. Our definition also contains elements of the contending interpretations of black markets while drawing on the concept of transnational crime. As argued by Andre Bossard, former secretary general of Interpol, transnational crime is distinguished by two key characteristics. First, a border must be crossed, either by the perpetrators, their victims, the goods and services being transacted, or the orders directing such transactions. Second, the activity must be recognized as a criminal offense by at least two states, either by treaty, convention, or similar national laws.[31] While Bossard's definition can encompass activities from drug trafficking to murder, this volume focuses on one broad type of transnational crime: transnational economic activities deemed illicit by states in importing or exporting countries.

State laws, including trade regulations, tax provisions, and prohibitions, ultimately set the parameters of the illicit global economy. The activities falling within these parameters are diverse. The cross-border trade in stolen cars, for example, is a multibillion-dollar business and plays a leading role in smuggling from richer to poorer countries.[32] Smugglers do not limit their operations to stolen goods or illicit products such as drugs. Through clandestine trade in licitly produced commodities, smugglers also seek to circumvent trade duties or to take advantage of variations in domestic taxes on high-demand products. German border control officials, for example, worry about the mass smuggling of untaxed cigarettes—a highly profitable and sometimes violent business partly run by Vietnamese criminal organizations based in Berlin.[33]

With the current trend toward market liberalization and regional integration, violations of state prohibitions rather than evasion of quotas and tariffs distinguish the illicit global economy. As explored in the following section, however, state prohibitions are historically fluid and not all have been broadly shared or equally enforced. Ethan Nadelmann's analysis of state regulation in areas including slavery, drug trafficking, and whaling suggests that allowable practices need not always remain so.[34] Prohibited practices, such as U.S. policy on alcohol trafficking earlier this century, also are subject to change.

What makes the illicit economy global rather than simply international? For Stephen Gill and David Law, the global political economy is not limited to international dynamics involving nation-states and their governments. Transnational actors have facilitated changes in production, capital flows, and trade on a global scale.[35] While globalization has a long history, there has been a recent shift toward greater "scope, reach, and intensity" in transnational interactions.[36] Many of the contributors to this volume reveal a similar pattern in the illicit side of transnational economic activity.

For example, while drug trafficking networks are certainly not a new phenomenon, their "scope, reach, and intensity" (to use Gill's words) have greatly increased in recent decades. The illicit opium trade during the 1800s entailed British and U.S. traffickers shipping drugs from India and Persia, respectively, into China. Illicit trade networks during the early 1900s included heroin and cocaine produced in the United States and Europe and transshipped through Japan and Russia into China.[37] What has changed since the 1960s, Paul Stares shows, is the rise of mass markets and sophisticated trafficking networks for heroin, cannabis, and cocaine in the United States and Europe.[38]

During the 1920s, the Naarden case emerged as one of the largest incidents of ongoing illicit drug transshipment. German, Swiss, and French manufacturers funneled roughly 850 kilograms of morphine, 3,000 kilograms of heroin, and 90 kilograms of cocaine through the Naarden factory in the Netherlands and into East Asia in 1927–1928.[39] Roughly seventy years later, the uproar over Naarden pales in comparison to incidents involving Latin American, European, East Asian, and East European trafficking organizations and charges of state complicity in facilitating the trade. Similarly, seizure rates, estimated to account for anywhere between 4 and 30 percent of actual trade levels, suggest significant changes in the magnitude of drug trafficking.[40] For 1996, the U.S. Customs Service reported seizures at the Mexican border alone of over 18,200 kilograms of cocaine, 230 kilograms of heroin, and 272,300 kilograms of cannabis.[41] According to the 1997 United Nations' *World Drug Report*, worldwide seizures of illicit drugs reached approximately 228,200 kilograms of cocaine, 28,200 kilograms of heroin, and 3.7 million kilograms of cannabis.[42]

However, sheer volume is only one reflection of the global nature of the illicit economy. Increasingly, actors in the illicit side of the economy mirror the transnational business strategies of actors in the licit side, including subcontracting, joint ventures and strategic alliances, use of offshore bank accounts, and sectoral diversification. Just as the major transnational corporations employ lawyers, transportation and communications specialists, security guards, accountants, and distribution and sales managers, so too do some of the major trafficking organizations in the illicit global economy.[43]

It is important, however, to emphasize that trafficking organizations come in all forms and sizes. While they are often lumped together as organized crime, this is misleading due to the extreme variation in the levels of organization and degree of criminality. Traffickers range from independent entrepreneurs to loose networks of transnational gangs, to highly developed and vertically integrated criminal organizations. Thus, the popular image of a concentrated, octopus-like global network of crime syndicates is a fiction.[44] How organized and sophisticated the trafficking groups are often depends on what is being trafficked and the intensity and form of state controls. Indeed, greater state enforcement can turn disorganized crime into organized crime. This is evident, for example, in the case of migrant trafficking through Central America. As the International Organization for Migration reports, "as authorities in the region stepped up the border control and enforcement efforts, migrant traffickers have had to grow in sophistication in order to survive. Links to transnational crime syndicates have consequently been established."[45]

State Power and the Illicit Global Economy

Three broad and interrelated questions stand out in the scholarly debate over transnational challenges to state power that help inform the contributions to this volume. What has been the historical variance in state authority and control over transnational economic forces? What challenges does the intensification of transnational economic forces pose for state power? And, to what extent has the state retreated in the face of intensifying transnational economic forces? The illicit global economy reveals even greater fluidity in state power in relation to transnational economic forces than that suggested by prominent scholarly debates. The illicit global economy also suggests extensive variation in the challenges to state power and, in turn, the retreat, persistence, and reassertion of the state.

The Historical Variance in State Authority and Control

Too often, contemporary debates over the retreat of the state lack sufficient historical perspective. For example, if a core characteristic of the state is its "monopoly over the legitimate use of physical force in the enforcement of order" (as emphasized in Weberian definitions of the state), then any erosion of that monopoly implies not only that state power is being challenged but also that the state's very existence is at risk. Yet, as noted by Thomson, states—defined as "centralized bureaucracies"—only completed the process of wresting decision-making authority and ownership over the means of violence from nonstate actors as of the early 1900s.[46] Although the absence of such a monopoly poses a serious challenge to state power, the state as a centralized bureaucracy could still exist. The definition of the state used in this volume follows this convention; the state refers to the central decision-making institutions and personnel staffing such institutions within a given politically demarcated territory.[47]

Susan Strange argues that the state is an institution that was created to fulfill ten basic functions, including the monopolization of the legitimate use of the means of violence. Strange notes how "structural change in world society and economy" has led to the retreat of the state. Yet, in failing to adequately address the historical baseline for such a shift, specifically the extent to which the state was ever able to fulfill these functions, Strange overlooks the fluidity of baselines in state power that scholars such as Thomson capture.[48] Thomson notes further that there "never was a time" when state control over transborder flows, ranging from economic activities to violence, "was assured or secure."[49]

Thomson makes an important distinction between authority and control as two interrelated dimensions of state power. States claim metapolitical authority: the right to decide what is political and, as such, "subject to state coercion." The scope of this authority is dynamic, being shaped by negotiation between (and within) states, and between state and nonstate actors. However, the authority to make rules differs from the ability to enforce them. The latter entails state power to control and is shaped by capabilities including police and security forces.[50] Distinguishing between these two forms of state power is essential in our analysis of the illicit global economy.

State actors invoke metapolitical authority when they criminalize specific transnational economic activities. Through criminalization, activities such as money laundering and the trafficking in endangered species become subject to the policing apparatus of the state. Yet, state authority to decide what cross-border economic flows are legal or illegal has not gone unchallenged. Defeat in the Opium Wars of the 1800s, for example, forced Chinese officials to legalize the opium trade under British pressure. During the early 1900s, British officials shifted away from the trade in the face of domestic political pressure from anti-opium forces and their parliamentary allies.[51] Equally significant shifts toward legalization or criminalization in the United States are evident, for example, in the repeal of alcohol prohibition and the prohibition of the slave labor trade. Ethan Nadelmann writes that the criminalization of specific transnational practices reflects the "culmination of both external pressures and domestic political struggles." In this process, the security and economic interests of contending state actors vie with the interests and influence of international counterparts, powerful nonstate actors, and "domestic and transnational moral entrepreneurs."[52] At times state actors have triumphed in the defense of metapolitical authority, at others they have not.

Even when retaining metapolitical authority, state actors have faced challenges in controlling illegal transnational economic activities. The seriousness of these challenges has varied significantly. Nadelmann argues that successful evasion of control efforts is shaped by differences in the expertise and resources needed to engage in the illegal activity, the ease of concealment of the activity, and the willingness of victims to report the activity to enforcement authorities. Drug trafficking in this context becomes more difficult to control than slave trading.[53] But, even within the drug trade there are variations. Interdiction efforts against marijuana, for example, tend to be more effective than those against heroin and cocaine because marijuana is a much bulkier product.

It is important to stress that some of the challenges to state controls over illegal transnational economic activities are, in a sense, self-produced. Criminalizing activities for which high market demand exists inflates their profitability and encourages new market entrants. An ironic symbiosis thus emerges between state control efforts and the proliferation of actors such as crime syndicates willing to circumvent them.[54] The gap between the state's metapolitical authority to pass prohibition laws and its ability to fully enforce such laws is the space where clandestine transnational actors operate. Indeed, the illicit global economy is defined by and depends on the state exercising metapolitical authority to criminalize without the full capacity to effectively enforce its criminal laws.

Under conditions of criminalization, state controls may, in some cases, be displaced by those of nonstate actors. By defining markets as illegal, governments essentially withdraw themselves from basic aspects of market regulation. Gianluca Fiorentini and Sam Peltzman write, "organized crime plays its role as a substitute for the government employing the typical tools which characterize public intervention in the economy, from levying taxes to restricting entry in different markets, from regulating the quality of goods and services to the coercive provision of public goods."[55] In some cases, the regulation of markets by organized crime may actually serve state interests. As Diego Gambetta argues in the cases of Italy and Japan, the interests of the state and mafias occasionally become one: "In regions where the mafia is efficiently run, problems of law and order and public hazards are kept under control."[56] State officials in a wide range of countries have tolerated, and at times even facilitated, the illegal activities of transnational crime groups in exchange for control over new market entrants (freelance criminals) as well as political opponents.

Paradoxically, the corruption that emerges from the interaction between state actors and nonstate criminal actors in the illicit global economy expresses the limits of state controls, but also their power. On the one hand, corruption reflects the penetration of the state, undermining the implementation of controls. But on the other hand, corruption expresses the penetration by the state, imposing an informal tax on illicit cross-border economic activities. Nonstate criminal actors must bribe corrupt state officials because they cannot entirely bypass or bully them.[57] Deeper levels of corruption, of course, can link state and criminal nonstate actors to such a degree that it becomes difficult to distinguish between the two. These cases are exceptional, and are largely limited to the drug trade. Such was the case, for example, in the Garcia Meza regime in Bolivia and the Noriega regime in Panama in the 1980s, where drug trafficking and other criminal activities essentially became a public enterprise.[58]

Challenges for State Power

Much of the recent scholarship on globalization stresses the pressure to facilitate rather than resist market forces. Robert Cox, for example, contends that "states are, by and large, reduced to the role of adjusting national economies to the dynamics of an unregulated global economy."[59] However, this imperative creates an awkward predicament for states, since the licit and illicit global economies are in many ways inextricably intertwined. Both the licit and illicit global economies benefit from the same cross-border transportation, financial, and communications networks. States thus face the increasingly difficult dilemma of how to facilitate legal cross-border economic flows while enforcing their laws against illegal cross-border economic flows. Opportunities for hiding illicit economic activities and clandestine actors lie in the sheer magnitude and global nature of licit trade flows, financial transactions, and migration. For example, opportunities emerged from the mid-1980s to the mid-1990s as annual world exports doubled to $4.1 trillion, daily foreign exchange transactions increased by a factor of 6.5 to $1.3 trillion, and annual immigration rates (not including tourism) doubled to 100 million persons.[60]

Most of the cocaine exported to the United States enters the country through legitimate ports of entry in commercial cargo conveyances and passenger vehicles. Technological innovations in the transportation of commercial cargo offer a striking illustration of the challenge to law enforcement. The shipping industry has turned to larger and larger container ships to facilitate the movement of cargo. During the mid-1990s, the per-ship carrying capacity on newer models increased from 4,000 to 6,000 TEU (one TEU equal to one 20-foot equivalent unit, such as a 20-foot cargo container).[61] For state law enforcement agencies to fully "weed out" illicit from licit shipments, each sealed container on a cargo ship requires inspection. Paul Stares notes that a thorough inspection of one container "takes five U.S. customs officers three hours." Thus, to process a single ship of this larger class would require the inspection of the equivalent of 6,000 cargo trailers and 90,000 man hours. Stares observes that under "streamlined" U.S. Customs inspection procedures, "only 3 percent of the nearly 9 million containers that enter the United States every year are checked."[62]

While increases in the magnitude of trade expand the pipelines within which illicit flows can hide, the global nature of the licit economy expands the routes such flows can take. Transshipment, the shipment of goods to a "third party en route to a final destination," of prohibited products has surged with globalization.[63] The monitoring capacity of customs officers and law enforcement agencies extends to only a "small

proportion of the cargoes and peoples coming into their territories."
Due to limited resources, enforcement officials often target their monitoring efforts on flows of prohibited transactions from known supplier
states. The monitoring of commercial air traffic, electronic wire transfers, and migrants from Colombia, Mexico, and Thailand for prohibited
transactions, therefore, tends to be more extensive than that from many
other countries.[64]

In this context, traffickers have taken advantage of the global economy to expand the complexity of transshipment operations. Louise
Shelley, for example, details a single drug transaction originating in
Pakistan and transshipped through Kenya, Israel, South Africa, and Ro-
mania before being disrupted in Slovakia, never reaching the final destination of Italy.[65] Similarly, money laundering operations through the
now infamous Bank of Commerce and Credit International (BCCI)
linked an array of financial networks in thirty-two countries including
Luxembourg, England, the United States, Canada, Colombia, the
United Arab Emirates, the Bahamas, the Cayman Islands, and Nigeria.[66]

The magnitude and global nature of migration create additional challenges for state control efforts by expanding the opportunities for transnational linkages between ethnic-based organized crime groups. Sociol-
ogists and immigration historians have long noted that as migrants
move to new countries, criminal organizations from their homelands
often follow. New immigrant communities, often ethnically isolated
from the surrounding society and wary of state institutions in their new
country, offer markets and bases of operations for ethnic crime
groups.[67] Perhaps the best historical example of this pattern is the linkages between Chinese Triads, local Tongs, and the opium trade in immigrant Chinese communities in the United States during the late 1800s
and early 1900s.[68]

Today, criminal groups continue to accompany immigration waves,
but on a more global scale. Albanian, Chinese, Colombian, Nigerian,
Russian, Chechnyan, Ukrainian, Jamaican, Italian, Sicilian, and other
ethnic criminal groups can be found working within new immigrant
communities across North America, Europe, and Asia. These communities also serve as potential intermediaries, providing personnel who can
link members of transnational criminal organizations with counterparts
in indigenous crime groups. In the cocaine trade and money laundering,
Colombian communities in Europe have facilitated linkages between
the Cali and Medellín organizations, the Sicilian Cosa Nostra, and the
Calibrian 'Ndrangheta. Similar ties have been facilitated by Colombians
in the United States with Jamaican, Dominican, Mexican, and African
American gangs.[69]

In addition to pressures on control efforts, the illicit global economy poses challenges to broader state authority. For example, empowered through the illicit global economy, transnational organized crime groups can threaten the state's authority over the use of violence within and emanating from its territory. Moreover, pressures from criminal groups, moral entrepreneurs and epistemic communities, other states, and intergovernmental organizations can threaten the state's authority to determine the nature, extent, and enforcement of legal prohibitions over cross-border economic activity.[70]

Transnational criminal organizations can increase the level of violence within societies through turf wars with rival organizations and attacks on state enforcement agencies, political officials, and journalists. The proliferation of nonstate violence, a threat to state authority in and of itself, begins to erode civil society as people question the ability of state officials to offer protection, further undermining the authority of the state.[71] Violence by transnational criminal organizations is not perpetrated only within their countries of origin. Turf wars between rival organizations and attacks on state officials often extend abroad, eroding state authority over violence emanating from its territory.

The linkage between the illicit global economy and expanding violence lies in the potential for increased access by criminal groups to money and, in turn, firepower. In some cases, the combination results in criminal organizations being better equipped with high-powered weaponry than the state agencies charged to curtail them. In one particularly extreme example, Patrick Clawson and Rensselaer Lee note the arsenal of Colombia's Medellín cartel during the 1980s, which included automatic weapons, rocket launchers, and an array of ground and air-launched missiles. The cartel's victims by the early 1990s speak to the potential levels of violence that can be generated. The list of those killed within Colombia includes nearly 500 policemen, 40 judges, a minister of justice, an attorney general, a governor, 3 presidential candidates, a number of leading journalists, and over 500 civilians (to car bombs alone). Abroad, turf wars between the Medellín and Cali cartels and with rival organizations also generated high levels of violence, sometimes with open street battles in major cities such as Miami and New York.[72]

However, the impact of the intensification of transnational market forces on state authority is not limited to the enhanced potential for nonstate violence. Transnational crime groups empowered through their expanding role in the illicit global economy have at times also sought to expand their political influence over the state. Clawson and Lee, for example, note the "nearly ten-year dialogue" between the Medellín and Cali cartels and Colombian officials over "matters of judicial and criminal procedures" such as extradition and the nature of imprisonment for drug trafficking offenses.[73] Importantly, however, transnational criminal organizations have been less likely to challenge state authority to determine what economic practices are legal and illegal. Simply put, since crime groups benefit more from prohibition than legalization there is little reason to push for the latter. Indeed, criminal organizations depend on the maintenance of prohibition. Their primary concern is not prohibition per se but how strongly it is enforced and against whom.

Other nonstate actors challenge the state's metapolitical authority to determine what is and is not prohibited, and how severe the prohibition laws and their enforcement may be. Part of the globalization process has been an increase in the ability and interests of transnational moral entrepreneurs, epistemic communities, and others in building cross-border coalitions that seek to alter the parameters of and penalties for engaging in prohibited economic activities. Thomas Princen, for example, notes the impact of professional and public opinion, and transnational environmental coalitions, ranging from the World Wildlife Fund to Greenpeace, in shaping the prohibition of the rapidly growing world ivory trade during the late 1980s. Opposed to the adverse impact of the ivory trade on elephant populations, these organizations turned to pressuring state officials in African ivory-producing countries to agree to a ban on the trade.[74]

While some transnational coalitions push for expanding the parameters of the illicit global economy (as in the case of banning the ivory trade), other coalitions seek to shrink the parameters of the illicit global economy through selective legalization. For example, during the 1990s, U.S.-based organizations such as the Drug Policy Foundation and the Lindesmith Center (both funded by billionaire philanthropist George Soros) have been instrumental in building transnational coalitions committed to the reform of prohibitionist drug laws. These coalitions lobby policymakers in the United States and Europe with demands ranging from selective decriminalization to full legalization of the drug trade.[75] One recent initiative, for example, successfully lobbied for the acceptance in a number of U.S. states of the medical use of marijuana, despite strong federal-level opposition.

Challenges to state authority also emanate from foreign states. During the 1980s and 1990s, for example, U.S. officials applied strong pressure on foreign counterparts to expand and toughen their prohibitions against drugs and related activities. To gain compliance with U.S. wishes to criminalize drug money laundering, for example, American officials threatened informal and formal sanctions through bilateral deliberations and multilateral forums such as the Financial Action Task Force (FATF) of the Group of Seven and the United Nations. The United States also pushed initiatives to increase the drug enforcement capacities of their foreign counterparts. Signatories to the 1988 UN Convention Against Illicit Traffic in Narcotic Drugs and Psychotropic Substances were obligated to adopt enforcement provisions against money laundering and the drug trade vigorously advocated by the United States, such as asset forfeiture.[76] The global drug prohibition regime, backed by the United States and other powerful states and institutionalized internationally through the UN system, helps inhibit states from exercising their authority to relax national drug laws.

To What Extent Has the State Retreated?

Nuanced globalization arguments question universal claims of a pervasive erosion of state power in the face of transnational market forces. The state's control efforts and metapolitical authority have always faced challenges from nonstate and foreign state actors. To varying degrees prior to the contemporary era of globalization, the state retreated, persisted, and expanded in the face of such challenges. With recent trends in globalization, the challenges have intensified but variation continues to distinguish state power. The contributors to this volume reveal that this variation has been greater and more complex than is recognized by much of the international relations literature.

Louise Shelley (chapter 2) provocatively argues that transnational crime groups have coopted or displaced the state to the extreme point of facilitating the emergence of a new form of nonstate authoritarianism. This pattern is especially evident in, but not confined to, transition states such as those that comprised the former Soviet Union. In contrast, Eric Helleiner (chapter 3) suggests that the retreat of the state has been much more selective and at times strategic. Helleiner's analysis of illicit activity in global finance stresses that the selective retreat of the state in some areas—as in the control over tax evasion and capital flight versus money laundering—is often the choice of powerful state and private financial actors. Moreover, state authorities have utilized international cooperation as a means of enhancing the domestic regulatory power over selected criminalized capital flows.

Jennifer Clapp (chapter 4) explores how parameters of the illicit global economy change and the ramifications of such shifts for state authority and control efforts. Trade in toxic waste and chloroflourocarbons (CFCs) reveals that these parameters are highly selective. Clapp notes that toxic waste itself is not prohibited but rather states have criminalized certain forms of disposing of it, such as dumping. Similarly, Helleiner points out that money is not prohibited but certain forms of trafficking of funds such as money laundering increasingly have become the focus of regulatory efforts by state and financial institutions.

Explanations of what is and is not prohibited are not automatically reducible to considerations of social harm. Clapp suggests that new knowledge about the adverse effects of a product or practice (often revealed by a broad epistemic community) may lead to efforts to establish national controls and international prohibition regimes. However, harm is only one of many considerations leading to the designation of what is licit or illicit. Clapp explains that, information on harm aside, different interests held by developed and developing country governments concerning the necessity and nature of regulating the trade in toxic waste and CFCs resulted in different regulatory regimes. Similarly, Helleiner reveals how considerations of norms, narrow self-interests of societal groups, and the interests and impact of hegemonic states differ in the extent to which they have shaped the variation in the criminalization of money laundering, tax evasion, and capital flight.

The final three chapters of this volume turn to more detailed country studies exploring the extent to which the state has retreated in the face of intensifying transnational economic forces. Prominent arguments on the retreat of the state have tended to focus on the trend toward deregulation and market liberalization while ignoring the important trend toward state reregulation through market criminalization. Helleiner and especially Peter Andreas (chapter 5) explore the latter, noting the reassertion of the state through its law enforcement apparatus. Admittedly, the success of such policing in practice often has been limited. For Andreas, one source of difficulty lies in the contending international pressures states face for compliance with neoliberal economic policies and prohibitionist drug measures. Mexico illustrates the contradictions found at this intersection of the licit and illicit economies. Andreas contends that pressure from the United States to roll back the state from regulating the economy has facilitated the very drug trade U.S. authorities are calling on Mexico to curtail. To comply with its international drug control obligations, the Mexican state is "rolling forward" in the realm of law enforcement with limited success.

William Walker III (chapter 6) reveals that Colombian drug policy is less illustrative of a state in retreat in the face of the international drug trade than of a state seeking room to maneuver against international pressures from the United States and domestic political challenges. In this sense, Walker suggests that drug trafficking in and of itself is not the core issue from the standpoint of Colombian state officials. Trafficking organizations become a threat only to the extent that they are politically ambitious and become politicized alternatives to the state. U.S. diplomatic pressure and assistance in this context is primarily used by the Colombian government to curtail these domestic political challenges.

Finally, H. Richard Friman's account of organized crime in Japan (chapter 7) suggests that the tendency of the prominent literature to posit the state in retreat in the face of transnational actors is misleading in that it discounts the role of domestic societal groups and their relations with the state as barriers to market access. Friman argues that state accommodations with Japanese organized crime have facilitated the rise of extensive drug distribution networks, organized and controlled by domestic crime syndicates. These private networks have continued to inhibit market access to foreign competitors, despite Japanese immigration practices that have eased the ability of transnational criminal organizations to evade state controls at the border.

Conclusion

This book argues for the inclusion of the illicit global economy in the central debates within the international relations literature. The dynamics of the illicit global economy provide a new and powerful, if rather unconventional, lens through which to examine core issues of concern to international relations scholars: the changing nature of states and markets, the impact of globalization across place and issue areas, and the sources of cooperation and conflict between and among states and nonstate actors. The volume's contributors do not adhere to a single theoretical approach nor are they drawn from a single disciplinary perspective, substantive focus, or country. Instead, the aim of this volume is to offer a wide-ranging impetus to scholarship on the illicit global economy. Such a focus offers fresh and provocative insights into the nature and scope of the transnational challenges to state power in a rapidly changing world.

Notes

1. David Bickford, former legal advisor to the UK Foreign Office, posits a "gross criminal product" generated by organized criminal groups, a figure that by 1996 had reached roughly $1.0 trillion. *Financial Times*, 14 February 1997.

2. Paul B. Stares, *Global Habit: The Drug Problem in a Borderless World* (Washington, DC: Brookings, 1996), 2, 123–24. Patrick Clawson and Rensselaer Lee place the figure for the illicit narcotics industry at between $100 and $300 billion. Patrick L. Clawson and Rensselaer W. Lee III, *The Andean Cocaine Industry* (New York: St. Martin's Press, 1996), 62. For a contending view, see Peter Reuter, "The Mismeasurement of Illegal Drug Markets: The Implications of Its Irrelevance," in *Exploring the Underground Economy: Studies of Illegal and Unreported Activity*, Susan Pozo, ed. (Kalamazoo, MI: Upjohn Institute, 1996), 63–80.

3. Myron Weiner, *The Global Migration Crisis: Challenge to States and to Human Rights* (New York: HarperCollins, 1995), 9–10; Richard Rothstein, "Immigration Dilemmas," in *Arguing Immigration*, Nicolus Mills, ed. (New York: Simon and Schuster, 1994), 53; and Jennifer Bolz, "Chinese Organized Crime and Illegal Alien Trafficking: Humans as a Commodity," *Asian Affairs* 22, no. 3 (Fall 1995): 147–58.

4. Jennifer Clapp, "The Toxic Waste Trade with Less-Industrialized Countries: Economic Linkages and Political Alliances," *Third World Quarterly* 15, no. 4 (1994): 505–18; and Gareth Porter and Janet Welsh Brown, *Global Environmental Politics* (Boulder: Westview Press, 1991), 85–88.

5. For example, see Donovan Webster, "The Animal Smugglers," *New York Times Magazine*, 16 February 1997.

6. For example, see Zachary Davis, "Nuclear Proliferation and Nonproliferation Policy in the 1990s," in *World Security: Challenges for a New Century*, Michael T. Klare and Daniel C. Thomas, eds. (New York: St. Martin's Press, 1994), 122; and Michael T. Klare, "Adding Fuel to the Fires: The Conventional Arms Trade in the 1990s," in *World Security*, Klare and Thomas, eds., 134.

7. For example, see Dick Ward, "The Black Market in Body Parts," *Criminal Justice International* 7, no. 5 (September-October 1991): 1; and Thomas W. Foster, "Trafficking in Human Organs: An Emerging Form of White Collar Crime," *International Journal of Offender Therapy and Comparative Criminology* 4, no. 2 (1997): 139–50.

8. For a discussion of these and other sources of money laundering, capital flight, and tax evasion, see R.T. Naylor, *Hot Money and the Politics of Debt* (Montreal: Black Rose Books, 1994), 434 (quote).

9. International Monetary Fund, "Tougher Measures needed to Counter Macro Effects of Money Laundering," *IMF Survey*, 29 July 1996, 246. Jeffrey Robinson argues that the figure ranges from $100 to $300 billion; see *The Laundrymen: Inside the World's Third Largest Business* (London: Simon and Schuster, 1994), 16.

10. For example, see Martin Edwin Anderson, "International Administration of Justice: The New American Security Frontier," *SAIS Review* 13, no. 1 (Winter/Spring 1993): 89–104; and Ethan A. Nadelmann, *Cops Across Border: The Internationalization of U.S. Criminal Law Enforcement* (University Park, PA: The Pennsylvania State University Press, 1993).

11. For example, see Samuel R. Berger, "A Foreign Policy Agenda for the Second Term," Address before the Center for Strategic and International Studies, Washington, DC, 27 March 1997; and R.T. Naylor, "From Cold War to Crime War: The Search for a New 'National Security' Threat," *Transnational Organized Crime* 1, no. 4 (Winter 1995): 37–56.

12. For example, see Rensselaer W. Lee III, *The White Labyrinth: Cocaine and Political Power* (New Brunswick and London: Transaction Publishers, 1989), 21–54; Susan George, *The Debt Boomerang: How Third World Debt Harms Us All* (Boulder: Westview Press, 1992), 34–62; and Wayne A. Cornelius et al., *Controlling Immigration: A Global Perspective* (Stanford: Stanford University Press, 1995).

13. Two important exceptions are Ethan Nadelmann, "Global Prohibition Regimes: The Evolution of Norms in International Society," *International Organization* 44, no. 4 (Autumn 1990): 479–526; and Janice Thomson, "State Sovereignty in International Relations," *International Studies Quarterly* 39, no. 2 (1995): 213–33.

14. Susan Strange, *The Retreat of the State: The Diffusion of Power in the World Economy* (Cambridge: Cambridge University Press, 1996).

15. Richard Cooper, "Economic Interdependence and Foreign Policy in the Seventies," *World Politics* 24 (January 1972): 159–81; Robert Morse, "Transnational Economic Processes," in *Transnational Relations and World Politics*, Robert O. Keohane and Joseph S. Nye, Jr., eds. (Cambridge: Harvard University Press, 1971), 23–47; and Robert O. Keohane and Joseph S. Nye, Jr., "Transnational Relations and World Politics: An Introduction," in *Transnational Relations*, Keohane and Nye, eds., xi–xvi.

16. Robert Gilpin, "The Politics of Transnational Economic Relations," in *Transnational Relations and World Politics*, Robert Keohane and Joseph S. Nye Jr., eds. (Cambridge: Harvard University Press, 1971), 48–69.

17. Robert Keohane and Joseph Nye, *Power and Interdependence* (Boston: Little, Brown, 1977).

18. For example, see Stephen D. Krasner, ed., *International Regimes* (Ithaca: Cornell University Press, 1983); and Robert Keohane, *International Institutions and State Power* (Boulder: Westview Press, 1989).

19. For example, see Peter J. Katzenstein, ed., *Between Power and Plenty: The Foreign Economic Policies of Advanced Industrial Countries* (Madison: University of Wisconsin Press, 1978); and Peter Evans et al., eds., *Bringing the State Back In* (Cambridge: Cambridge University Press, 1985).

20. See Hans-Henrik Holm and Georg Sorensen, "Introduction: What has Changed?" in *Whose World Order? Uneven Globalization and the End of the Cold War*, Hans-Henrik Holm and Georg Sorensen, eds. (Boulder: Westview, 1995), 4; and the special issue of *Daedalus* 124, no. 2 (Spring 1995) on the state and globalization.

21. James H. Mittelman, "The Dynamics of Globalization," in *Globalization: Critical Reflections*, James H. Mittelman, ed. (Boulder and London: Lynne Rienner, 1996), 7–9.

22. Janice Thomson, *Mercenaries, Pirates, & Sovereigns: State Building and Extraterritorial Violence in Early Modern Europe* (Princeton: Princeton University Press, 1994); and Thomson, "State Sovereignty in International Relations," 213–33. Other examples in this vein include Thomas J. Biersteker and Cynthia Weber, *State Sovereignty as Social Construct* (Cambridge: Cambridge University Press, 1996).

23. Holm and Sorensen, "Introduction," 7.

24. Mittelman, "The Dynamics of Globalization," 8–11; and James H. Mittelman, "How Does Globalization Really Work," in *Globalization: Critical Reflections*, James H. Mittelman, ed. (Boulder and London: Lynne Rienner, 1996), 238–39. In addition to the authors briefly discussed here, see Robert Boyer and Daniel Drache, eds., *States Against Markets: The Limits of Globalization* (London and New York: Routledge, 1996).

25. Exceptions include Susan Strange's chapter on "Organized Crime: The Mafias," in *The Retreat of the State*, 110–21.

26. *Webster's New World Dictionary* (New York: Times Mirror, 1972), 147.

27. Thomas C. Schelling, "Economic Analysis and Organized Crime," in *Task Force Report: Organized Crime*, The President's Commission on Law Enforcement and Administration of Justice, 1967, 116.

28. R.T. Naylor, "Loose Cannons: Covert Commerce and Underground Finance in the Modern Arms Black Market," *Crime, Law, and Social Change* 22 (1995): 1–57.

29. Kofi Buenor Hadjor, *Dictionary of Third World Terms* (London and New York: Penguin Books, 1993), 51 (quote), 161–64. In addition, see Hernando de Soto, *The Other Path: The Invisible Revolution in the Third World* (New York: Harper and Row, 1989).

30. Edgar L. Feige, "Overseas Holdings of U.S. Currency and the Underground Economy," in *Exploring the Underground Economy: Studies of Illegal and Unreported Activity*, Susan Pozo, ed. (Kalamazoo, MI: Upjohn Institute, 1996), 8–10.

31. Bossard as quoted in William F. McDonald, "The Globalization of Criminology: The New Frontier is the Frontier," *Transnational Organized Crime* 1, no. 1 (Spring 1995), 11.

32. For example, see *Tampa Tribune*, 16 February 1997.

33. For a discussion on the broader dynamics of smuggling, see Jorge I. Dominguez, "Smuggling," *Foreign Policy* 20 (Fall 1975): 87–96. The German example is drawn from interviews conducted by Peter Andreas with law enforcement officials, Frankfurt-Oder, Germany, 24 June 1996.

34. For example, see Nadelmann, "Global Prohibition Regimes."

35. Stephen Gill and David Law, *The Global Political Economy* (Baltimore: Johns Hopkins University Press, 1988), xxiii–iv.

36. Stephen Gill, "Globalization, Democratization, and the Politics of Indifference," in *Globalization: Critical Reflections*, James H. Mittelman, ed. (Boulder: Lynne Rienner, 1997), 209–10.

37. The literature here is extensive. For overviews and analysis, see William O. Walker III, *Opium and Foreign Policy: The Anglo-American Search for Order in Asia, 1912–1954* (Chapel Hill: University of North Carolina Press, 1991); and H. Richard Friman, *NarcoDiplomacy: Exporting the U.S. War on Drugs* (Ithaca and London: Cornell University Press, 1996).

38. Stares, *Global Habit*, 15–46.

39. Friman, *NarcoDiplomacy*, 31; and Marcel de Kort and Dirk J. Korf, "The Development of Drug Trade and Drug Control in the Netherlands: A Historical Perspective," *Crime, Law, and Social Change* 17 (1992): 130–31.

40. For the range of seizure rates, see the discussion in Clawson and Lee, *The Andean Cocaine Industry*, 6. For a discussion of data limitations in assessing the magnitude of the drug trade, see Stares, *Global Habit*, 9–11; and Peter Reuter, "The Mismeasurement of Illegal Drug Markets," 63–80.

41. Calculated from customs service data reprinted in the *New York Times*, 24 March 1997.

42. As reported in the *New York Times*, 26 June 1997.

43. For example, see Phil Williams, "Transnational Criminal Organizations: Strategic Alliances," *The Washington Quarterly* 18, no. 1 (Winter 1995): 57–72; and Phil Williams, "Transnational Criminal Organizations and Drug Trafficking," *Bulletin on Narcotics* 46, no. 2 (1994): 10–24.

44. For example, see Claire Sterling, *Crime Without Frontiers: The Worldwide Expansion of Organized Crime and the Pax Mafiosa* (London: Warner Books, 1995).

45. International Organization for Migration, "Trafficking in Migrants: Some Global and Regional Perspectives" (paper submitted for the Regional Conference on Migration, Puebla Mexico, 13–14 March 1996), 5.

46. Thomson, *Mercenaries, Pirates, & Sovereigns*, 3, 7–9.

47. This definition draws further on distinctions made by Stephen Krasner in "Power Politics, Institutions, and Transnational Relations," in *Bringing Transnational Relations Back In: Non-State Actors, Domestic Structures and International Institutions*, Thomas Risse-Kappen, ed. (Cambridge: Cambridge University Press, 1995), 258. In *Mercenaries, Pirates, & Sovereigns* (150), Thomson expands her definition conceptualizing the state "as simply the bureaucratic apparatus which claims ultimate administrative, policing, and military authority within a specific jurisdiction."

48. Strange, *The Retreat of the State*, 72–82, 184.

49. Thomson, "State Sovereignty in International Relations," 216.

50. Thomson, "State Sovereignty in International Relations," 223.

51. For example, see S.D. Stein, *International Diplomacy, State Administration and Narcotic Control: The Origins of a Social Problem* (Aldershot, UK: Gower, 1985); Bruce Johnson, "Righteousness before Revenue: The Forgotten Moral Crusade against the Indo-Chinese Opium Trade," *Journal of Drug Issues* 5 (1975): 307–17; and Friman, *NarcoDiplomacy*, 5–12.

52. Nadelmann, "Global Prohibition Regimes," 480–83 (first quote on page 480, second on page 483).

53. Nadelmann, "Global Prohibition Regimes," 512.

54. Strange, *The Retreat of the State*, 114. See also the evolutionary process of organized crime discussed in Naylor, "From Cold War to Crime War," 46; and Peter A. Lupsha, "Transnational Narco-Corruption and Narco-Investment: A Focus on Mexico," *Transnational Organized Crime* 1, no. 1 (Spring 1995): 84–101.

55. Gianluca Fiorentini and Sam Peltzman, "Introduction," in *The Economics of Organized Crime*, Gianluca Fiorentini and Sam Peltzman, eds. (Cambridge: Cambridge University Press, 1995), 1–30 (especially pages 9 and 12).

56. Diego Gambetta, *The Sicilian Mafia: The Business of Private Protection* (Cambridge and London: Harvard University Press, 1993), 2–4.

57. For a review of the literature on corruption, see Arnold Heidenheimer et al., eds., *Political Corruption: A Handbook* (New Brunswick: Transaction Publishers, 1990).

58. Peter Andreas, "Profits, Poverty, and Illegality: The Logic of Drug Corruption," *NACLA Report on the Americas* 27, no. 3 (November/December 1993): 22–28.

59. See Robert Cox, "Globalization, Multilateralism, and Democracy," in *Approaches to World Order*, Robert Cox with Timothy J. Sinclair, eds. (Cambridge: Cambridge University Press, 1996), 528.

60. The trade and exchange data are drawn from Thomas Lairson and David Skidmore, *International Political Economy* (Orlando: Harcourt Brace, 1997), 102. The immigration figures (for a shorter period of 1989–1992) are cited in Mittelman, "How does Globalization Really Work," 235. Paul Stares (*Global Habit*, 68) notes that total entry figures for the United States for 1994 equaled 451 million persons.

61. Philip Damas, "Big, Bigger, Super-Post-Panamax," *American Shipper* 38, no. 11 (November 1996), 61; and *Journal of Commerce and Commercial*, 6 and 30 January 1997.

62. Stares, *Global Habit*, 69.

63. The definition of transshipment is drawn from David Yoffie, *Power and Protectionism: Strategies of the Newly Industrializing Countries* (Columbia: Columbia University Press, 1993), 32.

64. Phil Williams, "Transnational Criminal Organizations and International Security," *Survival* 36, no. 1 (Spring 1994): 96–113 (quote 98); and H. Richard Friman, "Just Passing Through: Transit States and the Dynamics of Illicit Transshipment," *Transnational Organized Crime* 1, no. 1 (Spring 1995): 65–83.

65. Louise I. Shelley, "Transnational Organized Crime: An Imminent Threat to the Nation State?" *Journal of International Affairs* 48, no. 2 (Winter 1995): 472–73.

66. See Robinson, *The Laundrymen*, 276–90.

67. For example, see James M. O'Kane, *The Crooked Ladder: Gangsters, Ethnicity, and the American Dream* (New Brunswick: Transaction Publishers, 1992); Darnell F. Hawkins, ed., *Ethnicity, Race, and Crime: Perspectives Across Time and Place* (Albany: State University of New York Press, 1995); and William Kleinknecht, *The New Ethnic Mobs: The Changing Face of Organized Crime in America* (New York: Free Press, 1996).

68. For example, see Douglas Clark Kinder, "Shutting Out Evil: Nativism and Narcotics Control in the United States," in *Drug Control Policy: Essays in Historical and Comparative Perspective*, William O. Walker III, ed. (University Park: The Pennsylvania State University Press, 1992), 117–42; and David Courtwright, *Dark Paradise: Opiate Addiction in America Before 1940* (Cambridge and London: Harvard University Press, 1982).

69. For example, see Stares, *Global Habit*, 39; Clawson and Lee, *The Andean Cocaine Industry*, 62–86; and Williams, "Transnational Criminal Organizations and International Security," 103–5.

70. The focus on authority over violence and authority to "define the nature of an issue" is drawn from Thomson, *Mercenaries, Pirates, & Sovereigns*, 150. The concept of moral entrepreneurs is drawn from Nadelmann, "Prohibition Regimes." For a discussion of epistemic communities, see Emanual Adler and Peter M. Haas, eds., "Special Issue: Knowledge, Power, and International Policy," *International Organization* 46, no. 1 (1992).

71. Williams, "Transnational Criminal Organizations and International Security," 107–9.

72. Clawson and Lee, *The Andean Cocaine Industry*, 51–53; and Guy Gugliotta and Jeff Leen, *Kings of Cocaine* (New York: Simon and Schuster, 1989).

73. Clawson and Lee, *The Andean Cocaine Industry*, 91 (quote), 102–22. For additional examples, see Strange, *The Retreat of the State*, 115; and Stares *Global Habit*, 97–98.

74. Thomas Princen, "Ivory, Conservation, and Environmental Transnational Coalitions," in *Bringing Transnational Relations Back In*, Thomas Risse-Kappen, ed. (Cambridge: Cambridge University Press, 1995), 227–56. In contrast, a partial reversal of prohibition despite pressure from transnational organizations and state actors emerged in mid-1996. See, *New York Times*, 20 June 1997.

75. For example, see Diana R. Gordon, *The Return of the Dangerous Classes* (New York and London: W.W. Norton, 1994), 215–17; and the Drug Policy Foundation's *Newsletter*.

76. See Friman, *NarcoDiplomacy*, 82–84, 109–110.

2

Transnational Organized Crime: The New Authoritarianism

Louise I. Shelley

The collapse of the socialist system in Eastern Europe and the Soviet Union and the waning of communist power in China have been hailed as the end of authoritarianism. Likewise the end of military dictatorships in Latin America portended a new era of individual freedom and a transition from authoritarianism.[1] With the demise of Communism and military dictatorships, analysts concluded that citizens could no longer be denied access to information, restricted in their mobility, or compelled to obey by a powerful central state.

The pronouncements on the end of authoritarianism may have been premature. With the declining importance of the nation-state at the end of the twentieth century, the state is no longer the preeminent determinant of international politics or individual lives. But diminishing state sovereignty does not necessarily mean the disappearance of authoritarianism.[2] The demise of authoritarian states has not led to the decline of authoritarian practices because authoritarianism is not necessarily state-based. Transnational organized crime represents a new form of non-state-based authoritarianism.

Transnational organized crime groups have their greatest impact in their home country, but because they are transnational their authoritarian practices have repercussions outside their domestic base. The legal institutions of the world are still bound to the nation-state, but the forces of coercion are increasingly transnational. Existing state-based legal systems, therefore, cannot protect citizens from the new authoritarian threat provided by transnational organized crime.

Traditional authoritarianism is state-based and differs in many respects from the new transnational authoritarianism of organized crime. But both traditional and nonstate-based authoritarianism affect all aspects of society including economic relations, political structures, legal institutions, citizen-state relations, and human rights (see table 2.1).

Transnational crime groups, for the purposes of this chapter, are defined as organized crime groups (1) that are based in one state, (2) that commit their crimes in at least one but usually several host countries whose market conditions are favorable, and (3) in which the possibility of conducting illicit activity affords low risk of apprehension.[3] Transnational organized crime groups, like legitimate multinational companies, gravitate to areas where they can make significant profit. But unlike legitimate businesses, they must also seek locations where they will not be apprehended for their criminal conduct. These groups exploit the failure of state legal institutions to coordinate activities to combat transnational organized crime.

The Decline of the Nation-State and the Rise of Nonstate Actors

The increasingly global world has resulted in the decline of the nation-state in both developing and developed countries. The end of the Cold War and of superpower rivalry has focused attention on nonmilitary actors in international relations such as multinational corporations and their flipside, transnational organized crime groups.

Corruption and misrule have undermined the state in many third-world countries in Asia, Latin America, and Africa. The institutionalized corruption has facilitated the rise of international drug trafficking and other forms of illicit international trade. This highly profitable illicit trade has, in turn, exacerbated the existing corruption and undermined the integrity of basic state institutions.[4] States cannot protect their citizens from nonstate actors because they are compromised or collusive. International crime groups cannot be combated either on their domestic turf or by the international community because legal mechanisms are inadequate and jurisdictional problems impede cooperative efforts.

Nonstate actors are becoming major economic forces. Much attention has been paid to the growth of legitimate multinational businesses but not enough to the phenomenal growth in the illegitimate sector. The amount of illicit capital in the world's financial markets increases annually. The amounts compound because the illicit activity continues unabated, little of the money is confiscated, and much of it stays outside the reach of tax authorities, in offshore havens. The International Monetary Fund estimates that laundered money currently amounts to 2 per-

Table 2.1: Traditional Authoritarianism versus Authoritarianism of Transnational Organized Crime

Traditional Authoritarianism	Authoritarianism of Transnational Organized Crime
Ruling Structures	
◆ Based on concept of nation-state or empire	◆ Not state-based; predicated on demise of nation-state
◆ Centralized governmental control in monarchy, military government, or communist system	◆ Decline of centralized control; replacement by regional leaders beholden to or complicit with organized crime
◆ Controlled elections or absence of elections undermines democracy and results in impotent state	◆ Infiltration of organized crime into state structures
	◆ Presidential, executive, and legislative branches unable and unwilling to protect citizens' interests
State Relation to Its Citizens	
◆ Subordination of citizens' interests to the state	◆ Corruption undermines government integrity
◆ Compulsion of the citizen by state legal system	◆ Abnegation of state's obligations to its citizens
◆ Citizens often mobilized for state's objectives	◆ State cannot protect its citizens or residents from global reach of organized crime groups
◆ State limits civil society and denies human rights	
◆ State provides public services	

Table 2.1 (cont.)

Traditional Authoritarianism	Authoritarianism of Transnational Organized Crime
Ideological Control	
• Control by central state over film, art, mass media, and scholarship through state bureaucracy and legal means	• Intimidation of filmmakers, television, and print journalists, domestically and internationally • Acquisition of mass media to shape news coverage • Lawsuits against foreign media who seek to disclose organized crime activity • Intimidation of scholars
Economy	
• Under communist or socialist state, state ownership or control of economy • State domination of labor or labor unions • Disorganized areas not immune from organized crime • Use of economic levers to control other states • Strategic alliances with other authoritarian states • Government guarantees business transactions	• Organized crime groups control large sectors of economy at home base; invest transnationally • Exploit privatization process of state economies to gain control of key industries • Intimidation of labor force and cooperation of labor unions • Strategic alliances with crime groups for economic objectives • Cartel enforcement • Organized crime guarantees business transactions

Table 2.1 (cont.)

Traditional Authoritarianism	Authoritarianism of Transnational Organized Crime
Legal System	**Legal System**
• Legal system serves interests of state or controlling elite rather than welfare of citizenry • State maintains monopoly on forces of coercion and deployment of violence • Absence of independent judiciary • Extensive reliance on penal institutions and executions • State-sponsored violence remains unpunished	• Weakened state legal system serves interests of organized crime rather than state or citizens • Privatization of forces of state coercion by organized crime • Corruption by organized crime undermines law enforcement, judiciary in home country and in foreign countries • State penal institutions are rendered ineffective because of domination by transnational organized crime groups • Violence perpetuated by organized crime remains unprosecuted and unpunished by the state • Exploitation of weaknesses in legal structure

cent of global GDP, although it suggests that the total of laundered money is several times higher if tax evasion and illicit capital flight are factored in.[5] The impact of these billions in circulation is not equally distributed. In countries where this money represents a significant proportion of the money supply, the authoritarian impact of crime groups is most significant.

The billions generated by the illicit trafficking in human beings means that individuals are subject to violence in their home countries, in transit, and frequently at their destinations. The highly lucrative drug trade is predicated on collection of revenues internationally. Intimidation and reprisals across borders are tools to achieve the crime groups' financial objectives.[6] Large-scale illicit trade demands massive money laundering. Efforts to disclose the channels facilitating this process or efforts to limit these transactions can result in cross-border threats and intimidation.

Traditional Authoritarianism

Traditional theories of authoritarianism were based on the concept of the nation-state or the empire. There is no one definition of an authoritarian state or set of attributes that is common to all authoritarian societies. Rather there are a variety of features that characterize the governing structures, economies, and social conditions of these societies (see table 2.1).

In authoritarian states, centralized governmental control is exercised by a monarchy, a military government, or a communist system. The state is led by a long-term dictator, a governing coalition, or a hegemonic political party that permits no opposition. If elections are held, they are only for show because no individual or groups can challenge those in power. Citizens may be mobilized for elections to show their support for the existing power structures.

The modern authoritarian state coerces its population by means of a highly developed control apparatus that ensures compliance from the citizenry.[7] The military, law enforcement, the judiciary, and the penal system are important in guaranteeing conformity with state objectives.[8] The support of the military is central even in states that are not military dictatorships.

Authoritarian states often lack free and open markets. Communist states are the most extreme cases but are not unique. Dictatorships may cultivate or favor an economic oligarchy that will support its rule. Free flow of trade may be limited as part of the general control over the society.

The rule of law is absent. The execution of the law, particularly in the criminal arena, is subordinated to the interests of the ruler or the ruling elite. Objective enforcement of the civil law is also not assured because court decisions might favor supporters of the dictator, members of the military elite, or the ruling party.

Torture and human rights violations are often commonplace. Those who challenge state authority are singled out either through visible prosecutions, often widely publicized in the mass media, or through targeted executions or "disappearances." Intimidation of those who question the rulers is done either by the military, the security police, or other paramilitary groups.

Censorship and control of the media is central to the perpetuation of authoritarian states because there can be no competing sources of information differing from the official state position. Authoritarian states with a strong ideological base may mobilize the mass media to inculcate the citizenry with the leaders' views or aggrandize the threat of domestic or foreign enemies.

Education also assumes a crucial role in perpetuating authoritarian rule because citizens are not taught to challenge or question existing state policies or ideology. Control over curriculum and teachers is also common in many authoritarian states.

Civil society is emasculated or often coopted. Individual religious, social, and political organizations may be prohibited because they permit individual networks and associations outside of state control.

State paternalism often exists as the state provides for social and individual welfare, denying a role to civil society that might challenge its hegemonic control. Human rights are routinely denied because citizens are denied their labor rights, mobility, access to a free media, and right to individual expression.

The New Authoritarianism

Nonstate-based authoritarianism, like its state-based counterpart, affects all aspects of society, including economic relations, political structures, legal institutions, citizen-state relations, and human rights (see table 2.1). The diversified impact on individual rights and state institutions is not fully appreciated by most human rights specialists or analysts of organized crime.

Authoritarianism can exist without the state, an idea already recognized by enlightenment thinkers. Their analysis, based on man in a primitive state, also applies to the contemporary period beyond the nation-state because transnational organized crime groups often have their origins in a more primitive society.[9]

The authoritarianism of organized crime thrives in an environment with an absence of centralized control. This often occurs because of the collapse of the state or because corruption or organized crime groups have weakened the state. Power vacuums exist at the center of many former states because the communist parties have collapsed and no institutions exist to replace them. Many third-world governments have been weakened by years of endemic corruption. In the absence of a strong central government, power is often retained by regional leaders.[10]

Penetration of local authorities is more feasible and less costly than that of centralized states. Organized crime domination of regional governments is evident in such disparate countries as Russia, Mexico, Colombia, and Italy. In most cases, this phenomenon does not represent the decentralization of power but instead the rise of regional leaders beholden to organized crime or complicit with organized crime groups.[11] Regional leaders, enjoying the power of association with organized crime, are resisting the strong centralizing tendencies of the Mexican and Russian states. In Italy since unification, the power exercised by the Mafia in Sicily has diminished the controls exercised by the centralized state.[12]

Organized crime groups often supplant the state in societies in transition to democracy. Their representatives assume key positions in the incipient legislatures crafting the new legal framework. Organized crime groups' presence within legitimate state institutions undermines political stability because their goals are to further their own interests (illicit profits), not the interests of the populace at large. In this respect, they are not just a new form of leadership for the state but a self-interested group assuming power.

In traditional societies, the state is the source of the authoritarianism. In contrast, the authoritarianism of organized crime represents the abnegation of the state's obligations to its citizens. Citizens still live in fear but are now intimidated by nonstate actors in the form of organized crime groups. Organized crime represents such a potent threat because in many countries the government structures are often collusive and complicit in the organized crime activity, impeding the state's capacity or willingness to protect its citizens' lives and livelihoods. In collapsing states, like many to emerge from the former USSR, or poor countries in Latin America, the state cannot pay enough to keep and equip personnel to fight organized crime. In the absence of political will, the government does not invest the financial or human resources to address the growing threat posed by crime groups.

The traditional authoritarian state, limited by national boundaries, could only fully control its citizens within the nation-state or the empire. The organs of state control functioned within the country; rarely could or would the state reach outside its borders to control or punish its members who sought autonomy from the authoritarian state. The coercive capacity of the Cali and Medellín cartels is greatest in Colombia; of the Mafia, the Camorra, and other Italian crime groups in Italy; the Yakuza in Japan; and post-Soviet groups within the successor states. But their influence is by no means limited to these societies. The international reach of organized crime groups allows them to intimidate individuals and the media outside their home country.

Newspapers and television in the United States and Western Europe have refrained from providing exposés of organized crime groups following legal threats and the initiation of costly civil suits. Residents of democratic countries are intimidated by members of transnational crime groups. Most often the victims are emigrants who have ties to the countries where the crime group is based; they are the most likely but not the exclusive targets.

Organized Crime and the State

Transnational organized crime groups thrive in all kinds of states—democracies, declining superpowers, and rising economic powers. In all of the countries where they are based, they infiltrate government, assume governmental functions, and neutralize law enforcement. They undermine democratic institutions and the transition to free-market economies. Increasingly, transnational crime groups influence foreign states where they have large economic interests. In this respect, they mirror the legitimate multinational corporations that often corrupt third-world governments in efforts to obtain lucrative contracts and licenses.

Infiltration of Government

Transnational organized crime groups most often seek to penetrate the parliaments of their societies. Many also seek to corrupt or influence officials, most often at the regional level. The success of crime groups in infiltrating governments does not depend on the governmental structure. More often, their influence depends on the extent of their revenues and the contribution of the transnational crime group to the nation's economy.

Table 2.2 summarizes the diverse forms of government infiltrated by organized crime groups. Although democratic institutions may endure, as in Italy, serious damage is done to the integrity of government. In the most extreme cases, like Colombia and Russia, democracy is limited and the state becomes impotent.

Among the most blatant examples of a transnational crime group's

Table 2.2: Infiltration of Government

Examples	Locus of Infiltration	Impact of Infiltration
Democracy		
Italy	Parliament	Corruption
Colombia	Regional government	Undermine democracy
		Develop narcodemocracy
Rapidly Developing Economy		
Taiwan	Parliament	Influence legislation
		Officials corrupted
Former Socialist State		
Russia	Parliament	Influence legislators
Ukraine	Regional government	Limit democratic development

penetration of a domestic government is the Medellín cartel's participation in Colombian politics. Carlos Lehder-Rivas, a Medellín cartel leader, founded the Movimento Latino Nacional, which successfully elected candidates to regional office.[13] This visibility, however, backfired. During the last decade, the crime groups have participated more covertly than overtly.[14] The Cali cartel has been more successful by entering politics less obtrusively—it bribes candidates for parliament and other high positions. The current Colombian president, Ernesto Samper, stands accused of accepting campaign contributions from drug dealers. The issue has not been resolved. Many members of parliament are believed to have been bought off by organized crime.[15] The government, therefore, is ineffective in maintaining its democratically elected institutions.

In Taiwan, the justice minister reported that 4 to 10 percent of the elected officials in the legislature and National Assembly had gang affiliations. Many believe this figure to be significantly higher. The chairman of the judiciary committee is the most prominent of the gang-connected politicians. One independent lawmaker who challenged organized crime influence was kidnapped by gang members.[16]

The same phenomenon has been observed in Italy where the seven-time prime minister, Giulio Andreotti, the stalwart of the preeminent postwar Social Democratic party, has twice been deprived of his parliamentary immunity for charges of collaboration with the Mafia and is presently on trial. Five members of parliament from Naples were charged with collusion with the Camorra.[17]

The consequences of organized crime on the development of the state are particularly pernicious in the successor states of the former Soviet Union that are presently in transition. Organized crime, by undermining the electoral process, is shaping the development of the future legal system and the norms that will govern daily life and the operation of the economy.

The penetration of organized crime into the state exists from the municipal up to the federal level as organized crime has financed the election of candidates and members of the newly elected Russian parliament as well as those of other CIS states.[18] Candidates, once elected, acquire parliamentary immunity. The criminalized banking sector has financed different political campaigns as an insurance against postelection cleanup of the banking sector by the president or the parliament.

Transnational crime groups infiltrate state structures in their home states but are increasingly seeking to influence the policies of states in which they operate. Evidence of this has been the recent investigation launched in Israel and Italy to address the penetration of Russian organized crime groups into those countries' political processes. The 1996 Israeli elections were tainted by accusations that Russian organized crime groups financed candidates for local and national office. There were also reports that they had infiltrated the party that draws on the Russian immigrant community that is part of the ruling government coalition. [19]

Italian investigators carefully documented the success of a Russian crime boss in infiltrating the Italian government. The 900-page investigatory report culminated in the arrest of a Russian "thief-in-law," a member of the crime hierarchy, in the spring of 1997 in Italy. Simultaneous with the Russian's detention, a former leading Italian government official was arrested for Mafia association as were two former officials of the security service. The report reveals influence was sought with ministers and with senatorial staff.[20]

Transnational Organized Crime Assumes State Responsibilities

Organized crime assumes state responsibilities. In Asia, there is a long tradition of Triads and Yakuza performing social welfare functions.[21] In other countries such as Colombia and Russia, where organized crime groups have risen to prominence more recently, their assumption of state responsibilities is a newer phenomenon.

One of the most visible examples of this is the Yakuza's assistance to the 1995 earthquake victims in Kobe, Japan. The Yakuza compensated for the state's slow reaction by providing food, water, and supplies from their headquarters in nearby Osaka to needy victims.[22]

Drug traffickers in Latin America and the Caribbean have assumed many social welfare functions on a long-term basis. Pablo Escobar, the Medellín drug kingpin, financed educational facilities, schools, and sports plazas. In Bolivia, cocaine king Roberto Suarez provided sewing machines to needy women and college scholarships to those in need, and restored churches.[23]

Democracy Undermined by Transnational Organized Crime

The global reach of transnational organized crime is particularly harmful because it denies residents of even democratic countries the protection they expect from the state. With the mass movements of individuals around the globe, many individuals immigrate or even travel abroad for employment. Even when they obtain the legitimate right to residence and work in their new country, they often cannot escape the intimidation of the long arm of organized crime.

Chinese Triad groups intimidate both legal and illegal Asian migrants to the United States. This phenomenon was observed in Chinatowns in the United States at the turn of the century.[24] But the scale of this phenomenon has expanded in the United States, in Europe, and in many other regions of the world.

The smugglers demand large sums of money from individuals residing within Chinese communities, and if they cannot pay, the crime groups retaliate by violence, up to and including death. Law enforcement officials have not been able to stop this practice because members of the Chinese communities do not have faith in law enforcement nor do the local or federal police have personnel with enough language skills to successfully investigate these crimes. As Chinatowns grow in the United States, the presence of such large urban regions outside of the protection of the law undermines the legal order.[25]

The long reach of post-Soviet organized crime is evident in Europe, Canada, and the United States. Highly paid Russian émigré athletes in the United States are subjected to extortion threats. Organized crime intimidates the athletes and threatens family members in the former Soviet Union. Prostitutes in Western Europe are compelled to stay in prostitution because enforcers from the former Soviet Union threaten them and their families. Gangs based in Russia also intimidate Russian prostitutes in Israel.[26]

Legitimate businessmen who emigrated from the USSR in the 1970s and 1980s to Germany and the United States are now being extorted by organized crime groups; law enforcers are often unable to protect these businessmen from the intimidation.[27] These emigrants from an authoritarian state are still living in fear because the democracy in which they live is unable to protect them.

The State's Relations to Its Citizens

In the traditional authoritarian state, the citizens' interests are subordinated to the state and its ruling elite. Citizens are compelled by a legal system that does not uphold the rule of law but is a primary form of intimidation. Citizens are subjected to mass mobilization, often through governmental propaganda. Civil society is limited because the state discourages individual initiative.

Civil Society

Organized crime thrives in an environment in which there is limited civil society. As Robert Putnam has pointed out in his recent book *Making Democracy Work: Civic Traditions in Modern Italy*, Southern Italy lacked the civil society that had developed over centuries in Northern Italy.[28] Consequently, Southern Italy provided fertile ground for the development of organized crime.

Traditional authoritarian societies limit civil society because it undermines state control; likewise organized crime views civil society as a threat to its existence. Organized crime groups, therefore, undermine and coopt civil society. Organized crime can also be a manifestation of civil society, as in the Kobe earthquake example cited above. But this manifestation of civil society is not the bulwark against authoritarianism that theoreticians of civil society imagined.

Civil society has seemingly flourished since the collapse of the USSR. Yet recent research reveals that Russians believe charities are dominated by organized crime. Their assessment of this phenomenon is not misplaced. Many criminalized companies that have illegally privatized state resources support sports teams and other performance groups as a way of currying favor. Heads of crime groups have sponsored sports clubs. The significant role that the criminalized banking sector has assumed in the development of civil society has prevented the emergence of truly autonomous groups.[29] Many charity funds have been used to launder money. The recent indictment in New York of individuals who embezzled from the Chernobyl victims' fund raises serious questions about the propriety of the management of this Russian charity.[30]

The role of post-Soviet organized crime in civil society is not unique. As previously mentioned, members of the drug cartels have stepped in and provided resources for athletic programs, hospitals, and community programs. They have usurped and coopted citizen initiative.

Human Rights

Transnational organized crime undermines human rights in different ways from traditional authoritarian states. While international covenants are established to address the human rights violations of individual countries, they are not attuned to the threats to human rights caused by international crime groups. As will be discussed more fully later, the intimidation and assassination of journalists in different countries by international crime groups limits freedom of the press and individual expression. Their international trafficking in prostitutes and pornography demeans women and children, and the illegal smuggling of individuals to work situations where they are often exploited raises serious human rights concerns.[31]

Ideological Control

The modern totalitarian state maintained strict ideological controls.[32] This resulted in central state control over film, art, mass media, and scholarship. The legal system and the state bureaucracy were used to maintain this control. Censorship boards controlled expression, and errant writers and scholars could be threatened or even eliminated by the legal systems.[33]

Transnational organized crime groups also achieve ideological control. Like the authoritarian state, they seek to suppress all challenges to their economic and political power. Disclosure of organized crime activity is an essential first step to combating the phenomenon.[34] Suppression of this information is of paramount importance to leading crime groups. In transitional societies, organized crime groups seeking to shape the future development of their economies acquire newspapers and television stations to restrict citizen access to objective economic coverage. More blatant methods may be used in societies with a freer media. For example, a leading muckraking female journalist in Ireland was killed by a crime group after publishing reports of its international drug trafficking.[35]

Suppression of Information

In Russia, journalists and regional newspapers that attempt to confront organized crime are subjected to the strong-arm techniques of organized crime groups. Journalists are resisting the purchase of newspapers by the criminalized banking sector because it is subverting newspaper coverage. Newspapers and magazines unable to stay viable without injections of cash are often selling out to banks. This affects financial and banking reporting on television and in print.[36]

The significant financial resources of Russian organized crime are limiting press freedoms abroad by using intimidating law suits to stifle revelations in European and American newspapers. The *Wall Street Journal* was willing to assume the legal costs that followed the publication of an article revealing the significant role of former KGB personnel in a Russian bank. The suit against the *Journal* was dropped by the Russian side after it had spent millions of dollars in legal fees. Several Western newspapers have failed to publish articles that disclose the activities of Russian organized crime groups because they fear the costly suits that will follow.[37]

Despite the growing prominence of Mexican crime groups, there has been limited coverage of the subject, even after the killing of the Archbishop in Guadalajara by major narcotics traffickers. The explanation for this lies in the government's dominance of the mass media, the collusive relationships that exist between organized crime groups and local and national government, and the intimidation of muckraking journalists. In the late 1980s, a renowned columnist, Manuel Buendia, was executed in the presence of many witnesses. A high official in the Interior Ministry was subsequently convicted of his murder.[38]

Intimidation

In Japan, a leading filmmaker, Juzo Itami, was severely mutilated after preparing a serious and critical film on the Yakuza. Unlike his other films that circulate broadly internationally, this film is not readily available. Moreover, other Japanese cinematographers have not attempted to provide accurate depictions of organized crime.[39]

Intimidation of scholars by organized crime is rare but not unknown. Olga Kristanovskaya, a Russian researcher, received threats after publishing her sociological research on the criminalized banking sector. The journal *Sociological Research* was subsequently forced to issue a disclaimer. Pino Arlacchi, a leading Italian scholar of organized crime and a popular commentator on organized crime in the mass media, was issued a death threat by Toto Riina, the imprisoned head of the Cosa Nostra.[40] The leading Israeli scholar of organized crime once had to take refuge abroad temporarily after he was threatened by a particular group that he had studied.[41]

The Economy

Modern authoritarian states controlled, if they did not directly own, the economies of their societies. The mobilization of the corporate and industrial elite for state interests resulted in control even over private capital. Under the corporatist model, observed in many parts of Latin America, coercive force was used to restrict autonomous organizations and to structure strategic elements of the working class.[42] In other authoritarian states, a compliant labor force was assured through coaptation, domination, or control of labor unions.[43] Strategic economic alliances were made with other authoritarian states through such trade organizations as COMECON (Council for Mutual Economic Assistance). The corporatism of Latin America led to insular trading relationships among these countries rather than full integration into world markets.

The court systems, although denying individual liberties, usually protected commercial transactions. Under the communist system, in the absence of private property, the role of government in protecting transactions was less important than in a capitalist system with competing business interests.[44] Nonetheless, the state-controlled court and arbitration system ensured predictability and stability.

Despite state control and domination of the economy, a shadow economy existed in many authoritarian states. This economy usually prevailed in consumer areas, not in strategic military areas or the corporate sector of paramount interest to the state. Therefore, even in an authoritarian state, formally disorganized areas of the economy were not immune from an organized or parallel economy.[45] These shadow economies often laid the seeds for the future development of organized crime after the collapse of the authoritarian state.

Cartels and Illicit Global Trade

Contemporary global markets prevent the extent of control that states once enjoyed over their national economies. Yet organized crime groups attempt to replicate the controls of an authoritarian state. Serious debate exists regarding whether the international drug traffickers are actually operating cartels. But the mere use of the term reveals the concern that individuals have for the monopolistic tendencies of organized crime.

Illicit trade is following the ever-expanding legitimate trade on world markets.[46] Because this trade is international, the domestic laws of the country where the international crime group is based cannot regulate its activities. Neither can the international community control this activity because illicit trade is even less conducive to control than legitimate international commerce.

Investment: National and International

Transnational crime groups have acquired billions of dollars in the last few decades. Highly speculative estimates of the extent of the illicit global economy range up to $1 trillion. With this newly acquired and highly unregulated wealth, crime groups have been able to acquire key sectors of their national economies. In Colombia, organized crime groups have acquired significant urban real estate and large ranch areas.[47] In Italy, crime groups own billions in real estate holdings and resorts and increasingly have purchased large sectors of burgeoning light industry.[48] In Russia, possibly the most extreme case, organized crime groups have acquired or dominate a very significant share of the total economy, including the banking sector, joint ventures, and the highly lucrative export sector of natural resources.[49]

With such significant assets at home, mature transnational organized crime groups diversify their portfolios, investing very significantly overseas.[50] This same investment approach is pursued by legitimate multinational corporations.[51] Transnational organized crime groups do not necessarily globalize their portfolios because they are shrewd investors. In the Soviet successor states, the export of capital and the purchase of real estate and businesses abroad reflect the insecurity of domestic financial institutions and of private property.[52]

Intimidation of Businessmen and the Labor Force

Private property, according to John Locke, is to be the citizens' bastion against state authoritarianism. But in many states with large transnational organized crime groups, citizens do not possess the property they need to be autonomous actors. With organized crime's acquisition of businesses, they have moved from one kind of control to another. The labor force once controlled by the state or state-dominated trade unions will instead be subject to the intimidation of organized crime, which now operates as a major employer.

Organized crime groups do not use the usual rules of business to eliminate rivals. Foreign and local businessmen are threatened to force them to relinquish their financial holdings or to abandon their market niche to the benefit of their rivals. Russia and Ukraine represent the most extreme cases where hundreds of businessmen have been killed as a result of business rivalries. Most of these murders have occurred in Russia and Ukraine, but with the international reach of these crime groups, business rivals have also been killed in other foreign countries.

Exploitation of Privatization

Privatization of state enterprises was viewed as a major means of restructuring economies to heighten efficiency. The benefits of this process were widely touted but few foresaw the problems that would result from privatization without adequate transparency. The much heralded process of privatization of state resources in many countries is proving a growth industry for organized crime groups internationally.

State ownership or domination of the economy is being exchanged for control of key economic sectors and resources by organized crime groups who have the capital resources to acquire significant shares of denationalizing economies. Because transnational crime groups thrive in transitional or weakened states, these countries rarely have effective safeguards against the criminalization of the privatization process.

In Colombia, the privatization of state banking organizations has enabled drug lords to both covertly and overtly influence the operation of certain banks. Moreover, "the placement of foreign exchange markets in the hands of private financiers" has facilitated the entry and control of financial markets by the drug lords. Integration with the Venezuelan economy, already strongly affected by Colombian money laundering, represents a strategic alliance between criminalized banking sectors.[53]

Former socialist economies have gone from state authoritarianism and closed economies to nonstate authoritarianism and economic oligarchies comprising former members of the political elite, the control apparatus, and organized crime. The domination of these economies by criminal elites has precluded citizens acquiring a stake in their societies. These groups now have the financial resources to execute their illicit activities both domestically and internationally.[54]

The problem is by no means confined to the former Soviet Union. The absence of transparency in the privatization process in Eastern Europe permitted the transfer of resources to both domestic and international crime groups.[55] Italian authorities have been concerned about the purchase of real estate and banks in the Czech Republic and the former East Germany, as well as other Eastern European countries, by Cosa Nostra and 'Ndrangheta members.[56]

Strategic Economic Alliances

Strategic alliances exist among different international organized groups but the idea advocated by Claire Sterling of a Pax Mafiosa is premature.[57] The cooperation among the organized crime groups from different regions of the world enhances drug trafficking capacities and permits the smuggling of nuclear materials and the trafficking in human beings. These contacts are facilitated by increasing international trade, personal mobility, and the porousness of borders. Geographical proximity explains many of the alliances, such as the ties among Latin American drug traffickers or Asian organized crime groups and criminals in the Soviet Far East.[58]

The alliances are not explained solely by proximity because African crime groups are establishing alliances with groups on other continents and Colombian groups work with their Italian colleagues.[59] In these cases, the criminals are exploiting the weaknesses of the international legal system that permit them to forge alliances unimpeded by the laws or enforcers of their respective societies.

The economic alliances of the transnational crime groups are not yet a consolidated threat to the world order. Yet these alliances may become an authoritarian threat as transnational crime groups acquire more of the world's resources and extend their control over a larger share of the world's labor force and international markets.

The Legal System

Authoritarian societies depend on their legal systems and their institutions of social control for the maintenance of their power. In these societies, the state does not respect the rule of law. Instead, the legal system serves state interests and the controlling elite. Citizens' needs and interests are subordinated to those of the state.

The state maintains the monopoly of the forces of coercion. There is no room for private police or security. The state relies on violence as an instrument of control. Random and calculated violence ensures a submissive population. Death squads and arrests in the middle of the night are hallmarks of these regimes. These state-sponsored acts of violence remain unpunished because there is no accountability of the law enforcers to legal norms.

The independence of the judiciary, a key enlightenment idea, cannot exist because the interests of the state are paramount. Legal institutions are highly repressive, with reliance on severe and lengthy punishments. Executions are frequently used against both common and political offenders.

Weakened State Institutions

With the collapse of traditional authoritarian states, existing state institutions are weakened and subject to manipulation by individual interests. Organized crime through bribes and coercion corrupts the already weakened legal institutions. This is the case in many of the former socialist countries where the low-paid police are bribed or collusive in organized crime activity.[60] Strategic bribes to judicial personnel preclude effective action against organized crime.

States with limited traditions of rule of law have legal institutions highly susceptible to infiltration by organized crime. Law enforcement bodies in Mexico are notorious for their cooperation with the drug traffickers. Antinarcotics investigations were thwarted by associates of the former president. Raids did not take place and drug traffickers were set free because law enforcement personnel had been bribed and/or coerced.[61] Legal investigations of the former Mexican drug czar, General Gutierrez Rebollo, revealed that he and some of his senior associates conducted raids for one crime group against their competitors.[62]

Even established democracies such as Italy can have weak legal institutions. The corruption of the Italian legal apparatus is no longer confined to Southern Italy because organized crime groups bribe judges in Rome and even in Northern Italy to thwart investigations and prosecutions. In Southern Italy, the fight against the Cosa Nostra has been constantly impeded by police, magistrates, and judges in the pay of organized crime. Numerous courageous judges and police have paid with their lives for their perseverance in investigating and prosecuting organized crime.[63]

In Japan, there have been several highly publicized incidents of Yakuza bribery of police in the Osaka area. Law enforcement in port areas has been neutralized, facilitating Yakuza arms trafficking from China.

Privatization of Law Enforcement

The privatization of law enforcement and the legal system is a phenomenon common to different states where organized crime has acquired immense financial resources. The law enforcers are not only filling a power vacuum but also capitalizing on their ability to share some of the immense profits of the crime groups.

The privatization of law enforcement in the former socialist states and Mexico has some similarities to the phenomenon Diego Gambetta described in Sicily. Gambetta pointed out that the Mafia provided private protection in Sicily in the past century in a transitional period of the redistribution of property rights. Organized crime offered the protection needed by businesses that the courts and the law enforcement apparatus could not provide.[64]

As in the Italian case, in both many successor states to the former USSR and in Mexico, the central state is incapable of providing protection. The state is not relinquishing this function out of choice or duress. In contrast to the Italian case, private law enforcement in Mexico and the successor states has capitalized on the absence of state control to exploit its experience in control. Collusion of state authorities with privatized law enforcement has created potent auxiliaries of crime groups.[65]

Privatization of law enforcement in the socialist context has not meant the same as in the Western countries. Rather than representing a new form of policing, privatization merely continued the worst of Soviet policing practices while freeing private police forces from legislative and institutional controls. In Russia, approximately 800,000 individuals work in security bodies comprising former law enforcement, security, and military personnel. They do not just protect businesses, they intimidate honest citizens and business competitors.[66] A similar problem exists in many of the other Soviet successor states, Poland, and to a lesser degree, in other Eastern European countries.

International Reach

The global reach of transnational crime groups also undermines the administration of justice in foreign countries. In the United States, local sheriffs have been bribed in southern states to ignore Colombian air deliveries in their territories. Law enforcers in different European countries have been bribed by foreign crime groups to ignore alien smuggling, drug trafficking, or prostitution rings. The failure of compromised regulators to enforce money laundering legislation is particularly detrimental to the regulation of financial markets.[67]

Law enforcement cannot apprehend many transnational criminals because they and their money are highly mobile. Criminals exploit the inconsistencies in the international legal system by wiring money through many countries, impeding investigations of their financial activities. They avoid capture by traveling to countries that do not have extradition treaties with the country in which their crime was committed.[68]

Penal Institutions Rendered Ineffective

Even when states manage to convict and incarcerate members of transnational crime groups, their efforts often prove ineffective because the resources of the criminals permit them to bribe even top correctional officials. In Colombia, top drug officials have carried on their international criminal activity often from special prisons with all the comforts of home. In Russia, transnational crime groups operate unimpeded from penal institutions, even recruiting new members for their operations.[69] Therefore, even the most coercive actions of the government cannot protect its citizens from the threat of organized crime.

Unpunished Violence

Unpunished violence by organized crime groups is perhaps the most visible sign of state impotence. Thousands of contract killings committed by transnational crime groups on their home territory or abroad remain unprosecuted. In Russia and the other successor states, few of the hundreds of contract killings have been solved.[70] Neither the U.S. nor European governments have been successful in prosecuting the Russian hit men who make short trips to their countries to execute contract killings.[71]

Italy has never satisfactorily solved the bombing of the Ufizzi and the concomitant loss of life. Nor has it prosecuted the murderers of hundreds of victims in Sicily during the early 1990s. Colombia has been unable to solve the numerous murders committed as part of the internecine drug warfare, or to punish the perpetrators, even when these killings have targeted high governmental officials.[72] Just as the killings of the authoritarian state remained unpunished, transnational crime groups can perpetrate violence both at home and abroad with impunity.

In many countries or small communities within large societies (such as Chinatowns in the United States), citizens who confront organized crime groups still live in fear. Individuals often rightfully believe that law enforcement is incapable or unwilling to protect them from the retaliation of organized crime. Therefore, citizens will not report crimes committed by organized crime nor will they serve as witnesses. Citizen passivity, not just the corrosive impact of organized crime, impedes the rule of law. Citizens, therefore, become complicit in the perpetuation of the rule of organized crime just as they contributed to the perpetuation of authoritarian states.

Conclusion

The authoritarianism of transnational organized crime is predicated on a weak state. Organized crime groups, by corrupting the state, undermine its credibility and lessen its responsibility to its citizens. Presently, the impact of the transnational crime groups is most pronounced in their home countries, but as they become increasingly important actors in the global economy, crime groups' authoritarian practices will be felt increasingly in other countries. Recent examples of intimidation of foreign journalists and infiltration of foreign governments are evidence of the broadening reach of transnational organized crime groups.

The authoritarian threat posed by transnational organized crime is not presently as dangerous as that of traditional authoritarian states. Citizens of the global world cannot be sealed within the closed borders of a traditional authoritarian state nor subject to its controls. But the increasing wealth and power of transnational organized crime groups has the potential to undermine even the strongest democracies and impede the transition to democracy in transitional states.

Individuals who live in fear of organized crime may welcome authoritarian controls and the enhancement of state power in the name of fighting transnational organized crime. Therefore, transnational organized crime represents a double threat. Transnational organized crime groups intimidate individuals, promote violence, corrupt governmental structures, limit free markets, circumscribe expression, and undermine the rule of law. At the same time, the comprehensive and transnational measures needed to combat the phenomenon may lead to the reduction in civil liberties.

Weak and collusive governments are unable and unwilling to address the transnational organized crime problem. The coordinated international effort needed to combat transnational organized crime does not presently exist. In its absence, transnational crime may grow unimpeded internationally in the coming decades. The present international passivity against the growing power and entrenchment of organized crime may usher in a new form of authoritarianism with very severe long-term consequences for much of the world's citizenry.

Notes

1. Hans Binnendijk, ed., *Authoritarian Regimes in Transition* (Washington, DC: Foreign Service Institute, 1987); and Juan Linz and Alfred Stepan, *The Breakdown of Democratic Regimes: Latin America* (Baltimore: Johns Hopkins University Press, 1978).

2. For a discussion of state sovereignty see, for example, Michael P. Fowler and Julie M. Bunck, *Law, Power and the Sovereign State* (University Park: Penn State University Press, 1995); and Raymond Vernon, *Sovereignty at Bay: The Multinational Spread of U.S. Enterprises* (New York: Basic Books, 1971).

3. Phil Williams, "Transnational Criminal Organizations and International Security," *Survival* 36, no. 1 (Spring 1994): 96–113.

4. Kevin Jack Riley, *Snow Job?: The War Against International Drug Trafficking* (New Brunswick, NJ: Transaction, 1996); Francisco Thoumi, *Political Economy and Illegal Drugs in Colombia* (Boulder, CO: Lynne Rienner Publications, 1995); and Jeremy Pope, ed., *National Integrity Systems: The TI Source Book* (Berlin: Transparency International, 1996).

5. International Monetary Fund, "Tougher Measures Needed to Counter Macro Effects of Money Laundering," *IMF Survey*, 29 July 1996.

6. For an illustration of this phenomenon see testimony of Roy Godson,

"Threats to U.S.-Mexican Border Security," Subcommittee on Immigration and Claims, Committee on the Judiciary, U.S. House of Representatives, 23 April 1997. He points out that cross-border kidnapping occurs almost weekly. In one notable case, an individual was kidnapped in McAllen, Texas, and transported to the state of Guerrero where the individual was held. The drug traffickers claimed the individual had lost $250,000 in the United States.

7. Amos Perlmutter, *Modern Authoritarianism* (New Haven: Yale University Press, 1981).

8. Hannah Arendt, *Totalitarianism* (San Diego, New York, London: Harcourt Brace, 1976); and Adam Podgorecki and Vittorio Olgiati, eds., *Totalitarianism and Post-Totalitarian Law* (Aldershot, U.K.: Dartmouth, 1996).

9. E.J. Hobsbawm, *Primitive Rebels* (New York: Praeger, 1959).

10. Kenichi Ohmae, *The End of the Nation State: The Rise of Regional Economics* (New York: Free Press, 1995).

11. Vladimir Brovkin, "The Emperor's New Clothes: Continuity of Soviet Political Culture in Contemporary Russia," *Problems of Post-Communism* March/April (1996): 44–45.

12. Raimondo Catanzaro, *Men of Respect: A Social History of the Sicilian Mafia* (New York: Free Press, 1992); and Pino Arlacchi, *Mafia Business: The Mafia Ethic and the Spirit of Capitalism* (London: Verso, 1986).

13. Howard Abadinsky, *Organized Crime* (Chicago: Nelson Hall, 1994), 239.

14. Rensselaer W. Lee III, *The White Labyrinth: Cocaine and Political Power* (New Brunswick: Transaction, 1990), 130–39.

15. Douglas Farah, "Colombian President Took Drug Funds, Aide Says," *Washington Post*, 23 January 1996, A1, 11.

16. Julian Baum, "Perilous Politics: Public Interest Suffers as Gangs Infiltrate Government," *Far Eastern Economic Review*, 1 May 1997, 18.

17. The results of the investigation were published in "Camorra & Politica," *La Repubblica* (supplement), 15 April 1993.

18. "Duma Adopts Anticorruption Bills," *FBIS Daily Report*, 16 May 1994, 32; and A. Uglanov, "Prestupnost'i vlast'," *Argumenty I Fakty* 27 (July 1994): 1–2.

19. Menachem Amir, "Organized Crime in Israel," *Transnational Organized Crime* 2, no. 4 (Winter 1996): 34.

20. M. Antonietta Calabro, "La Mafia Russa," *Corriere della Sera*, 19 March 1997, 13; and Massimo Lugli, "In trappola il padrino russo," *La Repubblica*, 18 March 1997, 19.

21. Catanzaro, *Men of Respect*; and Arlacchi, *Mafia Business*.

22. Susan Maier, "After the Quake," *World Press Review* 42, no. 3 (March 1995): 24.

23. Lee, *The White Labyrinth*, 5.

24. Sterling Seagrave, *Lords of the Rim: The Invisible Empire of the Overseas Chinese* (New York: G.P. Putnam, 1995).

25. John Huey-Long Song and John Dombrink, "Asian Emerging Crime Groups: Examining the Definition of Organized Crime," *Criminal Justice Review* 19, no. 2 (Autumn 1994): 228–43.

26. Amir, "Organized Crime in Israel," 30–31.

27. Interviews with American law enforcement and BKA (German National Police) officials in Wiesbaden, Germany, August 1993.

28. Robert Putnam, Robert Leonardi, and Raffaella Nanetti, *Making Democracy Work: Civic Traditions in Modern Italy* (Princeton: Princeton University Press, 1993).

29. Igor Baranovsky, "To Jail in America from Russia—With Love," *Moscow News* 26, 25 June 1993, 13; and Paul Khlebnikov, "Joe Stalin's Heirs," *Forbes*, 27 September 1993, 131.

30. The indictment was issued in March 1996.

31. *Maritime Security Report*, U.S. Department of Transportation, Maritime Administration, no. 2, April 1996 discusses the large-scale problem of alien smuggling.

32. According to Juan Linz, ideological control differentiates totalitarian and authoritarian regimes. See Juan Linz, "Totalitarian and Authoritarian Regimes," in *Handbook of Political Science, vol. 3, Macropolitical Theory*, F. Greenstein and N. Polsby, eds. (Reading, MA: Addison-Wesley, 1975), 175–412.

33. See various contributors in Carl J. Friedrich, *Totalitarianism* (New York: Universal Library, 1964).

34. Interview with Jonathan Winer, Deputy Assistant Secretary of State, Bureau of International Narcotics and Law Enforcement Affairs, U.S. Department of State, on 1 December 1995.

35. Marjorie Rosen, Jeffrey Klinke, Ellin Stein, and Lydia Denworth, "Death of a Reporter," *People*, 22 July 1996, 40–43.

36. Elizabeth Tucker, "The Russian Media's Time of Troubles," *Demokratizatsiya* 4, no. 3 (Summer 1996): 443–60.

37. Author interview with Michael Waller who wrote the article for the *Wall Street Journal, European Edition* and was subsequently a party to this legal suit, March 1996, Washington, DC.

38. Roberto Blum, "Corruption and Complicity: Mortar of Mexico's Political System," Presented at the conference on the "Challenge of Corruption," Hacienda San Antonio, Mexico, March 1997.

39. Abadinsky, *Organized Crime*, 253.

40. He has entered national politics and subsequently served as Vice-Chair of the Parliament's Anti-Mafia Commission.

41. Professor Menachem Amir spent a year in Canada in the 1970s after being threatened by his research subjects.

42. For a discussion of this, see Perlmutter, *Modern Authoritarianism*, 123, and the major analysts of Latin American authoritarianism, including Alfred Stepan, ed., *Authoritarian Brazil* (New Haven: Yale University Press, 1973); David Collier, ed., *The New Authoritarianism in Latin America* (Princeton: Princeton University Press, 1979); and Guillermo O'Donnell, *Modernization and Bureaucratic Authoritarianism* (Berkeley: Institute of International Studies, 1975).

43. For example, see Daniel Levy and Gabriel Szekely, *Mexico Paradoxes of Stability and Change* (Boulder: Westview Press, 1987), 56–57; Robert E.

Scott, *Mexican Government in Transition*, rev. ed. (Urbana: University of Illinois Press, 1971), 24–25; and Leonard Bertram Shapiro and Joseph Godson, eds., *The Soviet Worker: From Lenin to Andropov*, 2d ed. (New York: St. Martin's Press, 1984).

44. For a discussion of the importance of the legal system in guaranteeing transactions see Diego Gambetta, *The Sicilian Mafia* (Cambridge: Harvard University Press, 1993). In the absence of these guarantees, organized crime can flourish.

45. See, for example, Maria Los, *Communist Ideology, Law and Crime: A Comparative View of the USSR and Poland* (London: Macmillan, 1988); and K.M. Simis, *USSR: The Corrupt Society* (New York: Simon and Schuster, 1982).

46. Williams, "Transnational Criminal Organizations," 96–113.

47. Thoumi, *Political Economy and Illegal Drugs in Colombia*.

48. "Mafia Money Laundering Practices Explained," Italian Federation of Public Enterprises reprinted in *Trends in Organized Crime* 1, no. 4 (Summer 1996): 96–102.

49. Timur Sinuraja, "Internationalization of Organized Economic Crime: The Russian Federation Case," *European Journal on Criminal Policy and Research* 3, no. 4 (1995): 34–53.

50. Thoumi, *Political Economy and Illegal Drugs in Colombia*; and Ernesto U. Savona, ed., *Mafia Issues Analyses and Proposals for Combating the Mafia Today* (Milan: International Scientific and Professional Advisory Council of the United Nations Crime Prevention and Criminal Justice Programme [ISPAC], 1993).

51. Vernon, *Sovereignty at Bay*.

52. Sinuraja, "Internationalization of Organized Economic Crime."

53. *Colombian Economic Reform: The Impact of Money Laundering within the Colombian Economy*, Financial Unit of the Strategic Intelligence Section, Drug Enforcement Administration, Washington, DC, September 1994, reprinted in *Trends in Organized Crime* 1, no. 4 (Summer 1996): 42–43.

54. Louise I. Shelley, "Privatization and Crime: The Post-Soviet Experience," *Journal of Contemporary Criminal Justice* 11, no. 4 (December 1995): 248–54.

55. Duc V. Trang, ed., *Corruption and Democracy* (Budapest: Institute for Constitutional and Legislative Policy, 1994), 73–85.

56. Material from the Anti-Mafia Commission of the Italian parliament, publication entitled "Espansione Territoriale e Devianze"; and Alison Jamieson, "The Transnational Dimension of Italian Organized Crime," *Transnational Organized Crime* 1, no. 2 (Summer 1995): 151–72.

57. Claire Sterling, *Thieves' World: The Threat of the New Global Network of Organized Crime* (New York: Simon and Schuster, 1994).

58. A.G. Korchagin, V.A. Nomokonov, and V.I. Shul'ga, *Organizovannaia prestupnost' I bor'ba s nei* (Vladivostok: Law Institute, Far East State University, 1995), 68–95; Observatoire Geopolitique des drogues, *Geopolitiques des drogues 1995* (Paris: La Decouverte, 1995), 59–60; and conference on orga-

nized crime in Irkutsk sponsored by the organized crime study center of the law faculty of Irkutsk State University, 30 May 1996.

59. Observatoire Geopolitique des drogues, *Geopolitiques des drogues 1995.*

60. Louise I. Shelley, *Policing Soviet Society: The Evolution of State Control* (London: Routledge, 1996), 173–76.

61. For a discussion of Mexico see the book by the former chief aide to the Mexican Attorney General for Narcotics, Eduardo Vale Espinosa, *El Segundo Disparo-La narcodemocracia mexicana* (Mexico City: Oceano/Edicion el Dedo en la Llaga, 1995).

62. Sam Dillon and Craig Pyes, "Court Files Say Drug Baron Used Mexican Military, A History of Collusion," *New York Times*, 24 May 1997, 1, 6.

63. Alexander Stille, *Excellent Cadavers: The Mafia and the Death of the First Italian Republic* (New York: Pantheon, 1995).

64. Gambetta, *The Sicilian Mafia*, 251–56.

65. See Blum's discussion of the growth of corruption as the justice system is privatized.

66. Interview with Viktor Iliukhin, head of the Russian State Duma Committee on Security, Moscow, July 1994.

67. Margaret E. Beare, "Money Laundering: A Preferred Law Enforcement Target for the 1990s," in *Contemporary Issues in Organized Crime*, Jay Albanese, ed. (New York: Criminal Justice Press, 1995).

68. The present federal indictment of a lawyer for Colombian drug traffickers suggests that he was hired by the Cali cartel because he had written the extradition legislation with Colombia while a high-level U.S. Justice Department official. See Meredith K. Wadman, "Cocaine and Abbell," *Washington City Paper*, 3 November 1995, 17–32.

69. V.I. Seliverstov, "Nekotorye voprosy preduprezhdeniia organizovannoi prestupnoi deiatel'nosti v mestakh lisheniia svobody," *Aktual'nye problemy teoriii praktiki bor'by s organizovannoi prestupnost'iu v Rossii*, 4 (Moscow: Institute of Ministry of Internal Affairs, 1994).

70. For a discussion of a recent conference sponsored by the Ministry of Interior on contract killings see "MVD nazyvaet avtorov zakaznykh ubiistv," *Interfaks-AIF*, 3–9 June 1996, 1, 29.

71. For a full discussion of the transnational crime activities of post-Soviet organized crime, see George J. Weise, Commissioner, U.S. Customs Service, "Statement before Committee on Governmental Affairs," Senate Permanent Subcommittee on Investigations, Hearings on Russian Organized Crime in the United States, 15 May 1996.

72. F. LaMond Tullis, *Unintended Consequences: Illegal Drugs and Drug Policies in Nine Countries* (Boulder: Lynne Rienner, 1995), 94–95.

3

State Power and the Regulation of Illicit Activity in Global Finance

Eric Helleiner

As the contributors to this volume note, economic globalization has encouraged the growth of a wide variety of illicit international economic transactions.[1] It is not surprising that an increase in illicit financial activities should be a particularly prominent aspect of this phenomenon. Money has always been one of the commodities that is most mobile and easiest to hide from state authorities. The financial sector is also where globalization has been most dramatic in recent years. As technological developments and financial liberalization have given money new mobility, the opportunities for illicit financial activity have grown dramatically.

Despite their increased attention to financial issues, scholars of international political economy (IPE) have been slow to show interest in the study of illicit activity in global finance. Particularly neglected has been a focus on the response of states to the growth of this activity.[2] This neglect is unfortunate since the state response has been considerable. Over the last decade, states have begun to construct an elaborate "global prohibition regime" that seeks to curtail certain kinds of these financial movements.[3] A study of states' willingness and capacity to take these steps has much to contribute to broader debates about state power in global finance as well as in the global political economy more generally. In particular, it calls into question the common view that the regulatory authority of the state is declining in this age of globalization.

This chapter aims to fill this gap in the literature by examining the nature and significance of the response of states to the growth of illicit international financial activity. In the first section, I describe the growth of three kinds of illicit financial activity and offer several explanations for why states have focused most of their attention on the regulation of only one of these activities. In the second, I analyze the specific regulatory strategy that states have chosen to curtail illicit financial activity and I place this strategy in an historical context of past initiatives of this kind during the League of Nations and Bretton Woods periods. In the third section, I examine the relevance of this study for two prominent causal arguments that attempt to link financial globalization to the decline of the regulatory power of the state. The chapter's principal arguments are then summarized in the conclusion.

Illicit Global Finance and Selective State Response

The globalization of finance is often seen as a process linked to the reduction of the regulatory authority of the state in the financial sector. This association is understandable given that the globalization trend has been accompanied by a dramatic liberalization of capital controls, a trend that has signalled a substantial withdrawal of state power from the arena of international finance. As noted in the introduction, however, the study of state responses to the illicit side of the global financial system calls into question this association. At the same time that states are liberalizing capital controls, they have begun reasserting their regulatory authority in other ways in an effort to curtail illicit financial activity that has grown alongside the globalization trend. Indeed, the reregulation of illicit finance is not the only example of this trend. As Ethan Kapstein highlights, states have also recently reregulated international banking markets through the 1988 Basle Accord on capital adequacy standards.[4] The relationship between financial globalization and state regulatory behavior is, thus, clearly more complicated than it first appears.

The story appears even more complicated when one explores the selective nature of state responses to the growth of illicit international financial flows. As this section explains, three different kinds of illicit financial activities have expanded dramatically alongside the financial globalization trend: money laundering, tax evasion, and capital flight. But states have been much more concerned about regulating the growth of the first kind of activity than the growth of the two others. What explains this selective pattern of state regulation and liberalization? After describing the growth of illicit financial activity, I suggest several explanations for this pattern of state behavior.

Financial Globalization and the Growth of Illicit Activity

The causes of the globalization of financial markets since the 1960s are still hotly debated.[5] What is not controversial, however, is the fact that this trend has encouraged a rapid growth in three kinds of illicit financial activity. The first is money laundering, which, in John Drage's words, is "the process by which criminals attempt to conceal the true origins and ownership of the proceeds of their criminal activities."[6] It is not difficult to understand why money laundering has been encouraged by the globalization of finance: illegally earned funds can be more easily concealed from state authorities if they can be moved to foreign financial systems. Historians of money laundering suggest that Meyer Lansky was the first to exploit the opportunities that the international financial system held for this activity.[7] Beginning in the early 1960s, he created offshore accounts—primarily in secrecy havens such as the Bahamas and Switzerland—that could be used to hide earnings from illegal activities in the United States. The path he blazed was then followed by a growing number of criminals around the world as they sought to hide what was estimated by the early 1990s to be close to $500 billion of illegally earned money worldwide.[8]

The activities of these criminals were facilitated not just by the globalization of financial activity. Developments in telecommunications technology have also greatly enhanced the ease and speed with which assets can be moved from place to place to escape state regulation. Money laundering activity has also obviously been facilitated by the proliferation of offshore havens around the world where the tracing of the ownership of assets is made difficult by bank secrecy laws or other similar legal provisions. Indeed, small secrecy havens such as the Cayman Islands have become among the top ten financial centers in the world and, according to some estimates, as much as 50 percent of the world's money resides in or flows through such offshore secrecy centers each year.[9]

The second category of illicit financial activity encouraged by the globalization of finance is tax evasion. This activity involves funds that were legally earned but that have become illicit because they are placed in such a way as to evade tax authorities. As in the case of money laundering, international tax evasion has grown dramatically alongside the general growth of international financial activity as individuals and companies have found ways to place funds abroad beyond the scrutiny of domestic tax authorities. Although most governments do attempt to tax the foreign income of their citizens, they have much greater difficulty obtaining accurate information about income earned abroad than that earned at home. As early as the 1960s, a large proportion of Euromarket activity was already associated with various kinds of tax evasion.[10] International tax evasion became even more widespread as capital controls were eliminated completely and technological developments facilitated the movement of funds worldwide in this new liberal environment.[11]

The proliferation of offshore secrecy havens also played a key role in fostering the growth of tax evasion since it is much more difficult for governments to obtain information about their citizens' income when the funds are earned and held in these locations. It is important to highlight, however, that tax evasion does not take place only in offshore secrecy havens. Throughout this period, the United States has offered what Vito Tanzi calls "among the most important" tax loopholes for international investors: the absence of a withholding tax on income from nonresident savings deposits in U.S. banks.[12] Latin American investors, in particular, took advantage of this loophole during the 1970s and 1980s, ensuring that their money was taxed neither by the U.S. government nor by their home governments who could not obtain accurate information about the billions of dollars held in these deposits. After 1984, the U.S. government also encouraged further tax evasion by foreigners in its financial markets by abolishing its 30 percent withholding tax on interest payments to foreign holders of domestic bonds and by beginning to issue government bonds in bearer (i.e., anonymous) form to nonresidents.[13]

Capital flight is the third category of illicit financial activity that has grown alongside the globalization of finance. "Capital flight" is a phrase that is defined in many different ways by different people. Some definitions, for example, include the financial activities of tax evasion and money laundering. In this chapter, I am using it in a quite limited and legalistic way to describe only the cross-border movement of financial capital which evades national capital controls. Unlike tax evasion and money laundering, there is no illicit financial activity *within* a country that corresponds to capital flight. It is illicit only because it breaks a law concerning the movement of money across the borders of a country.

For this reason, the relationship between financial globalization and the growth of this illicit financial activity is more complex than in the first two cases. On one hand, the elimination of capital controls has reduced the volume of capital flight (in the sense that I am using the term) because it makes cross-border financial movements that were previously illegal now legal. At the same time, however, the emergence of an increasingly open global financial marketplace has encouraged capital flight from countries that retain capital controls by providing greater opportunities for the evasion of these controls. This latter phenomenon has been particularly visible with respect to countries in the developing world where the size of capital flight has been enormous in the 1970s and 1980s. As Organization for Economic Cooperation and Development (OECD) financial markets liberalized in this period, wealthy individuals in these countries found what Carlos Diaz-Alejandro calls "comfortable possibilities for . . . exit" from their regulated national financial systems.[14] Since the late 1980s, capital flight of this kind has also grown dramatically from Russia and other ex-Eastern bloc countries.[15]

Why Have Some Illicit Flows Generated More Concern Than Others?

Financial globalization has thus been a major—though clearly not the only—cause of the growth of illicit financial transactions worldwide. This relationship has, in turn, generated the regulatory initiatives with which this chapter is concerned.[16] And yet, the link between the growth of illicit transactions and regulatory initiatives to curtail these activities is not a clear one. State policymakers have been more concerned with curtailing some illicit financial activities than others. Most attention has been given to the task of preventing money laundering activities, while much less has been devoted to the curtailment of tax evasion and especially capital flight. What explains this difference? And how does this explanation help us to understand the complicated pattern of both financial liberalization and reregulation in this age of globalization?

Three explanations can be offered. Each of these is closely related to an important interpretation of why the financial liberalization trend took place in the first place and thus provides part of the answer to the question why reregulation and liberalization strategies can coexist. The first explanation focuses on the role of liberal ideology. Most explanations of the financial liberalization trend over the last two decades give at least some role to the increasing ascendancy of liberal ideology among financial policymakers during this period. Given the considerable influence of liberal ideas in financial policymaking circles today, it seems logical that they also provide an important clue to help us account for the pattern of reregulation. And indeed they do. For liberals judge the relative merits of the regulation of the three kinds of illicit financial activity quite differently. Specifically, the regulation of international money laundering generates much less controversy in liberal circles than does the regulation of international tax evasion and capital flight.

This pattern of preferences helps provide an explanation for state behavior in this area. From the standpoint of many policymakers working within a liberal framework of thought, international tax evasion and capital flight do not necessarily require regulation. They may, after all,

simply reflect the reaction of individuals to government policies that
liberals disapprove of, such as excessively high taxation, inflationary
spending, or inadequate provisions for the protection of private property. Moreover, some kinds of tax evasion and capital flight are often
seen by liberals as having the positive effect of disciplining these governments and encouraging them to pursue more "appropriate" policies.[17] In the case of capital flight, liberals also disagree with the very
laws that these criminals are evading: laws that inhibit the free flow of
financial capital across borders.

Arguments of this kind defending tax evasion and capital flight have
a long-standing status in liberal circles.[18] This is not to suggest, however, that liberals today or in the past have ever been in complete agreement on the issue. Their equivocal position toward these illicit financial
flows stems from the fact that there are several powerful counterargu-
ments on liberal grounds to the arguments presented above. One is that
many individuals involved in international tax evasion and capital flight
are clearly not escaping from the kinds of government policies described above. Moreover, even when the motive for tax evasion and
capital flight is a justifiable one from a liberal standpoint, some liberals
argue that the negative consequences of these activities for the community outweigh the benefits they may provide to the individuals involved.
For some, this is an argument about equity: those with the ability and
wealth to move assets out of a country should not be permitted to leave
the rest of the population behind with an increased tax burden or with
their money held in a devalued currency.[19] A macroeconomic case is
also made by many liberal economists: tax evasion and capital flight can
severely undermine stabilization initiatives by eroding public finances,
encouraging volatile exchange rate movements, and exacerbating balance of payments crises.[20] In addition, tax evasion and capital flight can
cause financial capital to move internationally in ways that distort the
efficient allocation of capital worldwide.[21]

The lack of consensus within liberal circles concerning the desirabil-
ity of capital flight and international tax evasion has weakened efforts
to obtain agreement within and between states to prohibit these flows
in an age when liberal ideology is triumphant. By contrast, much less
controversy has been generated in contemporary liberal circles over the
objective of stopping money laundering. The lack of controversy is interesting since there is not a long tradition of thought on this subject in
liberal theory. Even the term "money laundering" is a relatively recent
one. As the phenomenon has been named and identified, however, contemporary Liberals have become increasingly convinced that the regulation of money laundering is not only justifiable but also necessary for
the maintenance of a liberal society for two reasons.

First, anti–money laundering initiatives are viewed as part of an effort to reduce criminal activities that liberals can largely agree are undesirable, such as drug trafficking, terrorism, and arms smuggling.[22] Although they may introduce unwanted regulation into the financial system, these regulations are viewed as necessary for the preservation of law and order, a task that is central to the liberal vision of a "nightwatchman" state. Second, liberals recognize that money laundering can pose a potentially serious threat to financial stability. When financial institutions or markets are found to have close links to individuals involved in these kinds of serious crimes, the public confidence on which financial systems depend can be rapidly undermined because of concerns about financial fraud or corrupt regulatory practices. Thus, as Tom Sherman explains, "Combatting money laundering is not just a matter of fighting crime but of preserving the integrity of financial institutions and ultimately the financial system as a whole."[23]

The different levels of concern generated by the rise of international money laundering, tax evasion, and capital flight in the current age cannot be explained entirely with reference to liberal ideology. A second set of explanations relates to the economic interests of private actors and public authorities in the markets. In almost all countries, the financial liberalization trend was driven at least in part by private actors operating at the international level who sought to rid themselves of cumbersome regulations as well as by financiers and public authorities who sought to bolster the competitive position of financial firms and financial centers. For this reason, initiatives to regulate illicit financial flows have often found strong opposition from these same groups.[24] And yet, this opposition has been much less in the face of initiatives to curtail money laundering than those aimed at tax evasion or capital flight.

One explanation for this difference touches on a point raised already: involvement in money laundering activities can undermine public confidence in financial institutions. Financial institutions, thus, have a self-interest in complying with money laundering regulations in order to preserve their "reputation" for trust and security in the marketplace for noncriminal financial business.[25] The same is true for entire financial centers since lax enforcement of anti–money laundering regulations can undermine confidence in the stability and reliability of financial transactions in that jurisdiction. This is even true—perhaps even more true—for the offshore secrecy havens that go to great lengths to promote an image of stability and reliability in order to attract business to their territory.[26]

The private interests who participate directly in each of these three illicit activities also have different abilities to influence government policymaking. Those with the least ability to lobby against regulatory initiatives are the groups involved in money laundering who are already being chased by the law and who, thus, must keep a low profile. By contrast, those involved in international tax evasion and capital flight are often individuals and corporations with considerable power in elite circles who are able to bend the ear of government policymakers considering a crackdown on these activities.[27]

In addition to these ideological and economic explanations, one final reason—indeed, probably the most important reason—why efforts to curtail money laundering have been pursued more vigorously is that the United States has shown greater interest in this issue. Analysts of the recent international anti–money laundering initiatives are unanimous in describing them as U.S.-led initiatives and the U.S. role has been crucial to their success for reasons explained in the third section of this chapter. The importance of U.S. leadership should come as little surprise to anyone who is familiar with the recent literature on the political economy of international finance. In this literature, few dispute the central role that the United States has played in promoting the recent financial liberalization trend and there is little question that the United States retains enormous "structural power" to influence current developments in international financial regulation.

But why has the United States pursued the regulation of money laundering more strongly than that of tax evasion and capital flight? The U.S. interest in regulating the international money laundering issue has stemmed largely from its campaign against illegal drug use domestically, a campaign that became particularly intense during the 1980s when the war on drugs was declared a "national security" issue. As other efforts to curb drug use have proven less than fully effective, U.S. policymakers have increasingly sought to prohibit drug money laundering—both domestic and international—as a central pillar in this campaign. Foreign governments have been strongly encouraged to follow the U.S. lead in a variety of ways described later in this chapter.[28]

The United States has also taken some important steps to combat international tax evasion, but the kind of consistent leadership shown in the drug money laundering field has been missing in this area.[29] No doubt, this partly reflects a recognition among U.S. policymakers that it will be much more difficult to build consensus within and outside the United States for anti–tax evasion initiatives for the reasons already outlined above.[30] It has also, however, resulted from the growing dependence of the United States on foreign capital inflows—including tax-evading flows—to help finance its twin deficits. Its 1984 decisions to issue bearer bonds and eliminate its withholding tax—both of which encouraged international tax evasion rather than reduced it—were driven by this concern of attracting foreign capital.[31] An attempt to crack down on tax avoidance involving foreigners investing in the United States by ending an income tax agreement with the Netherlands Antilles in June 1987 was also reversed two weeks later when it became clear the move would hurt foreign capital inflows into the United States.[32]

The same concerns contributed to an almost complete lack of U.S. interest in international regulatory or information-sharing initiatives to combat capital flight. The United States has been a major recipient of flight capital from the developing world, and these inflows have helped to finance its twin deficits. U.S. government behavior in this area has also been influenced by the opposition of American financial institutions to any regulatory efforts that might curtail the lucrative business of handling this flight capital. The kinds of liberal arguments that support capital flight, outlined above, also have been very influential in U.S. policymaking circles during the 1980s and 1990s.[33]

In sum, three factors can explain why states have shown more interest in regulating some illicit financial flows than others: liberal ideology, the economic concerns of private interests and public authorities, and U.S. goals. That these three factors should play a central role in determining outcomes is quite natural given the fact they also played a key role in explaining the financial liberalization trend. This overlap, in turn, helps to account for why states are both reasserting their regulatory authority in some areas of international finance and withdrawing it from others in this age of globalization. These two kinds of state behavior, which appear contradictory on the surface, seem less so once it is recognized that they are each driven by the same three factors.

One further conclusion may be drawn from this discussion. It seems less and less useful to debate whether financial globalization is or is not associated with a decline in the regulatory authority of the state. As the different pattern of state responses to illicit flows highlights, there is in fact no clear trend one way or the other. The more interesting issue is what drives the pattern of selective state retreat and reregulation in the context of globalized financial markets. In explaining state behavior with respect to illicit flows, I have suggested three central factors to explain this pattern. They may also be useful in explaining patterns in international financial regulation outside of the illicit sphere.

For example, like the move to curtail money laundering, the Basle Accord on capital adequacy standards derived much of its political support from the fact that it was compatible with liberal goals (in this case, to minimize financial instability), U.S. goals, and the "reputational" concerns of private interests and public authorities.[34] By contrast, support for the Tobin tax has been more difficult to mobilize not only because liberals view it more skeptically, but also because U.S. officials have shown little interest in it and it conflicts directly with the profit and competitive considerations of many private and public authorities with influence in financial policymaking circles. Patterns of state reregulation and retreat in international finance, thus, are linked less to the trend of "globalization" than to the political influence of powerful ideas and interests.

Reasserting State Authority: The Pattern of Reregulation

States have, thus, shown a growing interest in curtailing illicit financial movements—albeit some kinds more than others—that have been unleashed by financial globalization. But how have they gone about curtailing these flows? In what way have they chosen to reassert their regulatory authority given their commitment to financial liberalism? And what does the pattern of state response tell us about the nature of states' regulatory authority in global finance? To answer these questions, I suggest that it is useful first to place current regulatory initiatives in a longer historical context. The contemporary period is, after all, not the only one in which states have attempted to curtail illicit international financial activity. These historical precedents then set the stage for an examination of the ways in which contemporary responses are unique.

Regulation of Illicit Finance in the Past

The first time that the regulation of illicit financial flows was addressed in a substantial way within a multilateral setting was during debates that took place under League of Nations auspices in the 1920s. After World War I, capital flight and tax-evading international financial movements grew to a volume never seen before 1914. These movements were responding both to the new tax regimes and exchange controls that emerged during and after the war, as well as to the broader economic and political uncertainties of the period.[35] They caused enormous concern in policymaking circles, concern that was first expressed formally within multilateral circles at the 1922 International Financial Conference at Genoa.

Given the commitment to liberal values in financial circles at the time, delegates to that conference were wary of adopting regulatory approaches to curtailing these troublesome capital movements. Indeed, at the Brussels International Financial Conference only two years earlier, a resolution had been passed condemning all barriers to the international movement of capital.[36] Attention focused instead on the possibility of arranging exchanges of information between governments to recover illicit flows after they had taken place. The director of the German Reichsbank, in particular, suggested this course of action as an alternative to capital controls and a resolution was passed at the Genoa conference calling for its study by a committee of the League's Financial Commission.[37] The resolution made clear that the focus of the study was to be on the task of reducing tax-evading flows. The other kind of illicit flow—capital flight—was seen to be evading exchange controls that most of the delegates did not approve of in the first place.

The resolution also had an important caveat attached to it: any such initiative could interfere neither with the free movement of capital nor bank secrecy laws. The latter provision was likely insisted upon by the Swiss delegation, which had not wanted the entire issue studied at all.[38] It ensured that the committee's work would be largely ineffective. For if information-sharing agreements were to work, the domestic laws of all countries would need to be harmonized to a degree that overcame commitments to such things as bank secrecy or the confidentiality of tax information. The committee was thus left simply to recommend in a 1925 report that governments make every effort both to exchange information and to help recover taxes in their own territory that were due to foreign governments. To facilitate the latter, the League agreed in 1928 to two model treaties that countries could follow in pursuing such mutual judicial and administrative assistance in tax matters. A number of bilateral treaties were signed along the lines of these models before World War II, although their provisions relating to tax evasion were quite limited.[39]

The next moment when the issue of curtailing illicit financial flows was discussed prominently in a multilateral forum was during the negotiations that led up to the 1944 Bretton Woods conference. Here the focus was on the prevention of not just tax-evading flows but also various kinds of capital flight that might evade domestic exchange control regulations. With the rise of Keynesian economics and more interventionist financial practices during the 1930s and World War II, the negotiators were much more sympathetic to governments' desires to employ capital controls. Indeed, in contrast to the 1920 Brussels conference, the Bretton Woods conference endorsed the right of every government to use capital controls.[40]

This "embedded liberal" orientation was also clear in the manner by which governments chose to curtail illicit flows. In contrast to what Murphy calls the "liberal fundamentalist" policymakers during the 1920s, the Bretton Woods negotiators adopted a decidedly interventionist approach to this problem.[41] Illicit financial movements were to be prohibited through regulatory means at national borders. To this end, governments were to be entitled to use comprehensive exchange controls in which all transactions—capital account *and* current account—could be scrutinized for illegal financial flows (as long as current account flows were not restricted). The negotiators also endorsed the idea that each government might help to enforce the capital controls of other governments. As in the 1920s, this kind of cooperation could take the form of helping a foreign government retrieve the assets of its citizens that had already been sent illegally abroad (although, once again, no provision was made to override bank secrecy rules). It could also involve a more preventive approach whereby capital inflows that were considered illegal in a sending country would not be accepted by the receiving country.[42]

State Responses in the Contemporary Era

The efforts of governments to curtail illicit financial flows today bear more similarity to the initiatives in the 1920s than those at Bretton Woods. To begin with, international efforts to prohibit capital flight have been almost nonexistent. This is not to say that the possibility of such efforts has not been raised. In the context of the international debt crisis after 1982, many proposals were advanced to stop capital flight using the kinds of cooperative approaches endorsed at Bretton Woods. These proposals, however, have generated little interest in international policymaking circles for the reasons outlined in the first section of the chapter. Instead, the consistent recommendation from multilateral meetings has been for governments to pursue more "appropriate" domestic policies as the best way to eliminate capital flight.[43]

More international attention has been given to the problem of tax evasion. In 1977, the OECD approved a set of recommendations aimed at countering international tax evasion and avoidance. Both the UN and OECD also subsequently produced model bilateral conventions aimed at fostering international cooperation in this area. In addition, the OECD and Council of Europe opened for signature in 1988 a more ambitious "Multilateral Convention on Mutual Administrative Assistance in Tax Matters" (although only a small number of members have ratified it to date).[44] At a regional level, the countries of the European Community (EC) also decided in 1988 to begin to cooperate more closely in countering tax evasion.[45] In addition to these multilateral initiatives, hundreds of bilateral tax treaties have also been created in recent decades. Although their aim is primarily to minimize double taxation, they also often include provisions relating to the prevention of tax evasion.[46]

These various international initiatives, taken as a whole, have adopted a very similar approach as did the League of Nations to the problem of tax evasion. Instead of reversing financial liberalization decisions, they encourage governments to cooperate more closely in sharing information and providing legal and administrative assistance for each others' efforts to counter cross-border tax evasion.[47] At the same time, these initiatives also share the same limitation as was encountered in the 1920s: almost none of the agreements override domestic regulations concerning bank secrecy or confidentiality provisions with respect to tax information.[48]

They are also weakened in two further ways. One is the fact that many offshore financial centers lie outside the network of various bilateral and multilateral treaties. The other is that little effort has been made to harmonize domestic rules relating to this issue. For example, some states, such as Switzerland and the Cayman Islands, still do not criminalize nonfraudulent tax evasion, which greatly inhibits legal cooperation with them. Governments are also usually required by treaties only to share the information that they would normally collect themselves, information that might vary considerably from one country to the next. Cooperation between governments is also undermined by diverse administrative techniques used by governments in collecting and storing tax information.[49]

While these limitations have rendered international efforts to curtail tax evasion quite ineffective,[50] initiatives to prohibit money laundering have been much more ambitious. As in the tax field, a number of different initiatives have been pursued in this area. The first key multilateral initiatives took place in Interpol, which set up a special unit in 1983 to combat money laundering and which adopted a set of model legislation in this area in 1985.[51] In 1988, two more significant initiatives followed: the UN Convention Against Illicit Traffic in Narcotic Drugs and Psychotropic Substances (the "Vienna Convention"), and a code of conduct for banks issued by the Bank for International Settlements. A further important step came in 1990 when forty recommendations were issued by the Financial Action Task Force (FATF), a free-standing body that had been set up by the G-7 the previous year to address the money laundering issue. In 1992, the International Organization of Securities Commissions (IOSC) also passed a resolution recommending that its members observe the FATF recommendations in securities markets. These actions have then been bolstered and supplemented by many regional initiatives since the early 1990s—in bodies such as the Council of Europe, the EC, the Caribbean, the Organization of American States (OAS), and the Commonwealth—as well as by many bilateral and multilateral legal assistance treaties.[52]

Each of these various initiatives has complemented the others. Many of the procedures developed in Interpol for handling this issue, for ex-

ample, were adopted in the Vienna Convention and supported by
FATF.[53] Compliance with the UN Vienna Convention is also advocated
or required in most of the other agreements. In addition, many of the
regional initiatives attempt to persuade governments to adopt the FATF
recommendations. Both the Vienna Convention and the FATF also encourage the various kinds of regional and bilateral initiatives. Because
of this kind of complementarity, it seems appropriate to refer to these
various initiatives collectively as an increasingly cohesive anti–money
laundering "regime" at the international level.[54]

What are the key features of this global prohibition regime? The first
point to highlight is that it is focused primarily on curtailing one specific kind of money laundering: that associated with the drug trade.[55]
This focus has been justified on the grounds that drug money laundering
is by far the largest form of money laundering in most countries.[56] It
also has reflected U.S. goals. As we have already seen, the principal
U.S. interest in pressing for international action on money laundering
was to aid its domestic antidrug campaign.[57]

The second key feature of the regime is that, contrary to the approach
adopted at Bretton Woods, it does not focus on controlling illicit financial movements at the border. Indeed, initiatives such as the EC's 1991
anti–money laundering directive are designed explicitly to prevent governments from being tempted to use capital controls to control money
laundering.[58] This does not mean that borders have been neglected entirely as "intervention" points to curtail money laundering, however.
Some countries—namely the United States and Australia—have begun
to monitor cross-border capital flows as a way of gathering information
about money laundering activities.[59] When FATF was established in
1989, they also pressed other countries to adopt this same practice. The
majority of FATF members, however, opposed this request at that time.
As a compromise, the FATF members agreed simply to study the issue
in more detail "subject to strict safeguards to ensure proper use of the
information and without impeding in any way the freedom of capital
movements."[60]

Instead of controlling money laundering at borders, the anti–money
laundering regime seeks to bolster the ability of governments to crack
down on money laundering domestically. It does this by encouraging
international information sharing and legal cooperation with respect to
investigation, prosecution, confiscation, and extradition in money laundering cases. This approach is obviously similar to that pursued in the
tax field in the 1920s and the current day, but it also goes much further
in three respects.

The Novelty of the Anti–Money Laundering Regime

First, governments have agreed, beginning in the Vienna Convention, to ensure that bank secrecy provisions will not interfere with these forms of international cooperation. This important provision has finally enabled governments to overcome the barrier that bank secrecy laws have presented to effective international cooperation since the 1920s. It has also been implemented quite effectively. The Vienna Convention had been ratified by seventy-five countries as of 1994 and FATF members have also been successful in pressuring states to abandon various kinds of banking practices that seemed to contravene this principle of the Vienna Convention.[61]

The money laundering regime also actively promotes a significant harmonization of domestic laws and practices that are designed to combat money laundering. All governments are required under the Vienna Convention to criminalize money laundering and to allow for the seizure and forfeiture of the proceeds of this crime. Several initiatives, including the Bank for International Settlements (BIS) code of conduct and the FATF recommendations, also prompt governments to ensure that their financial institutions report all "suspicious" transactions to domestic authorities.[62] To prevent money laundering from taking place in the first place, governments have also been encouraged to prohibit their financial institutions from engaging in transactions where the identity of the customers involved is unknown by the institutions. Again, compliance with these various provisions has been quite high, although many states are still in the process of implementing them.[63] This level of compliance is particularly impressive given that so many of the initiatives that have promoted these provisions—such as the FATF recommendations, the BIS code of conduct, and the various model legislations—have no binding force on governments.

This ambitious initiative to harmonize domestic laws and practices is partly designed to facilitate international cooperation in legal matters and information sharing. Without all governments criminalizing money laundering, international legal cooperation on issues such as investigation, prosecution, confiscation, or extradition would be very difficult. A second objective is to ensure that all governments around the world become equally serious in their efforts to crack down on money laundering domestically. Without controls at the border, each country is vulnerable to a growth in money laundering activities abroad if any one foreign government chooses not to crack down on money laundering within its borders. The harmonization of domestic practices is designed to reduce this risk of "regime leakage."[64]

The final way in which the anti–money laundering regime goes beyond past and present anti–tax evasion initiatives is that it makes an active effort to be global in its geographical reach. States that have not yet agreed to join the regime have been subject to very strong lobbying efforts from those that have.[65] The FATF, in particular, has made enormous efforts to encourage nonmember states to adopt its forty recommendations through various missions, seminars, and the fostering of regional groupings with an associative relationship to the FATF.[66] Moreover, if this peer pressure and moral suasion are ultimately unsuccessful, FATF members also have agreed to take two tougher approaches to encourage recalcitrant states to adopt the recommendations.

One is a limited effort to apply some of the recommendations extraterritorially. One of the forty FATF recommendations asks financial institutions to apply FATF principles, such as those concerning the reporting of suspicious transactions and "know-your-customer" requirements, to majority-owned subsidiaries and branches abroad, "especially in countries which do not or insufficiently apply these [FATF] recommendations." But this suggestion is also accompanied by a key qualification that undermines its potential force. This extraterritorial application of FATF recommendations shall be done only "to the extent that local applicable laws and regulations permit."[67] In other words, if a non-FATF country has bank secrecy laws that prevent the reporting of suspicious transactions, financial institutions are not required to break these laws. With this clause, FATF members have demonstrated that they are not yet willing to undermine the sovereignty of non-FATF members. Instead, financial institutions faced with situations such as these are simply required to inform their home governments of their inability to apply FATF recommendations in this jurisdiction.

FATF members have also raised the prospect that financial movements between them and non-FATF members might be treated in a special way. They have agreed that the study of the possibility of monitoring financial movements from non-FATF countries is "of special importance," especially if peer pressure is unsuccessful in convincing these countries to adopt FATF recommendation.[68] Such monitoring would not only help to detect money laundering activities deriving from these noncomplying jurisdictions. It would also, in FATF's words, "increase the cost of transactions with them and thus compensate for the competitive advantage of the financial institutions located in the noncooperative country or territory."[69] The prospect of financial movements involving non-FATF members being not just monitored but also controlled has been raised in several places as well.[70]

These mechanisms have been quite successful in expanding the geographical reach of the regime to date. The core membership of FATF had expanded to twenty-six member governments (as well as the European Commission) by the mid-1990s.[71] FATF's forty recommendations have also been endorsed by many more nonmembers, such as the countries that belong to the Caribbean Financial Action Task Force. This latter group includes all the key offshore financial centers in that region, many of whom have refused to cooperate in international anti–tax evasion initiatives. One by-product of the expanding geographical coverage of the regime has been the growth of money laundering in financial centers that still remain outside the regime's reach, such as Thailand, the Seychelles, Sri Lanka, Russia, and Eastern Europe.[72] Once again, however, the FATF has begun to try to plug these holes in its coverage by lobbying these countries to adopt its recommendations.[73]

To sum up, initiatives to curtail money laundering have been much more extensive than those aimed at tax evasion or capital flight in the contemporary era. Indeed, the anti–money laundering regime should be closely scrutinized by those who believe the regulatory power of the state is in decline in this age of globalization. In her recent book *The Retreat of the State*, for example, Susan Strange cites the growth of international money laundering as evidence to support her broader thesis that the state's power within the world economy is eroding.[74] A focus on the anti–money laundering regime, however, can produce a somewhat different interpretation. Rather than signalling the retreat of the state, the growth of money laundering can be seen to have acted as a catalyst for a considerable reassertion of state authority in the ways that have just been described.

This reassertion of regulatory power, however, differs from the kind of authority states exerted in the financial sector during the post-1945 period in two ways. First, it eschews external controls at the border in favor of increased internal surveillance and regulation of the domestic financial systems. Some of the kinds of domestic surveillance and regulation that the regime has encouraged are in fact quite unprecedented, especially with respect to the overriding of bank secrecy laws. This pattern of regulatory action has been pursued in order to enable states to curtail illicit financial movements effectively without undermining their commitment to financial liberalism. In fact, the tension between financial liberalism and the prohibition of illicit financial activity has not been entirely eliminated. The regime has, in effect, displaced this tension from the international level to the domestic: a reimposition of capital controls at the border has been avoided by increasing the state's domestic surveillance and regulation in an internationally coordinated fashion.[75]

The way that international cooperation is used to bolster the regulatory power of the state represents the second important manner in which the reassertion of regulatory authority is distinctive from postwar practice. The Bretton Woods agreement did in fact endorse this kind of practice: international information sharing and legal cooperation were encouraged as a means to bolster the capacity of states to implement exchange controls. But such international cooperation was rarely forthcoming in the postwar period. The anti–money laundering effort has actually operationalized in an effective way this principle of using international cooperation to strengthen the state's regulatory power in finance. The objective, however, has also been both different and more ambitious than that at Bretton Woods. It is different in that international cooperation is designed to bolster the capacity of states to regulate and monitor illicit transactions within the domestic financial system rather than those that contravened external exchange controls. And it is more ambitious in that the regime has established technical and legal assistance programs that are designed to build up the regulatory power of states that have little capacity or experience with financial regulation of this kind.

Although the pattern of regulatory activity against money laundering is not the same as that which was characteristic of the post-1945 years, we have seen that it does bear some similarities to that advocated with respect to tax evasion within the League of Nations during the 1920s. In that era, Liberals advocated international information sharing and legal cooperation in order to enhance the ability of each government to combat tax evasion domestically. At the same time, however, the anti–money laundering regime has also overcome many of the difficulties that left international cooperation with respect to tax evasion quite limited and ineffective both in the 1920s and in the contemporary era. Bank secrecy rules have been overridden; the harmonization of domestic anti–money laundering practices has been encouraged; and provisions have been made to foster the worldwide extension of the regime. This provides yet one more reason to question the argument that the growth of money laundering is leading to an historically dramatic "retreat of the state." In a long historical context, the growth of money laundering in the contemporary period has encouraged states to pursue a much more extensive form of regulatory intervention than they were willing to consider in the last era of "fundamentalist" liberal internationalism during the 1920s.

Globalization and Declining State Regulatory Power?

In the previous two sections, I have argued that a study of the regulation of money laundering calls into question the conventional view that the regulatory power of the state is declining in this age of financial globalization. Up until this point, however, I have not yet directly engaged the arguments of those who advance this conventional view (aside from some brief comments about Susan Strange's views at the end of the previous section). What are the most prominent arguments put forward to defend the view that financial globalization is eroding the regulatory power of the state? And what lessons does the study of the regulation of money laundering hold for these arguments? In this final section, I attempt to address these questions by focusing on two key arguments that exist in the literature to explain why globalization might be eroding the state's regulatory power in finance.

Overcoming Competitive Deregulation Pressures

The first of these arguments focuses on a powerful competitive deregulation dynamic that is said to have been unleashed by the financial globalization trend. Phil Cerny has developed this argument most effectively. He argues that states are increasingly compelled to abandon existing financial regulations in order to avoid losing increasingly mobile financial capital and business to foreign markets. This same competitive dynamic is also said to cripple potential reregulatory initiatives. Unilateral reregulatory efforts are inhibited by a fear that they will render the national financial system uncompetitive. Similarly, cooperative reregulatory initiatives are seen to be almost impossible because they are scuttled by individual financial centers, which attempt to attract financial business and capital to their markets by not participating. Cerny concludes that the regulatory capacity of the nation-state in finance has thus been "gravely challenged." Moreover, he suggests that the competitive deregulation dynamic has begun to encourage an internal fragmentation of states, which only further undermines their capacity to take decisive regulatory action. From his viewpoint, only a turn to supranational reregulatory initiatives is likely to succeed in bringing finance back under some degree of control.[76]

Cerny's argument is an important one. Competitive deregulation pressures have played an important role in undermining international efforts to curtail tax evasion and capital flight. I and others have also argued that they played an important role in scuttling other reregulatory initiatives in the 1970s and 1980s as well as encouraging states to liberalize financial markets throughout this period.[77] At the same time, however, the influence of competitive deregulation pressures should not be overstated. As Kapstein points out, the Basle Accord on capital adequacy standards demonstrates that states can overcome competitive deregulation pressures to agree on a common international regulatory regime.[78] Cerny has recognized this countercase to his thesis but suggested that it was an aberration.[79] The success of the anti–money laundering regime, however, presents a second such aberration.[80]

Indeed, it is a more difficult aberration to explain away since states have reasserted their regulatory authority in this instance with a much more "market constraining" objective than was the case with the Basle Accord.[81] Moreover, it is worth highlighting that supranational bodies have played little role in the implementation and enforcement of the anti–money laundering regulations. The institution at the center of the anti–money laundering regime, the FATF, has no power over its member states and it is not even intended to be a permanent body. All of the efforts to promote international cooperation with respect to information sharing and legal assistance are also designed to bolster, rather than supplant or undermine, the regulatory power of the state. Furthermore, as noted above, the regime has also respected the regulatory authority of nonmember states, even when their behavior threatens to undermine the effectiveness of the regime.

How were states able to overcome competitive deregulation pressures to build this anti–money laundering regime? Interestingly, some of the explanations that Kapstein puts forward to explain how states were able to construct the capital adequacy regime also are relevant in accounting for the money laundering case. To begin with, in both cases the United States has been able to use its dominant position in the international financial system to push states toward cooperating to regulate international finance. In the case of the Basle Accord, the United States pressured foreign governments by threatening to cut off their access to the U.S. financial system unless they complied with the new standards. Because of the centrality of U.S. financial markets in the global financial system, this threat was very effective in encouraging foreign governments to comply.[82]

The same threat was made by the United States to encourage foreign states to begin to crack down on money laundering. It was in fact much more explicit in the money laundering case. The Kerry Amendment to the 1988 Anti-Drug Abuse Act empowered the U.S. government to cut foreigners off from access to the U.S. financial system, including its clearing systems, if their governments refused to reach specific anti-money laundering agreements with the U.S. Treasury. Foreigners had to take this threat seriously, especially since the U.S.-based clearing systems CHIPS and Fedwire handle roughly 95 percent of all wire transfers sent and received in the world.[83] In Mario Possamai's words, the threat was thus "a hefty club, since those systems are the underpinning of world trade and finance. A haven that was not plugged in would not survive long."[84] In fact, no country has yet had its access to the

U.S. financial system cut off under this provision and the Treasury has only negotiated a few agreements of the precise kind that the amendment requires.[85] Still, the threat was undoubtedly effective—as it was in the Basle Accord negotiations—in focusing foreign governments' attention on the seriousness with which the United States viewed the issue.[86]

The United States has also used other forms of power in pushing foreign governments to cooperate in combatting money laundering. In the early 1980s, the United States flirted briefly with the use of extraterritorial application of its laws, particularly with respect to the Caribbean offshore havens. As part of a drug investigation in 1983, the U.S. government demanded access to financial information from branches of the Bank of Nova Scotia in the Bahamas and the Cayman Islands. When the bank refused, a U.S. court assigned it heavy contempt of court charges (that reached $1.8 billion) and threatened to seize its U.S. assets. International protests made the United States more wary of pursuing this tactic again, but it did have the effect of encouraging not only the bank to give up the information requested, but also the Cayman Islands (and the Bahamas) to sign a mutual legal assistance treaty with the United States to combat money laundering.[87] More recently, the United States made its aid and tariff concessions under the Caribbean Basin Initiative conditional on their cooperation in helping to trace money laundering.[88] Foreign bankers who have not been fully cooperative with U.S. government authorities in this area have also had their visas revoked.[89]

The important role that U.S. leadership can play in overcoming competitive deregulation is acknowledged by Cerny. But he argues that this leadership role will be rare because of the internal fragmentation of the U.S. state, a fragmentation that he suggests has been exacerbated by the competitive pressures unleashed by financial globalization. But in the case of the fight against international money laundering, the U.S. state has in fact shown a high degree of cohesion and unity of purpose. This characteristic of U.S. policymaking is undoubtedly related in part to the fact that the anti–money laundering campaign has been linked to a cause that was declared a "national security" issue: the war on drugs. As other scholars have noted, when national security issues are at stake, the U.S. state has often intervened dramatically and decisively in international financial markets irrespective of the immediate consequences for the "competitiveness" of its financial markets and firms.[90] In instances such as these, the logic of Cerny's "competition state" appears to be overwhelmed by a pattern of politics associated with the more traditional "security state."

The decisive U.S. leadership role can also be attributed to a second factor. Cerny explains well how the competitive deregulation pressures can undermine the cohesion of state policy, especially in an already fragmented state such as the United States. But the examples of U.S. leadership with respect to capital adequacy standards and the anti–money laundering regime also show that the very same pressures can encourage decisive and coherent leadership in the international arena. Once it has become clear that a decision to reregulate is going to be made domestically in a leading state, that state has a large incentive to encourage other states to do the same in order to avoid losing financial business and capital to them. In the capital adequacy case, as soon as the U.S. Congress had decided to impose capital adequacy standards on its own banks, U.S. banks and various U.S. state officials quickly moved to ensure that these standards would be imposed on foreign banks as well. The same dynamic has encouraged the United States to play a lead role in pushing for international regulation of money laundering. In other words, the very competitive deregulation pressures that often work against decisive and coherent U.S. leadership can also promote it very rapidly once the tide is turned against deregulation domestically.

A further way in which competitive dynamics can encourage reregu-lation instead of deregulation is outlined by Kapstein in his explanation of the success of the Basle Accord. He notes that international financial markets themselves have played an important role in encouraging com-pliance with the standards. Financial institutions and financial centers that are not abiding by the new standards have been perceived within the markets to be less stable and secure than those that have adopted the standards. This, in turn, has encouraged the exact opposite of the competitive deregulation dynamic: financial institutions and govern-ments have been keen to adopt the new regulations in order to maintain their reputation within the financial markets. "Reputational" effects have, in other words, driven a kind of upward harmonization.[91]

This "competitive reregulation" dynamic has also encouraged fi-nancial institutions and governments to comply with the new anti–money laundering regulations. A growing number of financial scandals and crises involving money laundering have drawn the attention of "clean" market actors to the risks of doing business with financial insti-tutions and jurisdictions that have a reputation for money laundering activity. To preserve their business, financial institutions and govern-ments have thus been prompted to comply fully with the standards and regulations outlined in the new anti–money laundering regime. Of course, some institutions and financial centers may be tempted to base their livelihood mostly on money laundering activities. In this case, the "reputation" they seek is best cultivated by not complying. But the fact that most offshore financial centers have begun to cooperate in combatting money laundering suggests that it is more attractive to them to cultivate a reputation as "tax havens" or havens for capital flight than as magnets for money laundering.[92]

One final explanation that helps to account for the construction of the anti–money laundering regime in a context of competitive deregulation relates to the role of liberal ideas and norms that was analyzed in the first two sections of the chapter. In Cerny's analysis, international ideas and norms play little role in the determination of state behavior. I have argued, however, that liberal ideas and norms have been important in influencing both the choice of illicit financial flows to be regulated as well as the pattern of regulation pursued. Their impact, I would suggest, stems not just from the growth in the transnational influence of liberalism in recent years, as others have suggested.[93] Equally, if not more important, is the particular influence of shared norms and ideas within the narrow and quite insulated community of officials that dominates policy related to international financial regulation.[94]

Here again Kapstein's analysis of the capital adequacy standards is instructive. He explains how international support for such standards was bolstered by the common cognitive frameworks that central bankers working within the BIS share in analyzing problems of international finance.[95] In the case of money laundering, the transnational networks of officials involved in policymaking were wider, including not just central bankers but also other financial and law enforcement officials. Like central bankers, however, these latter two groups are also involved in increasingly tight and cohesive transnational policy networks, which are associated with the kinds of bodies that were involved in the construction of the anti–money laundering regime, such as the G-7, IOSC, the UN, Interpol, and various regional fora.[96] It was within these transnational policy networks that various officials—especially, but not exclusively, from the United States—began to promote the idea that money laundering should be seen as a "bad" to be regulated within the terms of liberal discourse. And the rapid manner in which an international consensus emerged on the issue can be attributed at least in part to the shared values and worldviews that are held by officials within these transnational networks. The high degree of compliance with such voluntary rules such as the FATF recommendations and the BIS code of conduct can also be attributed, at least in part, to the importance of shared norms and ideas among policymakers in this area.[97]

The influence of shared ideas and norms on international policymaking in this area should not, however, be overstated. The fact that the United States has felt compelled to use coercion to encourage money laundering regulation abroad highlights the limits of this explanatory variable. And recall, too, that it is not just the United States that has felt it necessary to threaten to cut off access to its financial markets to states that are outside of the "international consensus." Members of the FATF as a whole have suggested that they may soon monitor and even perhaps curtail financial flows from jurisdictions outside of their "community." In other words, FATF members are threatening to form a kind of liberal "zone of exclusion" within which capital movements take place freely but that is open only to those states that have joined the "consensus" and are adopting the responsibilities of policing money laundering.[98] This threat may ultimately be much more influential than the spread of any norms and ideas; if it were implemented, the various financial centers outside of FATF could not hope to attract significant financial business to their territories. It is also similar to the threat that the BIS central bankers have made with respect to those countries that do not supervise their financial systems according to BIS standards.[99]

To summarize, the construction of the anti–money laundering regime provides a second piece of evidence to question the argument that competitive deregulation dynamics are so powerful as to prevent states from regulating international finance in the contemporary age. To be sure, the pressures of competitive deregulation are influential ones in contemporary financial policymaking. But both the anti–money laundering regime and the Basle Accord suggest a number of reasons why these pressures do not always inhibit reregulation. One is that competitive concerns may actually encourage reregulation in some instances in the ways described above. A second is that hegemonic leadership can be decisive in overcoming collective action problems associated with competitive deregulation. And third, financial policymaking within key states is driven not only by competitive considerations but also by other considerations such as, in these two instances, liberal ideology and new "security" concerns.

Are Regulations Effective Anymore?

Arguments about the power of competitive deregulation are not the only ones questioning the regulatory authority of the state in this age of financial globalization. A second line of argument concentrates on states' apparent loss of even the technical capacity to regulate finance today. According to this view, even if states attempt to control financial capital, they will find it impossible to do so effectively for two reasons. First, global financial markets are said to have become so complex and innovative that any initiative to regulate one kind of financial activity will simply encourage diversion to new markets and financial products. Second, the information technology revolution, which has accompanied and promoted the financial globalization trend, is also said to have made regulation almost impossible. Because money has increasingly become simply a digital blip of information transmitted through sophisticated telecommunications channels, it is said to be enormously difficult for states to isolate the electronic blips that relate to money movements, let alone actually regulate them.[100] From this perspective, then, the issue is not whether states have found ways to cooperate in constructing an anti–money laundering regime. Instead, it is whether this regime has any chance of successfully prohibiting such money movements in practice.

Once again, this argument is an important one and the money laundering case might be seen at first sight to support it. All observers of recent regulations on money laundering agree that the new regulations have not come anywhere close to eliminating the phenomenon. Diversion to new financial markets and products has been considerable, forcing states to recognize the limited scope of their initial regulatory initiatives.[101] Similarly, it has become clear to regulators that the vast bulk of money laundering takes place through the very kind of electronic wire transfers that are said by many to be so difficult to control.[102]

But the experience of the anti–money laundering regime should not be seen as providing evidence to support this view so quickly. To begin with, it is important not to overstate the degree to which states have ever been able to control finance. Well before the current age of financial globalization, states also had enormous difficulties attempting to regulate finance, and especially international movements of finance. During the 1930s, for example, when most states began to experiment with comprehensive capital controls for the first time, these difficulties were very apparent. In that era, countries such as Germany discovered that even the threat of the death penalty did not stop people from finding ways to evade extremely tight exchange control regulations.[103]

The difficulties of controlling cross-border movements of finance were also actively discussed during the negotiations leading up to the 1944 Bretton Woods conference. Keynes, for example, had few illusions about these difficulties. He argued that unilateral efforts to regulate international financial movements were likely to be quite ineffective unless very draconian measures—such as postal censorship—were employed. For this reason, he argued that the more effective way to control finance was in a collective way where both sending and receiving countries cooperated in enforcing each other's capital controls.[104] Even in the age before financial globalization, then, it was recognized that states' authority over financial movements was relatively limited and that it could be bolstered more completely only if it were validated from the outside by foreign governments. This same lesson is being relearned today by those seeking to regulate international money laundering.

A second reason not to read too much into the experience of the anti–money laundering regime is that it is too early to judge its potential effectiveness. Many states are only just beginning to implement the new anti–money laundering laws that they have put in place. Domestic reporting and information-processing procedures are still being developed in many countries as are some of the mechanics of the various forms of international cooperation that have been endorsed. The scope of the regime itself is also still in the process of formation. The FATF, for example, has begun to extend the regime to cover a wider range of financial services and institutions than had been the initial target. This move has been taken to respond to the diversion of illicit flows toward as-yet unregulated sectors of the financial system. This diversion, rather than reflecting a weakness in the initial regime, however, suggests that the initial regulatory efforts have in fact been quite successful.

At this point, states have also not decided the extent to which they will attempt to regulate electronic wire transfers.[105] Interestingly, however, the first few tentative initiatives and investigations in this area suggest that their capacity to do so is in fact much higher than is often implied. Indeed, the effort to control money laundering suggests that information technologies have likely augmented, rather than undermined, state regulatory power. This can be seen in several ways.

First, electronic fund transfers, unlike transactions in hard cash, leave an electronic trace that can be monitored. For this reason, most analysts and regulatory authorities argue that efforts to discover and control money laundering will be helped enormously by the declining use of cash.[106] Where Keynes envisioned governments being forced to open mail to search for secret movements of cash, governments today need only monitor the limited number of electronic payments systems that increasingly dominate the financial services industry.

Second, the payments systems through which international movements of finance travel are also highly concentrated and very distinct from those carrying other electronic information flows. As mentioned already, almost all of these movements are channelled through the CHIPS and Fedwire clearing systems based in the United States. Equally important is SWIFT, which transmits the instructions to execute a large portion of the electronic funds transfers that take place through CHIPS and Fedwire.[107] Any initiative to monitor and regulate international financial transactions can thus accomplish an enormous amount simply by focusing on movements within these three systems. As part of its effort to encourage financial institutions to know the identity of their customers, for example, the FATF pressed SWIFT to broadcast a message on July 30, 1992, to all its users asking them to include the names and addresses of all senders and receivers of electronic messages who were not financial institutions.

Initiatives of this kind may signal the first step along a potential route of transforming CHIPS, Fedwire, and SWIFT into "closed-circuit systems" that can be used only by those willing to adopt certain responsibilities vis-à-vis the regulation of money laundering. Such a move would be very effective in controlling money laundering around the world. In Zamora's words: "If the world community adopts a closed-circuit system, it will be essential to enter that system in order to take part in the Western financial system."[108] Some might argue that such a move will encourage diversion to other clearing systems, but there are not many trustworthy alternatives for market actors to turn to and regulatory initiatives can quickly be extended to them.[109] For this reason, the new international electronic payments systems have in fact likely made the multilateral regulation of financial flows easier.

Finally, technological developments have also increased the potential for individual states to monitor suspicious financial movements in and out of their territory. As noted in the second section of the chapter, the FATF has encouraged states to investigate the potential for such monitoring. To date, Australia has been the pioneer in this regard. It has been experimenting with new software—developed initially for the U.S. Air Force to track incoming missiles—that can monitor an enormous number of cross-border electronic funds transfers and then report suspicious patterns that may emerge. This software has already proved its efficacy in several important money laundering incidents and the United States is expressing interest in introducing the system as well.[110]

The creation of the anti–money laundering regime, thus, has demonstrated not only that states have not been completely debilitated in the regulatory field by competitive deregulation pressures. It has also encouraged state policymakers to recognize and demonstrate for the first time that new technologies can be used to bolster, rather than undermine, their regulatory power in finance. This should give further pause to those who have predicted the erosion of the regulatory power of the state in this age of financial globalization.

Conclusion

As other contributions to this volume highlight, the financial sector is not the only sector of the world economy in which policymakers are confronted by a growth of illicit economic transactions in the new liberal international economic order. It is, however, a particularly interesting sector in which to examine state responses to this phenomenon. This is not only because financial activities have become among the most prominent of illicit activities in the global economy. It is also because issues related to the regulatory power of the state in the financial sector are at the center of broader debates in IPE about the relationship between states and globalization. What lessons does this study of state responses to the growth of illicit international finance bring to these broader debates?

First, it has called into question the view that globalization is linked to the decline of the regulatory authority of the state. My arguments here, of course, are not the first to raise doubts about this line of argument. Some critics have questioned whether a process that has been authored by the decisions of states to liberalize capital controls can be seen to undermine the regulatory authority of those same states. Others have highlighted how globalization has been accompanied by enhanced state regulatory powers in areas such as the defense of property rights or the preservation of financial stability.[111] Quite neglected in this critical literature, however, is a focus on how illicit economic transactions unleashed by the globalization trend have encouraged states to expand their policing power through reregulatory initiatives. As I have shown, these initiatives in the area of money laundering have resulted in a considerable reassertion of states' regulatory authority in the financial sector.

This study has also shown, however, that states have responded to the growth of illicit financial activity in a selective manner, regulating money laundering extensively but showing less interest and success in efforts to control tax evasion and capital flight. This observation led to a second argument that may have relevance to broader IPE debates. Given this diverse pattern of behavior, I argued that the central influence on the trajectory of state regulatory authority in finance today is not globalization per se, but rather three more specific factors: the influence of liberal ideology, the economic concerns of private interests and public authorities, and U.S. goals. I suggested that the identification of these specific factors can contribute to IPE debates on the politics of international financial regulation. Whether they have relevance beyond the financial sector in explaining patterns of state retreat and regulation is a more open question. The central point, however, is that the retreat or reassertion of states' regulatory authority is linked less to "globalization" than to the political influence of specific powerful ideas and interests.

The study of the manner in which states have attempted to curtail money laundering also has relevance to broader IPE scholarship. Although states have reasserted their regulatory authority in this instance, they have done so in a manner that is quite different from that which characterized the post-1945 years. Instead of focusing on regulation at the border, states have attempted to bolster their capacity to monitor and regulate transactions within their borders. Moreover, intensive forms of international cooperation have been developed to strengthen the state's power to regulate and monitor domestic financial activity in these new ways. This pattern of regulation is reminiscent of the intentions of regulators in the 1920s, as I have noted. It also provides an interesting solution to the problem of how the reregulation can take place in a context where global markets are deeply integrated and policymakers are strongly committed to liberal norms. Whether this solution has also been arrived at in other sectors of the world economy would be an interesting issue for future research by IPE scholars. What it does suggest, however, is that the regulatory authority of states, while not in decline, is certainly being exercised in new ways in this age of globalization.

Finally, I have suggested that this study also highlights some lessons for two prominent causal arguments that link financial globalization to an erosion of the state's regulatory power. Those who argue that competitive deregulation pressures undermine states' willingness to regulate finance need to explain why these pressures have not inhibited the reregulatory trend in the money laundering field. I have suggested several explanations that deserve more attention from advocates of this argument: the role of U.S. leadership, the fact that financial policymaking is not driven by competitive considerations alone, and the dynamic that encourages competitive pressures to act as a catalyst not just for deregulation but also reregulation. I have also questioned arguments that suggest that the technical capacity of states to regulate finance has declined in any significant way from earlier historical periods. Then as now, financial movements have proved difficult to control, especially in the absence of cooperation between states. Moreover, as anti–money laundering initiatives have become more extensive, they have begun to demonstrate that the new technologies that are said to erode state regulatory capacity today may in fact even enhance it. In short, state responses to the growth of money laundering point to the conclusion that predictions of the death of the state's regulatory power in this age of financial globalization are exaggerated.

Notes

1. For research help and/or comments, I am very grateful to Rob Aitken, Peter Andreas, Rich Friman, Albrecht Funk, Peter Katzenstein, Jonathan Kirschner, Tom Princen, Louise Shelley, Vincent Sica, Susan Strange, Gita Sud, Janice Thomson, William Walker, and Michael Webb. For helping to finance some of the research for this chapter, I am also very grateful to Human Re-

sources Development Canada, York University, and the Social Sciences and
Humanities Research Council of Canada.

2. As is evidenced by the endnotes in this chapter, writing in this area to
date has been dominated by lawyers, policymakers, financial journalists, and
practitioners in the financial markets.

3. For the term "global prohibition regimes," see Ethan Nadelmann,
"Global Prohibition Regimes: The Evolution of Norms in International Society," *International Organization* 44, no. 4 (Autumn 1990): 479–526.

4. Ethan Kapstein, *Governing the Global Economy* (Cambridge: Harvard
University Press, 1994). For discussions of regulatory initiatives in securities
markets, see also Geoffrey Underhill, "Keeping Governments Out of Politics:
Transnational Securities Markets, Regulatory Cooperation and Political Legitimacy" *Review of International Studies* 21, no. 3 (1995): 251–78; and Tony
Porter, *States, Markets and Regimes in Global Finance* (London: Macmillan,
1993).

5. See, for example, Benjamin Cohen, "Phoenix Arisen: The Resurrection
of Global Finance" *World Politics* 48, no. 2 (January 1996): 268–97.

6. John Drage, "Countering Money Laundering," in *Money Laundering*,
David Hume Institute (Edinburgh: Edinburgh University Press, 1993), 60.

7. See, for example, R.T. Naylor, *Hot Money and the Politics of Debt* (Montreal: Black Rose Books, 1994), 20, 40; and Rachel Ehrenfeld, *Evil Money*
(New York: HarperBusiness, 1992).

8. For this figure, see International Monetary Fund, "Tougher Measures
Needed to Counter Macro Effects of Money Laundering" *IMF Survey*, 29 July
1996, 245–48.

9. Mario Possamai, *Money on the Run* (Toronto: Viking, 1992); and Nick
Kochan, "Cleaning Up by Cleaning Up," *Euromoney* (April 1991), 73–77.

10. Eric Helleiner, *States and the Reemergence of Global Finance* (Ithaca:
Cornell University Press, 1994), 87 fn. 11.

11. See, for example, Vito Tanzi, *Taxation in an Integrated World* (Washington: Brookings, 1995).

12. Tanzi, *Taxation in an Integrated World*, 81.

13. Karin Lissakers, *Banks, Borrowers and the Establishment* (New York:
Basic Books, 1991), 153–54.

14. Carlos Diaz-Alejandro, "Latin American Debt," *Brookings Papers on
Economic Activity* 2 (1984), 379; and Lissakers, *Banks, Borrowers and the
Establishment*, Chapter 6.

15. Eric Helleiner, "Handling 'Hot Money': U.S. Policy Towards Latin
American Capital Flight in Historical Perspective," *Alternatives* 20, no. 1
(1995): 81–110.

16. Indeed, the link between decisions to liberalize capital controls and regulatory initiatives to curtail illicit transactions in the new liberal environment has
often been very close. In the European Community, for example, initiatives to
curtail tax evasion and money laundering began to be pursued at the very same
time that member countries had agreed to abolish capital controls. Helleiner,
States and the Reemergence of Global Finance, 158; and Peter Cullen, "The

European Community Directive," in *Money Laundering*, David Hume Institute (Edinburgh: Edinburgh University Press, 1993), 35.

17. Richard McKenzie and Dwight Lee, *Quicksilver Capital* (New York: Free Press, 1991); and Ingo Walter, *Secret Money* (London: Unwin, 1989), 306, 309–10.

18. Albert Hirschman, *The Passions and the Interests* (Princeton: Princeton University Press, 1977).

19. Naylor, *Hot Money and the Politics of Debt*, 16; Tanzi, *Taxation in an Integrated World*, 134; and Walter, *Secret Money*, 302.

20. Rudiger Dornbusch, "World Economic Problems for the Summit," Mimeo, 1988; and Alberto Giovannini, *International Capital Mobility and Tax Evasion*, CEPR Discussion Paper no. 231 (London: CEPR, 1988).

21. Tanzi, *Taxation in an Integrated World*.

22. Some liberals, however, oppose the criminalization of drugs, arguing that this move is not compatible with liberal ideology.

23. Tom Sherman, "International Efforts to Combat Money Laundering: The Role of the Financial Action Task Force," in *Money Laundering*, David Hume Institute (Edinburgh: Edinburgh University Press, 1993), 20. See also the views of the BIS and EC in W. Gilmore, ed., *International Efforts to Combat Money Laundering* (Cambridge: Grotius Publications, 1992) as well as the IMF in "Tougher Measures," 247. Peter Quirk (Peter Quirk, "Money Laundering: Muddying the Macroeconomy," *Finance and Development* 34, no. 1 [March 1997]: 7–9) of the IMF has argued that money laundering also threatens macroeconomic policymaking and economic growth.

24. For this opposition in the case of initiatives to control capital flight in the 1980s, see Helleiner, "Handling 'Hot Money.' "

25. Few financial institutions or financial centers attempt to rely on money laundering as their chief source of financial business. In cases such as these, however, obviously these "reputational incentives" would be quite different. Also, the enthusiasm of financial institutions for complying with money laundering regulations is dampened somewhat by the fact that this compliance often requires the implementation of expensive and burdensome monitoring procedures.

26. Susan Roberts, "Small Place, Big Money: The Cayman Islands and the International Financial System," *Economic Geography* 71, no. 3 (July 1995): 237–56; Alan Hudson, "Globalization, Regulation, and Geography: The Development of the Bahamas and Cayman Islands Offshore Financial Centres," Ph.D., Geography, Cambridge University, 1996; and Sol Picciotto, *International Business Taxation* (New York: Quorum, 1992), 131.

27. For the influence of such groups on policies toward capital flight, see for example, David Felix, "Latin America's Debt Crisis," *World Policy Journal* 7, no. 4 (Fall 1990): 761; and Jimmy Burns and Gillian Tett, "Probe Into Flight of Capital From Former Soviet Union Abandoned," *Financial Times*, 7 February 1994. For their influence on tax policy, see for example Picciotto, *International Business Taxation*, 126.

28. For example, see H. Richard Friman, "International Pressure and Do-

mestic Bargains: Regulating Money Laundering in Japan," *Crime, Law, and Social Change* 21 (December 1994): 253–66. As Blum (Richard Blum, *Offshore Haven Banks, Trusts and Companies: The Business of Crime in the Euromarket* [New York: Praeger, 1984], 227) notes, many foreign governments initially viewed the U.S. interest in controlling international money laundering as "a U.S. political and ideological attempt improperly to export the responsibility for U.S. crime. Unable to control or clean up its rampant onshore criminality, that is, drug traffic and financial crime, the U.S. blames other countries for it." See also Ian Taylor, "The International Drug Trade and Money Laundering: Border Controls and Other Issues," *European Sociological Review* 8, no. 2 (1992): 181–93.

29. For U.S. activities in the early to mid-1980s, see Blum, *Offshore Haven Banks, Trusts and Companies*; R. Elliot Rosen, "Treasury's Blunder in Paradise," *New York Times*, 4 October 1987; Hudson, "Globalization, Regulation, and Geography," Chapter 6; and Picciotto, *International Business Taxation*, 164–66. Even earlier, the U.S. 1970 Bank Secrecy Act, which imposed reporting requirements on banks for transactions over $10,000, was also driven in part by a desire to curtail international tax evasion. These requirements were not, however, applied at all consistently or rigorously. See Margaret Beare, *Tracing of Illicit Funds: Money Laundering in Canada* (Ottawa: Solicitor General, 1990), 78, 81–82.

30. For example, see Blum, *Offshore Haven Banks, Trusts and Companies*, 224; and Scott MacDonald, "Frontiers for International Money Regulation After BCCI: International Cooperation or Fragmentation?" *Proceedings of the 86th Annual Meeting of the American Society of International Law*, Washington, 1992, 207.

31. Naylor, *Hot Money and the Politics of Debt*, 283; Lissakers, *Banks, Borrowers and the Establishment*, 153; Helleiner, *States and the Reemergence of Global Finance*, 149; and Walter, *Secret Money*, 232–34.

32. Rosen, "Treasury's Blunder in Paradise"; and Picciotto, *International Business Taxation*, 168. Hudson ("Globalization, Regulation, and Geography," 252–53) provides further evidence that U.S. reluctance to crack down on tax evasion in Caribbean offshore havens has been linked to its fear that such a move would hurt foreign investment in the United States.

33. Helleiner, "Handling 'Hot Money.' "

34. Kapstein, *Governing the Global Economy*.

35. See for example, Barry Eichengreen, *Golden Fetters* (Oxford: Oxford University Press, 1992).

36. League of Nations, *International Financial Conference, 1920*, vol. 1 (Brussels: The Dewarichet, 1920).

37. For the resolution, see League of Nations, The Secretariat, "The Flight of Capital," Mimeo. Provisional Economic and Financial Committee, E-F-S, 282.A.165, 30 May 1922, League Archives, Geneva. In its final report in 1925, the committee noted some precedents for this kind of action. Germany, Czechoslovakia, and Austria had a limited agreement after World War I to share information for this purpose, and several similar agreements between European

countries had existed in the pre-1914 period. But each of these arrangements had involved only two or three countries and had very limited coverage. League of Nations, Technical Experts, *Double Taxation and Tax Evasion,* 7 February 1925, Financial Committee, F.212. League of Nations Archives (Geneva).

38. League of Nations, "The Flight of Capital," 1. For the role of Switzerland as a tax haven in the 1920s, see Ronen Palan and Jason Abbott, *State Strategies in the Global Political Economy* (London: Pinter, 1996), 171–72.

39. Picciotto, *International Business Taxation,* 22–27, 251–52.

40. Helleiner, *States and the Reemergence of Global Finance,* Chapter 2.

41. Quote from Craig Murphy, *International Organization and Industrial Change* (Oxford: Oxford University, 1994).

42. In the 1942 U.S. draft of the IMF Articles of Agreement, this latter kind of cooperation was in fact made mandatory. The final Articles of Agreement, however, included a much more limited provision, which required member governments to ensure only that all exchange contracts that contravened other members' exchange control regulations be made "unenforceable" in their territory. See Helleiner, *States and the Reemergence of Global Finance,* 38, 47–49.

43. See Helleiner, "Handling 'Hot Money.' "

44. R.A. Johns and C. Le Marchand, *Finance Centres: British Isle Offshore Development Since 1979* (London: Pinter, 1993), 83–89; and Picciotto, *International Business Taxation,* 256. The potential success of the convention has also been undermined by the fact that the United States has refused to sign on to the provisions of the convention that relate to mutual assistance in recovering taxes.

45. Helleiner, *State and the Reemergence of Global Finance,* 158; Age Bakker, *The Liberalization of Capital Movements in Europe* (London: Kluwer, 1996), 208–9; and Picciotto, *International Business Taxation,* 75.

46. Tanzi, *Taxation in an Integrated World;* and Michael Webb, "International Cooperation and the Taxation of Transnational Business" (paper presented at the annual meeting of the American Political Science Association, San Francisco, CA, 29 August—1 September 1996).

47. The UN Model Treaty is a partial exception in its endorsement of the use of withholding taxes to apply to income paid from "less developed countries" to "developed" countries. There was also considerable support in France and the European Commission for the introduction of an EC-wide withholding tax in 1988, but the opposition of Britain, Luxembourg, the Netherlands, and eventually Germany defeated this proposal. Helleiner, *States and the Reemergence of Global Finance,* 158; Tanzi, *Taxation in an Integrated World,* 129; and Picciotto, *International Business Taxation,* 74–75.

48. Picciotto, *International Business Taxation,* 262–72. Even the EC has been unable to overcome this limitation. A 1988 proposal to institute routine exchange of information concerning the interest incomes paid to nonresidents was rejected on the grounds that it would conflict with bank secrecy and other domestic legal rules (Tanzi, *Taxation in an Integrated World,* 129). Since 1988, the United States has been pushing for bilateral agreements with countries in Latin America and the Caribbean that are more ambitious in areas such as the overriding of confidentiality rules and the automatic sharing of information

(David Felix, "Suggestions for International Collaboration to Reduce Destabilizing Effects of International Capital Mobility on the Developing Countries," in *Monetary and Financial Issues for the 1990s: vol. 3* [New York: United Nations, 1993], 62).

49. See Tanzi, *Taxation in an Integrated World*, 86–89; and Picciotto, *International Business Taxation*, Chapter 10.

50. Tanzi, *Taxation in an Integrated World*, 89.

51. Michael Fooner, *Interpol* (New York: Plenum Press, 1989), 6; and Fenton Bresler, *Interpol* (London: Sinclair-Stevenson, 1992), 252. For the importance of Interpol's role in combatting money laundering, see also Bruce Zagaris and Sheila Castilla, "Constructing an International Financial Enforcement Subregime: The Implementation of Anti-Money-Laundering Policy," *Brooklyn Journal of International Law* 19, no. 3 (1993): 884–86. One previous multilateral initiative was a resolution passed by the Council of Europe in 1977, but it had little impact at the time (Konstantin Magliveras, "Defeating the Money Launderer," *Journal of Business Law* (1992): 163–64; and Gilmore, *International Efforts to Combat Money Laundering*, 169–76).

52. For an overview of these various initiatives, see for example, Johannes Dumbacher, "The Fight Against Money Laundering," *Intereconomics* (July/ August 1995): 177–86; Duncan Alford, "Anti-Money Laundering Regulation," *North Carolina Journal of International Law and Commercial Regulation* 19 (1993–94): 437–68; Berta Hernandez, "RIP to IRP: Money Laundering and Drug Trafficking Controls Score Knockout Victory Over Bank Secrecy," *North Carolina Journal of International Law and Commercial Regulation* 18 (1992–93): 233–304; and Gilmore, *International Efforts to Combat Money Laundering*.

53. Fooner, *Interpol*, 6; and Zagaris and Castilla, "Constructing an International Financial Enforcement Subregime," 884–86.

54. MacDonald, "Frontiers for International Money Regulation After BCCI"; Bruce Zagaris and Scott MacDonald, "Money Laundering, Financial Fraud, and Technology," *George Washington Journal of International Law and Economics* 26, no. 1 (1992): 61–107; and Zagaris and Castilla, "Constructing an International Financial Enforcement Subregime."

55. It is worth noting that this narrow focus has begun to show signs of widening. See Sherman, "International Efforts to Combat Money Laundering," 20; and Dumbacher, "The Fight Against Money Laundering."

56. Roughly one-half to two-thirds of money laundering in the United States is said to be drug money laundering. In Europe and Asia, the portion may be as high as three-quarters (Dumbacher, "The Fight Against Money Laundering," 177).

57. More recently, the United States has been pushing within the FATF to expand the definition of money laundering beyond its narrow association with drug activities (Theodore Greenberg, "Anti-Money Laundering Activities in the United States," *Commonwealth Law Bulletin* [October 1993]: 1870). The 1986 U.S. law that criminalizes money laundering defines the latter to include more than just drug money laundering. Indeed, "tax fraud" is even included as one

of the possible predicates for money laundering (Scott Sultzer, "Money Laundering: The Scope of the Problem and Attempts to Combat It," *Tennessee Law Review* 63, no. 143 [1995]: 176–77).

58. Gilmore, *International Efforts to Combat Money Laundering*, 244.

59. Australia has done this since 1988 and the United States since 1970. On these monitoring provisions, see Sultzer, "Money Laundering," 223–31.

60. Financial Action Task Force on Money Laundering, "Report-February 6, 1990," in *International Efforts to Combat Money Laundering*, W. Gilmore, ed. (Cambridge: Grotius Publications, 1992), 20. On the implementation of the compromise, see Quirk, "Money Laundering," 7.

61. Most recently, Austria has been pressured successfully in this way by the FATF. See "Austria Yields Over Accounts," *Financial Times*, 1 August 1996.

62. On disagreements within the FATF about how best to operationalize this notion, see FATF, "Report-February 6, 1990," 21; and Financial Action Task Force on Money Laundering, "Report-1990–91," in *International Efforts to Combat Money Laundering*, W. Gilmore, ed. (Cambridge: Grotius Publication, 1992), 42.

63. For levels of compliance, see Financial Action Task Force on Money Laundering, "Report-1993–94," *Financial Market Trends* 58 (June 1994): 21–53; and Financial Action Task Force on Money Laundering, "Report-1994–5," *Financial Market Trends* 62 (December 1995): 37–67.

64. Nadelmann ("Global Prohibition Regimes," 483) uses this phrase.

65. David Andelman ("Drug Money Maze," *Foreign Affairs* [July/August 1994]: 105) describes the efforts to expand the membership of FATF as an "intensive campaign that may at times have bordered on coercion."

66. See, for example, FATF, "Report-1994–5."

67. FATF, "Report-February 6, 1990," 20.

68. FATF, "Report-February 6, 1990," 20. For deliberations over the use of a "black list" and actions by individual states, see FATF, "Report-1990–91," 41, 48.

69. FATF, "Report-1990–91," 49.

70. See, for example, International Monetary Fund, "Tougher Measures Needed to Counter Macro Effects of Money Laundering"; Andelman, "Drug Money Maze," 107; and Scott Mortman, "Putting Starch in European Efforts to Combat Money Laundering," *Fordham Law Review* 60 (1992): S464, fn. 271.

71. This includes the G-7, the rest of the EU, Australia, New Zealand, Norway, Switzerland, Iceland, Singapore, Hong Kong, Turkey, and the Gulf Cooperation Council.

72. "Insert Money, Press Start," *The Economist*, 17 February 1996.

73. FATF, "Report-1994–5."

74. Susan Strange, *The Retreat of the State* (Cambridge: Cambridge University Press, 1996), 117–21.

75. For the tension between the reintroduction of controls and liberal arguments, see Hernandez, "RIP to IRP"; Alford, "Anti-Money Laundering Regulation"; Stephen Zamora, "Remarks," *Proceedings of the 86th Annual Meeting*

of the American Society of International Law (Washington, 1992), 202, 208; Lissakers, *Banks, Borrowers and the Establishment*, 158; and Felix, "Suggestions for International Collaboration."

76. Quote from Phil Cerny, "The Dynamics of Financial Globalization," *Policy Sciences* 27, no. 4 (1994): 320, 339. See also Phil Cerny, "American Decline and the Emergence of Embedded Financial Orthodoxy" in *Finance and World Politics*, P. Cerny, ed. (Aldershot: Elgar, 1993), 175–78; and McKenzie and Lee, *Quicksilver Capital*.

77. Helleiner, *States and the Reemergence of Global Finance*.

78. Kapstein, *Governing the Global Economy*.

79. Cerny, "The Dynamics of Financial Globalization," 337; and Cerny, "American Decline and the Emergence of Embedded Financial Orthodoxy," 175–77.

80. Recent initiatives to regulate international securities markets might be seen as a third, but they have been more limited and less successful. See, for example, Underhill, "Keeping Governments Out of Politics"; and Porter, *States, Markets and Regimes and Global Finance*, Chapter 4.

81. Cerny ("American Decline and the Emergence of Embedded Financial Orthodoxy") distinguishes regulatory initiatives designed to be "market constraining" and those that are designed to be market promoting.

82. Kapstein, *Governing the Global Economy*. The United States was also assisted by Britain in this instance who made a similar threat with respect to access to its markets. Porter (*States, Markets and Regimes and Global Finance*, 68–71), however, takes a more skeptical view than Kapstein of the importance of the U.S. role in this case.

83. Gerard Wyrsch, "Treasury Regulation of International Wire Transfer and Money Laundering," *Denver Journal of International Law and Policy* 20, no. 3 (1992): 518.

84. Possamai, *Money on the Run*, 136.

85. These agreements were supposed to require foreign governments to get their own banks to record all U.S. dollar transactions above $10,000 and make them available to the United States on request. Several agreements of this kind have been negotiated with Latin American countries, but even they allow foreign governments to withhold information with minimal justifications. See Sultzer, "Money Laundering," 209 fn. 404; and Possamai, *Money on the Run*, 136–37. Jonathan Beaty and Richard Hornik ("A Torrent of Dirty Dollars," *Time*, 18 December 1989, 50) note that the U.S. government has been reluctant to enforce the Kerry Amendment "for fear of hampering the U.S. banking industry."

86. See, for example, Friman ("International Pressure and Domestic Bargains," 258) on its role in encouraging Japan to adopt anti–money laundering legislation.

87. Naylor, *Hot Money and the Politics of Debt*, 301–4; Sultzer, "Money Laundering," 207; and Hudson, *Globalization, Regulation, and Geography*, 231–38.

88. Naylor, *Hot Money and the Politics of Debt*, 299.

89. Andelman, "Anti-Money Laundering Regulation," 97.

90. Mahvash Alerasool, *Freezing Assets: The USA and the Most Effective Economic Sanction* (London: MacMillan, 1993).

91. Kapstein, *Governing the Global Economy*, 13, 126, 190 fn. 40 (quote); and Porter, *States, Markets and Regimes and Global Finance*, 78, 157.

92. See, for example, Hudson, *Globalization, Regulation, and Geography*, 238–49. As Naylor (*Hot Money and the Politics of Debt*, 302) notes, this is especially true of older, more established secrecy havens, such as Switzerland.

93. Stephen Gill, "Globalization, Market Civilization and Disciplinary Neo-liberalism," *Millennium* 24, no. 3 (1995): 399–423.

94. See, for example, Helleiner, *States and the Reemergence of Global Finance*.

95. Ethan Kapstein, "Between Power and Purpose: Central Bankers and the Politics of Regulatory Convergence," *International Organization* 46, no. 2 (Winter 1992): 265–87.

96. For this phenomenon with respect to law enforcement officials, see Malcolm Anderson, *Policing the World: The Politics of International Police Cooperation* (Oxford: Clarendon, 1989), 13.

97. Moreover, the influence of norms may have been enhanced by the consensual way in which they have been enforced through practices such as the mutual evaluation procedure used in the FATF since 1991.

98. As a recent IMF report ("Tougher Measures Needed to Counter Macro Effects of Money Laundering," 248) put it: "This [international financial] market should become an exclusive club with benefits and obligation for those wishing to belong."

99. There is, however, one important difference. BIS members have threatened to prevent financial institutions from entering their markets if the institution's home government does not follow BIS supervisory practices (Porter, *States, Markets and Regimes and Global Finance*, 61, 72). FATF members are threatening instead to monitor or curtail financial transactions from jurisdictions that do not adopt the FATF recommendations.

100. See especially Walter Wriston, "Technology and Sovereignty," *Foreign Affairs* 67, no. 2 (Winter 1988): 63–75.

101. See FATF, "Report-1994–5."

102. Beare, *Tracing of Illicit Funds*, 243.

103. Charles Kindleberger, "A Historical Perspective," in *Capital Flight and Third World Debt*, J. Williamson and D. Lessard, eds. (Washington: Institute for International Economics, 1987).

104. Helleiner, *States and the Reemergence of Global Finance*, Chapter 2.

105. In its 1992 report, the FATF noted that it is beginning to study measures to detect and deter the use of international wire transfers for money laundering (Zagaris and Castilla, "Constructing an International Financial Enforcement Subregime," 890).

106. See for example, Possamai, *Money on the Run*, 46.

107. SWIFT's two operating centers are in the Netherlands and near Washington, DC. Close to 140 countries are linked by the SWIFT network.

108. Zamora, "Remarks," 203–4.

109. The FATF has, for example, already begun to discuss cooperation with Western Union as the latter has begun to grow in importance as a transmitter of information for financial flows taking place via wire transfers.

110. John Fialka, "Computers Keep Tabs on Dirty Money," *Wall Street Journal*, 8 May 1995; and Neil Jensen, "International Funds Transfer Instructions: Australia at the Leading Edge," *Journal of Law and Information Science* 4, no. 2 (1993): 304–29.

111. For these various arguments see, for example, Stephen Krasner and Janice Thomson, "Global Transactions and the Consolidation of Sovereignty," in *Global Changes and Theoretical Challenges*, J. Rosenau and E.O. Czempiel, eds. (Cambridge: Cambridge University Press, 1989); Kapstein, *Governing the Global Economy*; Leo Panitch, "Globalization and the State," in *Socialist Register 1994*, R. Miliband and L. Panitch, eds. (London: Merlin Press, 1994); Geoffrey Underhill, "Markets Beyond Politics?" *European Journal of Political Research* 19, no. 2–3 (1991): 197–225; and Helleiner, *States and the Reemergence of Global Finance*.

4

The Illicit Trade in Hazardous Wastes and CFCs: International Responses to Environmental "Bads"

Jennifer Clapp

With the rapid globalization of the world economy over the past few decades, there has been a rise in cross-border economic activity that is generally not sanctioned by states or by the general public because of its widely perceived negative impact on society, the economy, or the natural environment.[1] This "illicit" side of the global economy has only recently been recognized in international political economy literature as being an important phenomenon. The rise in undesirable economic activity, or "bads," is seen by many as a signal that state authority is weakened by its inability to stop such activity in an increasingly global economy.[2] But it is not clear that this rise in illicit activity is solely a result of the state's "retreat" from responsibility in the face of economic globalization. While this may be an important element, it seems that state response to the growth in cross-border bads has been somewhat selective, suggesting that in certain cases some states have perhaps been more unwilling than unable to stem the bad activity.

The labeling of certain economic activities as bad often originates with nonstate actors, who try to convince states that such activities are harmful.[3] As more activities are labeled undesirable, states as well as the global community have moved to regulate or prohibit them via national laws and international agreements. Ethan Nadelmann has argued that practices that are prohibited globally go through an evolutionary process from the activity originally being seen as entirely legitimate, to being defined as a bad, to being prohibited through national and international law. If successful, the prohibition regime leads to a significant reduction in the occurrence of the undesirable activity.[4] But the prohibition of a number of transnational economic activities has not necessarily led to their complete disappearance. It appears that certain undesirable economic activities continue to be risked by smugglers in part because the global nature of the world economy enables them to continue their business undetected despite prohibition of the activity, and also because states have chosen to police these activities on a selective basis.

The identification of and response to cross-border economic bads has been particularly evident in recent years with respect to environmental issues. The cross-border trade in two particular bads—the export of hazardous wastes from rich to poor countries and the production, use, and trade in chloroflourocarbons (CFCs)—has gained special attention in recent years. These two problems are different in scope, as the trade in hazardous wastes is largely seen as a transboundary pollution issue, while the emission of CFCs is linked to the more global problem of the destruction of the ozone layer. The political dynamics of the illicit trade in these areas is also different, with most of the concern over the hazardous waste trade being directed to the export of waste from rich to poor states, while the flow of illicit trade in CFCs is mainly from poor states to rich states.

While these are different environmental problems with different dynamics, there are some important similarities from which we can begin to understand state behavior with respect to cross-border economic bads. The trade both in hazardous waste and in CFCs has been seen as being harmful enough to the environment to spark movement toward their prohibition through international legal conventions, namely the Basel Convention and the Montreal Protocol. But the sets of global rules outlawing economic activities that contribute to these two problems have not been entirely successful. Hazardous wastes have continued to find their way to developing countries via a number of channels, and a thriving transnational black market in CFCs has emerged. States in response have tightened the rules and have stepped up their policing of the outlawed activities to varying degrees. But not all states have addressed these issues with an equal sense of urgency.

In this chapter, I examine the way in which states respond to the illicit trade in hazardous wastes and CFCs. I argue that the way in which states define such activities as bad, the scope of their efforts to outlaw them, as well as their willingness and capacity to police the illegal activity are influenced by three main factors. First, the extent of involvement of nonstate actors in identifying undesirable practices and the types of arguments they put forward in doing so seem to be important in determining states' willingness to label certain forms of economic activity as bad. Nongovernmental organizations (NGOs) in particular have gained importance as part of a growing "global civil society" in recent decades.[5] These groups have been extremely important actors in shaping public opinion and in turn have had some degree of influence over states' responses to international environmental issues.[6] As part of this growing importance of nonstate actors, epistemic communities of experts who possess specialized scientific knowledge have been important in shaping states' positions in global environmental politics.[7] International organizations, such as the United Nations Environment Program (UNEP), also have been key nonstate actors that influence the outcome of international environmental treaties.[8]

Second, the structural position of different states in the global political economy seems to have shaped their interests regarding whether or not to take steps to halt the particular bad as well as their ability to do so. Differences in interests and abilities between rich industrialized countries, or the North, and the less industrialized South have long been an important feature of international politics.[9] This point has been especially relevant to states' positions on global environmental issues. In particular, tensions between northern and southern states over the type of action to take on certain issues as well as over financing have arisen in the formation of international environmental regimes.[10] Northern states have been keen to address international environmental issues in ways that do not contravene the principles of global free trade, while the southern states have tended to focus more on their desire to preserve their sovereign rights, and to secure financial support from the North to enhance their capacity to implement environmental agreements.

Third, the stand taken by powerful industry players regarding particular undesirable economic activities has also influenced the degree to which different states have attempted to address them. The growing power of multinational corporations and business actors has been recognized as an important force in the international political economy literature since the 1970s. A main concern has been that states' economic and political sovereignty is eroded by increasingly powerful global corporations.[11] The influence of industry and global corporations is especially relevant today in the analysis of global environmental issues. There is growing attention being paid to the influence that industry has, not just in contributing to environmental problems in the first place but also in determining state responses.[12] Industry lobby groups, for example, have become an important force in the negotiation of environmental regimes in recent years.[13]

Although the emergence of illicit trade in hazardous wastes and CFCs appears to be primarily the result of declining state authority and competence in the face of economic globalization, the role of nonstate actors, the structural position of states in the global political economy, and the interests of industry were also extremely important in shaping state behavior. These influences were evident throughout state involvement in debates to define these practices as bads, and shaped the extent to which states were willing and able to police these activities. In the first section of the chapter, I examine the rise of the hazardous waste and CFC trades, the various actors involved, and arguments put forward in the debate over whether to label each activity as undesirable. In the second section, I outline the regulatory steps that have been taken by states to restrict these activities and examine the role that various actors had in influencing the outcomes. In section three, I look at the factors that are behind the continuation of the trades as illicit activities and the actions taken by states to police them.

The Emergence of Environmental Bads

The emergence of the North to South hazardous waste trade and the growth of CFC production, use, and trade are partially linked to the increasingly global nature of the world economy. In the case of hazardous wastes, however, regulatory differences, as well as differences in financial opportunities between rich and poor countries, were also key factors contributing to the emergence of the problem. Other factors were also at play in the case of CFC proliferation, such as the increased reliance on chemicals in manufacturing without extensive testing.

Nonstate actors were key, alongside states and industry, in the debate that eventually defined hazardous waste and CFC trade as undesirable. In the case of hazardous waste, environmental NGOs and the UNEP were important players alongside developing countries in convincing the global community that the practice was unacceptable. As the most seriously affected by the waste trade, the southern states were among the more vocal states in calling for it to end. Because the problem was a global manifestation of the "not in my backyard" (NIMBY) syndrome, the arguments used by southern states and environmental groups focused mainly on the injustice of exporting wastes to poor countries. In the case of CFCs as ozone-depleting substances, scientists were key players alongside environmental groups, UNEP, and northern states in arguing that these chemicals should be controlled for the greater good of the international community. The main tactic in defining CFCs as bad was to appeal to the broader public with scientific information about how depletion of the ozone would affect personal health. In both cases, industry players were reluctant to see these activities labeled as bad, as doing so would harm their profits.

Despite the resistance from industrial interests, the arguments made with regard to both hazardous waste and CFCs were eventually effective in garnering sufficient agreement from states on the need to regulate the cross-border trade. The degree of support for accepting these activities as bads was different for northern and southern states in both cases. The scientific arguments with respect to CFCs seem to have been more easily accepted by northern states as a basis for action than those based on justice, which were made regarding the North to South export of hazardous wastes. At the same time, the justice arguments with respect to hazardous waste were more readily embraced by southern states than the scientific arguments regarding CFCs. However, both activities were eventually accepted by the global community as warranting action to regulate them.

The Export of Toxic Waste to Developing Countries

Toxic waste disposal was relatively free from strict regulation in industrialized countries until the 1970s, when the disasters at Love Canal and Seveso changed the government attitudes in Europe and the United States on the need for stringent waste disposal regulation. But while the NIMBY syndrome gained momentum and lead to tighter domestic regulations on hazardous waste disposal, the export of hazardous wastes did not rouse concerns until the early to mid-1980s when it was disclosed that the developing countries were recipients of a growing amount of wastes produced in the North. This latter development in particular has raised concerns among international environmental groups because these countries are much less likely than advanced industrialized countries to be equipped to deal with hazards in a way that protects the local environment and human health.[14]

The generation of large amounts of toxic waste itself is linked mainly to industrialization and the increased use of chemicals in manufacturing since the Second World War. In the 1990s, some 300–500 million tons of hazardous waste are generated globally every year.[15] The liberalization of trade over the past twenty years appears to have facilitated the global trade in hazardous waste. It has become very easy to ship hazardous waste around the world, and to do so relatively unnoticed. Exports from rich countries to poor countries began in the 1980s when northern waste-generating firms began to face higher costs and tighter regulations for toxic waste disposal. For most waste-generating firms, the export of their toxic wastes to countries with less strict environmental regulations and lower dumping fees was a cost-saving measure.

Although the amount paid to recipients in the developing world was large given their need for foreign exchange, it was small compared to costs for disposal in advanced industrialized countries. The disposal cost per ton of hazardous waste in the United States in the 1980s was upwards of $250, while at the same time the high-end dumping fee for toxic waste in Africa was around $40 per ton.[16] This discrepancy was epitomized by the experience in Koko, Nigeria, where some 8,000 leaking barrels of chemical wastes, including polychlorinated biphenyls (PCBs), were dumped in a local farmer's backyard. This farmer had rented his yard to an Italian firm for $100 per month, and was not informed of the contents of the barrels the firm was storing there.[17] Following this incident, the Nigerian government adopted a law making hazardous waste importing punishable by death, and the Organization of African Unity adopted a resolution calling the dumping of hazardous waste on the continent a crime against Africa and its people.[18]

The generally weak or nonexistent environmental laws in less industrialized countries in the 1980s, and the poor enforcement of those environmental regulations that have since come into place, have been factors contributing to the inability of developing countries to stem the flow of hazardous effluents into their countries. Waste trade deals are for the most part contracted by individual entrepreneurs in the South, though in a number of cases, governments or government officials have also been involved.[19] The incentives for such deals were very strong, as the short-term economic benefits from taking the waste were often so attractive that the concerns over safe disposal were swept aside. The government of Guinea-Bissau, for example, was offered twice the value of its external debt if it would dispose of up to fifteen million tons of toxic wastes over a fifteen-year period. Lacking other opportunities to earn hard currency, the government originally agreed to the proposal, despite the fact that it did not have the capacity to dispose of the waste safely.[20] After strong pressure from other African governments and environmental groups, who argued that it was a new form of exploitation of the continent, the Guinea-Bissau government renounced the deal.

It is difficult to quantify with precision the extent of the toxic waste trade, as these transactions tend to be carried out covertly by individuals. This is especially true for the North to South trade in wastes, as much of it takes place clandestinely and thus goes unrecorded. In addition, no two countries have the same definition of hazardous waste, making a precise measurement of the waste trade nearly impossible. Despite these difficulties in measurement, it is estimated that some thirty to forty-five million tons of toxic waste cross borders every year.[21] At least 20 percent of this traded waste is estimated to make its way to less industrialized countries.[22] By the early 1990s, industrial country toxic waste had made its way to nearly every part of the developing world.[23] Developing countries in Africa, Asia, Latin America, and Eastern Europe have all been targeted by waste traders. A number of these contracts were canceled once the government in the recipient state discovered the plans, often tipped off by environmental groups and/or the media. How many deals have remained undercover and have resulted in the transfer of wastes from North to South is not known.

When the extent of the practice first came to light in the mid-1980s, there were no universally agreed upon international rules regarding the trade in toxic waste. Some industrialized countries had already begun to construct national laws on domestic disposal and the Organization for Economic Cooperation and Development (OECD) countries had set up guidelines on the export and import of waste among themselves.[24] Most developing countries had few or no laws governing imports or the disposal of hazardous wastes. Though there were no rules governing hazardous waste exports to developing countries, dealers who sought to dispose of wastes in those countries were careful to remain undercover. This was no doubt because they feared that it would be viewed as being undesirable by the general public, and because if the true nature of the export was discovered, they might be held liable for damages and be responsible for the waste's removal. Such firms sought anonymity and protected one another in maintaining their secrecy. Most generators of waste contracted out disposal of their toxic by-products to waste dealers, who often set up "umbrella companies" based in tax havens with bogus company directors. Once a transaction was complete, the firm in question was often dissolved, and the waste traders simply created another for the next waste deal.[25] These fly-by-night operations made tracing the waste to the dealer, much less to the generator, nearly impossible.

By the mid-1980s, developing countries, environmental groups, and UNEP sought to end this trade, or at least to give developing country governments the right to refuse these toxic imports. Many were outraged that the South was receiving toxic by-products from the North, as well as being outraged by the environmental and health risks associated with it, but without any of the benefits from the production that created those wastes. It was argued that the export of waste from North to South was an unjust practice, constituting "garbage imperialism" and "toxic terrorism."[26] Stemming from these concerns, UNEP began to develop international guidelines on the management of hazardous waste. This work resulted in 1987 in the adoption of the Cairo Guidelines on the Environmentally Sound Management of Hazardous Wastes, which sought to ensure the safe handling and disposal of hazardous wastes and encouraged states to acquire permission from importing states before wastes were shipped to them.[27]

While these rules were an important step, they were not binding.

Southern countries argued for further binding legal action to ban waste exports to developing countries. Northern environmental groups, in particular Greenpeace International, also began to campaign for a global ban on the waste trade with poor countries.[28] Exporters of hazardous wastes were obviously opposed to the idea of a ban and argued that international regulations were not necessary on the grounds that some countries have a comparative advantage in accepting wastes.[29] But the principal waste-exporting countries, having already established guidelines for the trade in toxic waste among themselves, did eventually recognize that some guidelines were necessary to ensure that wastes exported to developing countries were disposed of safely.

CFCs as Ozone-Depleting Substances

The first CFCs were invented for General Motors in 1928 for use as refrigerants. These chemicals were perceived as wonder products because their inert, nonflammable, noncorrosive, and nontoxic qualities gave the impression that they were extremely safe for use in a variety of applications. The number of applications for CFCs rapidly increased beyond refrigerants to also include their use in foam production, as propellants for aerosol spray cans, as coolants in air conditioners for cars and homes, and as solvents in the electronics industry. With this expansion in the number of uses, per annum production of the most popular CFCs, CFC-11 and CFC-12, grew from 1.2 million pounds in 1931 to 76.0 million pounds in 1950, to 2.0 billion pounds in 1974.[30] In the 1970s, about 50–60 percent of CFC use was in aerosol spray cans alone.[31]

The production of CFCs was initially very concentrated geographically, with the United States accounting for about 44 percent in 1974, and DuPont accounting for about half of that production.[32] Other countries with the capability to produce CFCs at that time included the UK, France, Germany, Italy, Holland, Japan, Spain, Greece, and several developing countries.[33] By the mid-1980s, a total of some seventeen firms in sixteen countries were producing CFCs.[34] In 1986, the regional breakdown of CFC production was still relatively concentrated, with 35 percent produced in the United States, 36 percent in Western Europe, 8 percent in the Soviet Union and Eastern Europe, 18 percent in Asia, and 3 percent in Latin America.[35] While nearly all U.S. production was used domestically, about half of Europe's production was exported.[36] Even though production of CFCs was relatively concentrated until the mid-1980s, their use became truly global as their applications multiplied and global demand for and trade in the chemicals grew throughout the 1970s and 1980s.

As the production and global use of CFCs expanded, a number of scientific studies were published in the 1970s that theorized that the chlorine in CFCs could damage the ozone layer.[37] Because these studies presented hypotheses that were not yet proven empirically, they sparked controversy over whether there was depletion of the ozone layer, and if so, whether CFCs were the main cause of that depletion.[38] Industry vociferously denied any connection. To make its point, DuPont announced that if CFCs were found not to be usable without harm to humans, it would cease to produce them.[39] The uncertainty about the effects of CFCs on the ozone layer led to further scientific research into the issue in the 1970s and 1980s.

Scientific evidence mounted throughout the 1970s that CFCs had the potential to cause great harm to the ozone layer, and were increasingly labeled as a "bad" by scientists and the general public, particularly in the United States. Fears grew as studies showed that a 1 percent decrease in the density of the ozone layer could lead to a 2 percent increase in ultraviolet radiation and thus a rise in skin cancer.[40] Other potential problems associated with ozone layer destruction included damage to crops, immune system disruption in humans and animals, and an increase in cataracts. There was still an active debate about whether these hypotheses could be proven, but nonetheless there was a growing acceptance that these chemicals could theoretically cause ozone layer destruction. By 1978, the United States banned the use of CFCs in aerosol spray cans, as this was a relatively easy way to substantially reduce the release of CFCs into the atmosphere. Several other countries followed suit, including Canada, Norway, and Sweden.[41] The United States under the Carter administration also threatened further legislation to control CFC production and use, prompting the largest manufacturers, such as DuPont, to begin research into possible alternatives.[42]

Calls for global action were made by scientists, environmental groups, and the general public in a number of industrialized countries. UNEP began to work on global cooperation on the ozone issue as early as 1976, shortly after the publication of the initial studies implicating CFCs as potentially damaging to the ozone layer. The organization held several conferences and created a coordinating committee on the ozone layer to study the issue. In 1982, UNEP began preparing a global treaty for the protection of the ozone layer, as recommended by its governing council the previous year. The result, after negotiations between 1982 and 1985, was the Vienna Convention for the Protection of the Ozone Layer. But the Vienna Convention did not impose any production or

consumption restrictions on signatories. Instead, it represented a broad
agreement to take "appropriate measures," which were not specified,
to protect the ozone layer.[43]

Though CFCs were increasingly determined to be bads by the general
public in industrialized countries, and domestic laws in some of these
countries regulated their use in spray cans, international trade in CFCs
was not regulated before 1987. American CFC manufacturers formed a
lobby group in 1980, the Alliance for Responsible CFC Policy, to fight
any regulations on production or trade in the chemicals. During the
early to mid-1980s, the CFC industry was given a boost in the United
States, as efforts toward further regulation of CFC use were stalled
during the Reagan administration, and research into alternatives by the
large producers was shelved.[44] At the same time, the production and
trade in these chemicals became increasingly global as more countries
gained the technology to produce them. Firms made little attempt to
hide their continued production and use in applications that were not
regulated.

In 1985, the tide of opinion shifted to the side of defining CFCs as
bads, particularly in northern industrialized countries. That year, a
widely accepted scientific study was published proving that a gaping
hole in the ozone layer over Antarctica had developed. Though CFCs
were not yet definitely linked to the destruction of the ozone layer at
this time, studies turned to seeking a connection, which they found by
1987.[45] CFC-producing firms had by then realized that if they wished
to save their reputation as responsible corporations, they should think
about curtailing their use of these chemicals. Many resumed their earlier research on alternatives in the face of further impetus at the global
level to strengthen the Vienna Convention via a protocol to control the
production, use, and trade in ozone-depleting chemicals.

Selective Prohibition: Outlawing Trade in Environmental Bads

Once the export of hazardous wastes to poor countries and the continued production of CFCs were broadly defined as bads by the general
public in both North and South, states began to take action to control
them through binding international legal conventions. The Basel Convention was established to regulate the trade in hazardous wastes, and
the Montreal Protocol set out to regulate the production and use of
CFCs. While some of the key states and industries were initially reluctant to back global treaties in both of these cases on the grounds that
such measures would compromise economic goals like global free
trade, regulations were put in place, if in a somewhat watered down

form from what those who fought hardest to define the practice as a bad had hoped for. The positions of the key states involved in the international negotiations again were affected by the arguments put forward by nonstate actors, states' relative position in the global political economy, and the interests of key industry players.

The negotiation of these treaties revealed some tensions between northern and southern states over the desire to preserve free-trade goals by the former, and a desire to respect state sovereignty and authority by the latter. In the case of the Basel Convention, developing countries desired a right to refuse unwanted imports of hazardous waste, and in the case of the Montreal Protocol they argued for their right to develop their own CFC industry and to have access to assistance for the purchase of alternative technologies. On the other hand, the industrialized countries appeared to be more concerned about the preservation of free-trade goals than about sovereignty in each of the treaties. In the case of the Basel Convention, northern countries argued for the least trade-restrictive regulations, and in the case of the Montreal Protocol they favored domestic production and consumption restrictions over trade measures as the main mechanisms for controlling ozone-depleting substances, although both were ultimately used.

Nonstate actors continued to be important players in the treaty negotiations. Greenpeace International played a central role in shaping the debate over the waste trade, creating an alliance with developing countries in negotiations. The epistemic community of scientists on the CFC issues also continued to be important in the negotiations of the Montreal Protocol, especially as new scientific evidence was introduced during the negotiations, prompting further tightening of the rules. The concerns of industrial interests also influenced the outcome of negotiations and in the end the relevant industries were pleased with the outcomes. The waste-exporting industry was opposed to a ban on the waste trade, while the CFC industry was supportive of an agreement regulating the production, use, and trade of ozone-depleting substances. These positions were influenced largely by each industry's immediate economic interests. Both industries were active in the relevant negotiations, attempting to influence states' positions toward the issues.

The Basel Convention and Other Rules

Many countries in the developing world began to refuse toxic waste imports in the late 1980s when the practice became widely publicized in the international media. They also began to enact laws to forbid such imports. Shortly following the adoption of the 1987 Cairo Guidelines,

UNEP began to work on a binding global treaty to govern the international waste trade. The treaty's particular aim was to control the illegal traffic in wastes by enabling countries to refuse unwanted waste imports. After less than two years of negotiation, the 1989 Basel Convention on the Transboundary Movement of Hazardous Wastes and Their Disposal was agreed upon.

Developing countries were active and largely united in the Basel Convention negotiations, arguing that a complete ban on hazardous wastes exports to developing countries was imperative. Environmental groups sided with developing countries in favor of an outright ban on the waste trade. Industrialized countries and industry lobby groups argued firmly against such a ban, which they saw as counter to the principles of free trade.[46] Because of the divergence of interests, and the short time frame for adopting the convention, concessions had to be made. In the end, the treaty was based on the regulation of the international waste trade rather than a full ban, but it also gave states strong rights to refuse imports if they so wished.

The principal form of regulation mandated by the Basel Convention allows recipient states to control imports of waste. Exporters are required to inform recipients of the nature of the export and receive written consent from the importer before the shipment is sent—a system known as prior informed consent (PIC). The waste must then be disposed of in a manner no less environmentally sound than it would have been disposed of in the country of export. Parties are also asked not to trade wastes at all with nonparties to the convention, unless a bilateral deal, which is consistent with the provisions of the Basel Convention, has been agreed upon.[47] Exports of wastes that do not receive prior informed consent, under which consent is obtained through fraud, which receive consent but which are not disposed of in an environmentally sound manner, or which are exported to a nonparty state that has not entered into a bilateral deal with another state are considered "illegal" under international law. Exporting states of such illegal traffic in waste are required to retrieve and dispose of it at their own cost.[48] The convention was signed by thirty-five countries at the time of its adoption in 1989, and came into force with the necessary forty ratifications by 1992. By early 1996, 100 countries and the European Community had ratified the convention.[49] The United States, however, as a major producer and exporter of hazardous wastes, has not yet ratified the treaty.

The Basel Convention took bold steps through strict trade measures in its attempt to control an environmental bad. But shortly after it was signed, the treaty was subject to criticism from a number of camps. The convention clearly called on states to discriminate against nonparties and allowed countries to ban certain imports. Industry and a number of industrialized states felt that these provisions, particularly the discrimination against nonparties, went against the spirit of the General Agreement on Tariffs and Trade (GATT).[50] This is widely perceived to be the reason that the United States has not yet ratified the treaty. At the same time, industry and northern states were somewhat relieved that the measures called for PIC rather than an outright ban on the trade with developing countries. At the opposite end of the spectrum, environmental groups and many developing countries complained that the convention's vague definition of "environmentally sound" and the lack of strict enforcement mechanisms made it difficult to ensure compliance and left developing countries just as vulnerable as they had been previously to unwanted waste imports.[51] More importantly, the fact that the convention did not ban the waste trade also upset environmental groups and developing countries. Many African countries, for example, refused to sign the convention for that reason.[52] Greenpeace also felt that the convention should have gone further in terms of providing incentives to reduce the production of hazardous wastes in the first place.[53]

Responding to the spate of dumping incidents on the continent in the late 1980s and the fact that the Basel Convention would not necessarily be able to stop such trade in the future, African countries decided in 1991 to draft the Bamako Convention, which bans the import of hazardous wastes. A ban on the waste trade between the European Economic Community (EEC) and the sixty-nine African, Caribbean, and Pacific (ACP) countries was also negotiated as part of the Lomé IV Convention, which came into force in 1991. A number of less industrialized countries, encouraged by environmental NGOs such as Greenpeace, have also enacted national laws and regional conventions banning the importation of hazardous wastes.[54] Regional agreements banning waste imports have been signed in Central America, South America, Southeast Asia, and the South Pacific. With stricter regulations and laws put in place every year, the export of hazardous wastes to developing countries of the sort that took place in the 1980s was by the early 1990s expressly forbidden by many states and by signatories to various environmental treaties.

The Montreal Protocol

With the growing scientific consensus that CFCs were a direct cause of ozone depletion and the news of greater than expected ozone losses in 1985, movement began right away on the negotiation of a protocol to the Vienna Convention to place controls on CFCs and other ozone-depleting substances. The Montreal Protocol was signed by twenty-four states and the EC in 1987. The negotiations of the Montreal Protocol benefitted from growing agreement, scientific and political, that the only way to stop the problem of ozone depletion was to drastically reduce and ultimately phase out the production and use of ozone-depleting substances, especially CFCs. Thus the main control provisions were placed on production and consumption. Trade provisions were also included in the agreement, but their primary purpose was to encourage states to join the regime, and they were not the principal measure of control.

The initial debates over the extent to which CFCs should be regulated were mainly among northern states. During the Montreal Protocol negotiations, the Toronto Group, which included the United States, Canada, the Nordic countries, and Austria and Switzerland, was in favor of strong controls on the production, use, and trade of CFCs and ozone-depleting chemicals.[55] But not all countries were willing to take such drastic control measures. European Community countries worried about tight controls because they exported about half of their production, and tight controls would mean a significant loss in export revenues. Out of this concern, the EC even consulted a legal expert at the GATT on whether the restrictions on trade with nonparties would be inconsistent with global trade norms. The response from the expert was that these measures were allowable under Article XX of the GATT because they were deemed "necessary to protect human, animal, or plant life and health" and also related to the conservation of natural resources.[56] The European Community countries eventually agreed on the need for such controls.

Many developing countries felt that the problem was caused mainly by the North, and that if the latter wanted the participation of the former in the agreement, it would have to make some concessions to them. In particular, developing countries wanted to ensure that they were not going to be denied their right to develop their own CFC industries or their right to import CFCs.[57] Trade restrictions on CFCs and the technology to produce them were thus seen as a threat to those rights. Industry was also initially against the negotiation of the Montreal Protocol and the strict provisions being discussed. But in 1986, the CFC industry reversed its position after DuPont unexpectedly announced its support for a strong protocol. Some have speculated that the reason DuPont changed its position was that it preferred global regulations to unilateral regulations in the United States,[58] and perhaps more importantly it saw a huge opportunity in marketing alternative chemicals if CFCs were eventually banned.[59] Scientists and NGOs continued to be important throughout the negotiation of the protocol in terms of shaping public opinion around the urgency of the problem and the need for action. All of these forces came together in the negotiations and ensured a strong agreement.

The Montreal Protocol agreement placed domestically controlled limits on both the production and consumption of ozone-depleting substances, including CFCs and halons. Production and consumption of CFCs were to be immediately frozen by each country at their 1986 levels and then to be cut to 50 percent of 1986 levels by 1999. Production and use of halons was to be frozen by 1992. The enforcement of these controls was left up to each individual state. Countries with less than 0.3 kilogram of CFC production per capita in 1986 (mainly developing countries) were given a ten-year grace period to meet the production and consumption provisions, as outlined in Article 5 of the protocol.[60] The protocol also included a number of trade provisions. Parties were to ban the import of controlled substances from any nonparty from 1990, and were not allowed to export controlled substances to nonparties from 1993. Parties were also to refrain from exporting controlled substances or technology used to produce controlled substances to any nonparty, and to ban, from 1992, the import of products containing controlled substances from nonparties. Parties were to study the feasibility of trade restrictions on goods produced with CFCs as well. To alleviate concerns raised about how compatible such restrictions were with the GATT, the protocol exempted nonparties who were in compliance with production controls from the import restrictions placed on parties.[61]

As new scientific evidence was introduced indicating a more rapid than expected rate of ozone depletion, the production and use controls of the agreement were tightened. The Montreal Protocol was amended at the London Meeting of the Parties in 1990 to reflect this new concern. The phaseout target for CFCs and halons was increased to a 100 percent phaseout by the year 2000 and a few more ozone-depleting substances were now controlled. Also in 1990, a Multilateral Fund was set up with $160–$240 million for countries consuming less than 0.3 kilogram of ozone-depleting substances per capita, and developing countries retained their ten-year delay for implementing reductions and phaseouts. Further amendments were made at the Copenhagen Meeting of the Parties in 1992, advancing the complete phaseout for CFCs to 1996 and 1994 for halons. The import of products containing ozone-depleting substances from nonparties began to be banned from 1992. The ten-year delay for developing countries in meeting these targets was kept, while the Multilateral Fund was made permanent. The parties decided not to impose further trade restrictions at this point on products produced with controlled substances.[62]

By mid-1996, 157 parties had ratified the Montreal Protocol, though fewer parties have ratified the 1990 London amendments and the 1992 Copenhagen amendments.[63] Though many developing countries initially argued that the trade restrictions against nonparties were an infringement on southern states' right to develop their own CFC industry, fears of a challenge to the GATT waned as many developing countries signed and ratified the treaty in order to avoid restrictions on their exports of goods containing ozone-depleting substances and to take advantage of the financial support available from the Multilateral Fund.[64]

Getting Around the Rules: Black Market Wastes and Contraband CFCs

Both the Basel Convention and the Montreal Protocol were heralded as path-breaking agreements, which sought to deal with environmental problems by adopting strict economic measures to stop undesirable transactions leading to environmental harm. But soon after both agreements were signed, it was clear that a significant portion of the activities that they sought to control was able to circumvent the rules. The weak ability of developing countries to exercise their right to protect themselves from unwanted waste imports, particularly those destined for recycling operations, resulted in a continuation of the North to South waste trade. The lag in implementation of the Montreal Protocol production and use of phaseouts for CFCs created a situation ripe for an illegal CFC trade. In both cases, the rise of illicit trade led to enhanced policing of the problem by states and nonstate actors. However, the process of gaining the support for tighter rules and enhanced policing, as well as the mechanisms chosen for doing so, was different in each case. Again, the North-South dynamics, the arguments put forward by nonstate actors about the nature of the bad, and the interests of industry were influential in determining the willingness and ability of states to respond.

Because the control mechanisms were different in each of the treaties, the ways in which the leaks were dealt with were different in each case. With hazardous wastes, measures were taken to tighten the trade restrictions by installing a complete ban on the waste trade between OECD and non-OECD countries who were parties to the Basel Convention. Environmental NGOs were key in leading this campaign to ban the waste trade and worked closely with developing countries on strategies to achieve this outcome. While this measure enhanced the South's enforcement capacity by forcing other states to support developing countries in exercising their right to refuse imports, it went against the North's desire to preserve free-trade goals. This helps to explain why some northern states and waste-exporting industry groups were outraged at the move and have subsequently softened their support for the treaty. In the ozone case, the onus for implementing the Montreal Protocol remained on the CFC-importing states, but measures were taken by some states to control illicit imports through enhanced policing operations at their borders. While such enhanced trade controls could be perceived as also going against free-trade goals, these arguments were not raised largely because these measures were encouraged and supported by the chemical industry in those countries.

Illegal Waste Exports and the Growth of Recycling

The signing of the Basel Convention and other regional and national legal initiatives did not put a stop to the export of hazardous wastes to less industrialized countries. Instead, it prompted waste traders in many cases to become more clever in their schemes to export wastes. While exports of toxic waste to developing countries for disposal purposes did decrease somewhat, a moderate black market in waste exports for disposal emerged, and there was a significant growth in exports of waste to developing countries for the purpose of recycling—much of which escaped the Basel rules.

Since the Basel Convention was adopted, there have been continued reports of illicit waste exports destined for disposal operations, indicating that incentives to continue this trade have not been eliminated.[65] In 1991, for example, Somalia received a waste shipment proposal in the midst of famine and war. This proposal was initially accepted by the health minister of the deposed government, who was allegedly offered a large bribe for letting in the wastes.[66] Although the deal was believed to have been canceled, it has been reported that several European waste trading firms had agreed to pay the Somali government $80 million to take up to 500,000 tons of toxic waste over a period of twenty years. The firms stood to make $8 to $10 million per shipment.[67] In another case, exporters attempted to disguise the toxic waste and sell it as a legitimate product. In 1992, Bangladesh received 1,000 tons of copper smelter furnace dust (containing high levels of lead and cadmium), which was mixed with fertilizer by several U.S. firms and individuals.[68] This mixture was subsequently sold to the government of Bangladesh with assistance from the Asian Development Bank. But some Bangladeshi farmers had already spread it on their fields before they were made aware of its contents.[69] The firms involved were eventually convicted by the U.S. government and forced to pay a fine of $1 million. Disguised waste has been a serious problem for developing countries, as most do not have the resources to ascertain the contents of every import container. The extent to which this continues to be a problem is not known for this very reason. This weakness on the part of developing countries represented an inability of the South to exercise its right to refuse unwanted imports.

The continuing problem of illegal exports was discussed at the first Conference of Parties (COP) to the Basel Convention in 1992. Developing countries were still in favor of altering the convention to include a ban on waste exports to developing countries, as they felt that it was the duty of the North to respect the sovereign rights of the South regarding waste imports. The industrialized countries were still hesitant, being more accepting of the argument for restrictions on disposal than for a ban on recycling in developing countries. No decisions were made on a ban at this time, but the final resolution of the COP requested that OECD states refrain from exporting wastes to developing countries for final disposal.[70] It was understood that a decision on whether or not to impose an outright ban on waste exports for disposal would be discussed at the next COP. While this was a strong stand to take on this aspect of the waste problem, the issue of recycling was left hanging. It was decided that the parties would discuss the issue of recycling at a later date after more study of the issue had been carried out.[71]

By the early 1990s, most of the hazardous waste trade with developing countries shifted from that destined for disposal to that headed for recycling operations. The Basel Convention makes no distinction between wastes for recycling and wastes for disposal, and all are thus theoretically subject to the PIC procedure outlined in the convention. But the rules of the convention have been difficult to enforce when hazardous wastes are not labeled as hazardous wastes. Even though these exports are technically covered by the Basel Convention and thus require prior informed consent, and exporting countries are required to ensure that they are dealt with in an environmentally sound manner in the country of import, many of the wastes that are exported for recycling do not follow these rules. The reason is that many exporting countries do not consider these wastes to be hazardous. Equally important, countries not yet party to the Basel Convention, such as the United States, have been able to export for recycling without restrictions. With such loopholes present, more firms in recent years have begun to relabel hazardous wastes as commodities to be recycled rather than as wastes to be dumped, which has enabled them, by and large, to continue their trade.

The terms "recycling" and "recovery" of hazardous waste tend to give the impression that such wastes are being dealt with in an environmentally friendly manner. But it is often the case that these recycling processes are extremely polluting. Because a large proportion of these wastes are not recoverable, they must still be disposed of either in landfills or by incineration, both of which often result in environmental hazards. Moreover, many hazardous wastes are exported to developing countries under the pretext of recycling, when in fact the waste is not recycled at all. Rather, such exports have in many cases been revealed as a disguise for waste disposal.[72] According to the environmental group Greenpeace, some 80–90 percent of all waste export schemes to developing countries are now under the label of products destined for recycling operations.[73]

The documented cases of environmentally unsound recycling of imported hazardous wastes in developing countries include waste-to-energy schemes and the recycling of plastics and heavy metals, which are carried out in dangerous circumstances.[74] Most of these cases were investigated and publicized by environmental NGOs. Greenpeace International was especially active on the hazardous waste trade issue and released a large number of reports and newsletters that exposed cases in an attempt to embarrass exporting countries. In the early 1990s, a number of developing countries began to take measures to impose national bans on the import of hazardous waste for recycling in addition to the existing ban on imports for disposal.[75] Though developing countries had the right to refuse hazardous waste imports as allowed in the Basel Convention, policing their national bans has proven extremely difficult given their weak resources, and they increasingly wanted assurance that the burden of implementing a ban did not rest entirely on the importing state. Developing countries thus sought a firm agreement from OECD countries that they too would assist the policing of this trade by banning its export to non-OECD countries for both disposal and for recycling.

At the Second Conference of Parties held in Geneva in 1994, developing countries and environmental NGOs argued again for a decision to ban the waste trade with developing countries. They wanted this ban to include waste destined for recycling, arguing that environmentally unsound waste disposal and dirty recycling of northern-generated hazardous wastes had become a growing problem in the third world. But a small number of OECD countries and industry groups were vocal in arguing against such a ban. They were insistent that not all exports of hazardous wastes for recycling had been carried out in an environmentally unsound manner, and argued that indeed recycling was beneficial for the South's development. While many OECD countries began to accept the wishes of the developing countries to incorporate a ban into the treaty, a group of seven OECD countries, including the United

States, UK, Australia, Germany, Canada, Japan, and the Netherlands, was set to stand firmly against a full ban.

The seven OECD countries in question, under international pressure from environmental groups, developing countries, and those OECD countries sympathetic to the ban, gradually increased their willingness to accept a ban on waste exports for disposal. But they were determined not to budge on the issue of recycling. As a growing number of OECD countries joined the full ban side, however, the small group of states was increasingly marginalized and eventually gave in. In the last moments of the 1994 COP meeting, a decision was adopted that effectively bans the toxic waste trade for both disposal and recycling between the OECD countries and non-OECD countries who are signatories of the Basel Convention. This decision was made on the grounds that such disposal and recycling was, according to evidence to date, highly unlikely to be carried out in an "environmentally sound manner" in non-OECD countries.[76] The ban decision, though nonbinding, applies to wastes exported both for disposal (effective immediately) as well as those destined for recycling (effective December 31, 1997). The U.S. government was upset at the decision, saying that it went too far and was counter to free-trade goals. The U.S. Chamber of Commerce pulled its support for the treaty, while the Bureau of International Recycling argued that the decision denied developing countries of much needed raw materials, and cost industry millions in lost exports.[77]

While industry and a small number of industrialized countries remained opposed to the idea of a binding ban on all waste trade between OECD and non-OECD countries, the momentum on the issue did not die. Greenpeace International stepped up its campaign for a ban throughout 1994 and 1995. The question of imposing a full ban was raised again at the Third Conference of the Parties to the Basel Convention, which met in Geneva in 1995. At this meeting, the Norwegian government put forward a proposal to formally amend the convention to incorporate the ban decision, which would make it legally binding on parties. Over the course of 1994–1995 the International Chamber of Commerce had attempted to round up non-OECD countries that imported wastes for recycling to oppose the ban amendment, but was unsuccessful.[78] The developing countries held firm, and although several of the OECD countries still opposed the ban amendment going into the meeting, they were pressured in the end to support it. A consensus was finally reached to adopt an amendment to the convention that incorporates a ban on waste exports to non-OECD countries for final disposal and recycling.[79] This amendment must now be ratified by 75 percent of the parties before it comes into force.

It is not clear whether the ban will lead to a decrease in the illegal traffic of hazardous wastes, as traffickers are much more careful to hide their trade now than they were in the 1980s. In an attempt to ensure that rules of the convention are enforced, the Basel Convention Secretariat has now begun to cooperate with the World Customs Organization and Interpol to crack down on illegal transfers of hazardous waste.[80] Although developing countries still lack the financial and technical resources to police their imports, the efforts on the part of the global community could be seen as a reinforcement of the authority of these countries from the outside by enabling them to exercise their rights and to fulfill their duties as required by the convention. Critics of the ban, however, have argued that the ban is in fact an infringement on the South's authority, as it is leaving decisions on which wastes to import in the hands of an international treaty.[81]

Following the ban decision there has been a growing debate on whether the ban is in fact "legal" under the GATT.[82] Though some of these analyses have argued that it does violate GATT's principles of free trade, as yet there have not been any formal challenges to the Basel Convention filed with the World Trade Organization (WTO). The hazardous waste recycling industry has come forward to express its displeasure at the ban decision.[83] In the meantime, the definition of hazardous waste itself is being more clearly defined in the annexes to the convention, a measure that is likely to avert any future complaints that might be filed at the WTO. This clear delineation of which wastes are and are not covered by the convention, based on their scientific properties and risk factors, seeks to reach agreement on what precisely is bad while at the same time preserving liberal trade goals.

The Emerging Black Market in CFCs

The Montreal Protocol and its amendments were also unsuccessful in stemming the bad transactions they sought to eliminate. A thriving black market in CFCs has emerged in the 1990s in direct response to the protocol's production and consumption control provisions. This illegal trade in CFCs really only emerged in full force once production phaseouts for industrialized countries were within a few years of coming into force. A number of smuggling schemes have been uncovered in Western Europe and the United States. There are several reasons for the emergence of this black market.

The delay in implementing the phaseouts between developing countries and industrialized countries, necessary in the first place to garner widespread agreement to the Montreal Protocol, has been the major force behind the illegal trade in CFCs. As outlined in the agreement and its amendments, countries with per capita production of less than 0.3 kilogram in 1986 are given ten years (or more, depending on which of the amendments they ratified) to phase out production and consumption of CFCs. Thus some countries, mainly developing countries, are able to legally produce CFCs, while others, mainly the industrialized countries, could not as of January 1, 1996 (or January 1, 1995 in the case of the European Union [EU]). This situation has been exacerbated as Russia and many Eastern European countries, originally scheduled to phase out production and consumption of CFCs along with other industrialized countries by January 1, 1996, as outlined in the Montreal Protocol, announced in 1995 that they were unable to meet that target.[84] Russia asked for a five- to ten-year extension for its phaseout.

Meanwhile, as phaseouts have been implemented in most industrialized countries, production in the developing world increased by some 87 percent between 1986 and 1993, while exports from the South have increased by seventeen-fold in the same period.[85] India and China are now major producers and exporters of CFCs, with production in each country rising by eightfold and fivefold, respectively, between 1986 and 1994.[86] But while restrictions were placed on production, consumption, and imports in industrialized countries, demand for CFCs in these countries has nonetheless remained strong. Though industrialized countries had by 1994 reduced CFC demand to about a quarter of its 1986 level, the remaining demand is expected to be both expensive and difficult to eliminate.[87] The recharging of existing refrigeration equipment has been a major source of this demand.[88] Small auto repair shops in particular have a strong demand for CFCs, which are used to recharge automobile air conditioners. Because they are small operations, it is difficult to trace where they purchase and use CFCs. Although cars manufactured in the United States after 1996 are equipped with CFC-free air conditioners, it is difficult to say when the old air conditioners, which still use CFCs, will be eliminated or replaced.[89]

A further important factor in the emergence of the black market was the way in which the domestic regulations to ensure implementation of the provisions in the agreement were undertaken, particularly in the United States. A system of allowances for production and imports of virgin CFCs was put into place in the United States, but CFCs that were reused or recycled did not count against firms' allowances. The United States also put in place a relatively steep tax on ozone-depleting substances such as CFCs at rates that rose as the phaseout date approached. This tax represented an attempt to ensure that alternatives were roughly the same price as CFCs.[90] This tax was $4.00 per pound in the early 1990s, and rose to $5.30 per pound in the mid-1990s.[91] At the same time, the cost of producing CFCs was only about $2.00 per pound.

These factors, combined with the high demand in the United States, made the United States ripe for illegal imports of CFCs. Contraband CFCs began to make their way to the United States, and are now the second most important illegal import into Miami, Florida, after drugs.[92] Sources of these illegal CFCs found in the United States include India, China, Russia, Eastern Europe, and Southeast Asia. Ozone Action, a U.S. environmental group, claims that some 22,000 tons of CFCs, the equivalent of one-third of U.S. production, is smuggled into the United States, while the U.S. government claims that illegal imports are only some 10,000 tons.[93] This translates into losses in tax revenues for the U.S. government of some $100–$200 million per year.[94]

The EU has also been plagued with illegal CFC imports. The EU did not tax CFCs or install quotas to meet its production and consumption targets, but smuggling emerged nonetheless as demand for the chemicals has remained high. Moreover, the earlier phaseout date for use of CFCs in Europe (January 1, 1995) and its proximity to Russia, which has expanded its exports and has not yet complied with required phaseout targets, has contributed to the problem.[95] Importers of illegal CFCs into EU countries have also been able to take advantage of a loophole in EU law, which allows the import of recycled CFCs.[96] This has led smugglers to disguise virgin CFCs as being recycled, or to bribe customs officials into certifying that they were recycled, in order to import their contraband. Some 12,000 tons of CFCs are reported to have entered France illegally in the first eight months of 1995, while some 4,000 tons are estimated to have entered the United Kingdom in that same time period.[97]

The illegal trade in CFCs has been significant, largely because there have been huge incentives to evade the payment of taxes on ozone-depleting substances in the United States coupled with the advantage of existing demand in a situation of short supply in both the United States and the EU. This growing trade in illegal CFCs has upset the large chemical producers such as DuPont, ICI, Alf-Atochem, and Allied Signal who are now phasing out their production of CFCs. The chemicals industry estimates that up to 20 percent of all CFCs in current use globally were bought on the black market.[98] Chemical producers have raised complaints to governments about these imports, and have demanded action be taken to stop them.[99] The Alliance for Responsible Atmospheric Policy (formerly the Alliance for Responsible CFC Policy), which once lobbied against regulation, is now lobbying the U.S. government to step up its crackdown on illegal CFC imports.

Not only are the chemical industry's sales of CFC alternatives in industrialized countries damaged by this trade, but also hurt is their legal sale of CFCs, which they are still allowed to produce for export and for "essential use" at home.[100] Their concern was raised by a growth in imports of "recycled" CFCs from countries that do not have the capacity to recycle them.[101] Russia, for example, exports a substantial amount of "recycled" CFCs, despite the fact that it lacks significant recycling facilities.[102] At the 1994 meeting of the parties to the Montreal Protocol, both the United States and the EU called for the international registration and regulation of recycling plants.[103] Another problem has been excessive imports into some countries far beyond their capacity to use them, which suggests that these countries are being used as points of transshipment for illegal CFCs into the United States and Europe. The Netherlands Antilles, for example, has been cited as importing between 1,500 and 2,000 metric tons of CFCs in 1994 and 1995, when its maximum consumption is about 99 tons per year.[104]

The recipient states of illegal CFCs, mainly the United States and the EU, but also other countries such as Taiwan and Canada, are increasingly on guard to catch CFC smugglers. This represents a move on the part of some parties to the Montreal Protocol to install border controls to capture illegal imports. Most action has been taken in the United States, where a loss of tax revenue is a large incentive for the government to crack down on smugglers. An interagency task force was set up in October 1994, which includes the U.S. Environmental Protection Agency (EPA), U.S. Customs, and the Internal Revenue Service, along with the cooperation of the departments of Commerce and Justice.[105] The task force, code-name Operation Cool Breeze, has been successful in capturing some of the illegal trade through its investigations. In its first year of operation, it confiscated 500 tons of illegal CFCs and recouped some $40 million in taxes.[106] The CFCs that are confiscated have been handed over to the U.S. Defense Department for its stockpiles, which it uses to recharge its older equipment.[107] Over a dozen cases have been tried so far, with eleven convictions having being made by the end of 1995.[108] The U.S. government has also taken measures to control the problems of recycled CFC imports and the illegal retention of CFCs, which were supposed to be reexported to developing countries. These measures include the requirement after 1995 of all importers of recycled CFCs to petition to the U.S. EPA.[109] A similar process is being sought by the EPA for imports of CFCs that are to be reexported.[110] Further cooperation between the EPA and U.S. Customs was announced in early 1996 to crack down on smuggling of illegal CFCs.[111]

While the U.S. government has taken elaborate steps to halt the illegal CFC trade, there has been much less action in Europe to do the same, probably because the incentive to collect tax is not present. Due to pressure from both the United States following its own enforcement successes and from industry in Europe, the EU established a working group in 1995 made up of industry and enforcement authorities. This working group, however, is reported to have had much less success than the United States in catching smugglers.[112] The EU has also stepped up restrictions on imports of used CFCs, even though these are permitted under the Montreal Protocol.[113] In addition, the EU has tightened regulations by requiring a license for imports of CFCs that are for reexport, which was not required before January 1, 1995.[114] Canada and Taiwan have also begun to take action to catch and convict CFC smugglers.[115] The meeting of the parties to the Montreal Protocol tried to address this growing problem at its 1995 meeting in Vienna, but there has been no agreement yet on what should be done to stop it. The parties decided to conduct a study on the illegal CFC trade.[116] At the Eighth Meeting of the Parties to the Montreal Protocol held in November 1996 in San José, Costa Rica, the parties adopted Decision VIII/20 on Illegal Imports and Exports on Controlled Substances.[117] This decision requests non-Article 5 countries to report to the Ninth Meeting of the Parties with respect to actions taken to establish a system for validating and approving imports, before they are imported, of all used, reclaimed, or recycled ozone-depleting substances. It also stated that importers of such substances should be able to sufficiently demonstrate to approving authorities that they genuinely had been previously used. Whether this step will be enough to halt the trade remains to be seen.

Conclusion

The export of hazardous wastes to developing countries and the production, use, and trade of CFCs have been defined as bads in the eyes of the global community. But the extent to which states have responded to these bads by outlawing and policing them has varied. It is not clear that it is just state inability to respond to these issues in the face of an increasingly global economy that has resulted in the proliferation of bads and their illicit trade even once measures are taken to outlaw them. Rather, three key factors appear to have had the most influence in determining how states responded to the definition of these particular bads, their prohibition, and state policing of the problem. These are first, the extent of involvement of nonstate actors and the type of arguments they used in defining the problem as a bad; second, the structural position of different states in the global political economy, which was affected by their interest in dealing with the particular problem, as well as their capacity to do so; and third, the interests of powerful industry players.

These dimensions were present in both cases, though the dynamics differed in each, resulting in different outcomes.

The rise of the waste trade was seen by southern states as a direct threat to their authority. The focus on the injustice of the transboundary relocation of wastes to poor countries by environmental groups, UNEP, and southern states led to the definition of the practice as a bad. Southern states called for a ban to the practice, which they felt would enhance their ability to exercise their sovereign right to refuse such imports. But the concern expressed by northern states and industry that banning the practice would run counter to principles of free trade led to a convention that regulated, rather than banned the trade, while attempting to preserve southern states' sovereign rights by allowing them to individually refuse imports. Though industry and some northern states felt that the regulations in the convention went against free-trade goals, they saw this as better than a ban. The Basel Convention, however, failed to stop illegal transfers of hazardous wastes to developing countries, because even though southern states had the right to refuse imports, they did not always have the ability to exercise that right. This led southern states and environmental groups to push harder for a complete ban on the trade, which while going even further against the principles of free trade and angering industry, would force northern states to assist them in exercising their sovereign right to refuse waste imports. Northern states eventually, under pressure, went along with this ban, but some key states as well as industrial interests have since softened their support for the treaty. Whether the treaty will be enforceable under these circumstances remains to be seen.

The problem of CFCs depleting the stratospheric ozone layer was perceived as a threat to all states' authority because of the global effects it would have on ecosystems and human health. Scientists, along with a number of northern states, relied on scientific arguments put forth by an epistemic community to define CFCs as bads that needed to be controlled. Industry, while initially against such controls, turned in favor of them as market opportunities for alternative chemicals became apparent. In formulating international regulations on CFCs and other ozone-depleting substances, northern states sought to control production and consumption at the domestic level and to preserve liberal trade policies as much as possible, though they did still suggest trade restrictions. Southern states were initially less concerned about the issue, until it was evident that the production, use, and trade controls might infringe on their right to develop their own CFC industries, and might make alternative technologies extremely expensive. The result was a treaty that focused primarily on domestic production and consumption controls, and that offered a grace period and financial assistance to developing countries as a way to relieve their concerns. But this agreement was not able to eliminate the problem of CFCs in the northern countries that were phasing them out. A black market in CFCs has emerged, which is a response to both the difference in the treaty provisions for northern and southern states and the way in which northern states implemented their phaseouts of these chemicals. The response of northern states was to step up policing of CFC imports, while southern states have done little to address the illicit export of CFCs. Though the northern states' actions represented a move against liberal trade goals, the actions were endorsed by industry because of its interest in selling CFC alternatives.

As these two cases show, the responses of states to the rise of environmental bads can be very different, with some states showing more interest in stopping certain activities than others. Thus it is very difficult to generalize about how states will respond to undesirable economic activities. However, certain factors do seem to be important, at least in these two cases, in explaining the variation in state responses. The role of nonstate actors, the relative position of states in the global political economy, and the interests of powerful industrial players were all influential in determining state responses to the rise of illicit, or bad economic activity. Thus while the increasingly global nature of the world economy may be contributing to the rise of undesirable economic activity, the response of states is not solely one of retreat from responsibility or incapacity to address the issue.

Notes

1. I would like to thank Nancy Palardy for research assistance, and Peter Andreas, Rich Friman, Derek Hall, Eric Helleiner, Peter Katzenstein, and Janice Thomson for helpful comments. I would also like to thank the Social Sciences and Humanities Research Council of Canada for financial support for this research.

2. Stanley Hoffmann, "The Crisis of Liberal Internationalism," *Foreign Policy* 98 (Spring 1995): 175; and Susan Strange, *The Retreat of the State* (Cambridge: Cambridge University Press, 1996).

3. Ethan Nadelmann, "Global Prohibition Regimes: The Evolution of Norms in International Society," *International Organization* 44, no. 4 (Autumn 1990): 481–82.

4. Nadelmann, "Global Prohibition Regimes," 484–86.

5. Ronnie Lipschutz, "Reconstructing World Politics: The Emergence of Global Civil Society," *Millennium* 21, no. 3 (1992): 389–420; and Thomas Wiess and Leon Gordenker, *NGOs, the UN and Global Governance* (Boulder: Lynne Rienner, 1996).

6. On global civil society and NGOs in global environmental politics, see

Ronnie Lipschutz, *Global Civil Society and Global Environmental Governance* (Albany: SUNY Press, 1996); Paul Wapner, *Environmental Activism and World Civic Politics* (Albany: SUNY Press, 1995); and Tom Princen and Matthias Finger, *Environmental NGOs in World Politics* (New York: Routledge, 1994).

7. Peter Haas, "Introduction: Epistemic Communities and International Policy Coordination," *International Organization* 46, no. 1 (Winter 1992): 1–35; and Peter Haas, "Do Regimes Matter? Epistemic Communities and Mediterranean Pollution Control," *International Organization* 43, no. 3 (Summer 1989): 377–403.

8. Gareth Porter and Janet Welsh Brown, *Global Environmental Politics* (Boulder: Westview Press, 1996).

9. Stephen Krasner, *Structural Conflict: The Third World Against Global Liberalism* (Berkeley: University of California Press, 1985).

10. See, for example, Marian Miller, *The Third World in Global Environmental Politics* (Boulder: Lynne Rienner, 1995); and Porter and Brown, *Global Environmental Politics*.

11. Raymond Vernon, *Sovereignty at Bay* (New York: Basic Books, 1971); and Robert Gilpin, *U.S. Power and the Multinational Corporation: The Political Economy of Foreign Direct Investment* (New York: Basic Books, 1975).

12. See, for example, David Korten, *When Corporations Rule the World* (West Hartford: Kumarian Press, 1995); and Richard Barnet and John Cavanagh, *Global Dreams: Imperial Corporations and the New World Order* (New York: Simon and Schuster, 1994).

13. Pratap Chatterjee and Matthias Finger, *The Earth Brokers* (New York: Routledge, 1994).

14. This is not to argue that all waste disposal and hazardous industries in the OECD countries are handled in an entirely environmentally sound manner. Disasters such as Love Canal and Seveso, as well as the continuing controversies over the cleanup of toxic dump sites in the United States, are reminders that even the OECD countries have problems with safe waste disposal and industrial hazards. But these countries do have access to technology that can improve the safety of hazardous waste disposal and industry. The irony is that rather than use this technology, these countries are increasingly exporting their hazards to the non-OECD world where access to technology to ensure environmentally sound handling of such hazards is distinctly lacking.

15. Mustapha Tolba, "The Global Agenda and the Hazardous Wastes Challenge," *Marine Policy* 14, no. 3 (1990): 205.

16. Tolba, "The Global Agenda and the Hazardous Wastes Challenge," 206.

17. For further details on this case, see Bill Moyers and the Center for Investigative Reporting, *Global Dumping Ground* (Cambridge: Lutterworth Press, 1991), 1–2; *New African*, no. 253 (October 1988): 22; and Economist Intelligence Unit, *Nigeria Country Report*, no. 4 (1988): 8–9.

18. Francois Roelants du Vivier, "Control of Waste Exports to the Third World," *Marine Policy* 14, no. 3 (1990): 268.

19. In Guinea, for example, government officials and the Norwegian ambassador were implicated in a hazardous waste trade deal. See Jennifer Clapp,

"Africa, NGOs and the International Toxic Waste Trade," *Journal of Environment and Development* 3, no. 2 (1994): 20.

20. Brian Wynne, "The Toxic Waste Trade: International Regulatory Issues and Options," *Third World Quarterly* 11, no. 3 (1989): 121; and Jim Puckett, "Dumping on Our World Neighbours," in *Green Globe Yearbook*, H. Bergesen, M. Norderhaug, and G. Parmann, eds. (Oxford: Oxford University Press, 1992), 95.

21. Christopher Hilz, *The International Toxic Waste Trade* (New York: VanNostrand Reinhold, 1992), 20; and see also *ENDS Report*, no. 223 (August 1993), 15.

22. Hilz, *The International Toxic Waste Trade*, 20–21; and Christopher Hilz and M. Radka "Environmental Negotiations and Policy: The Basel Convention on Transboundary Movement of Hazardous Wastes and Their Disposal," *International Journal of Environment and Pollution* 1, no. 1–2 (1991): 56. Because of difficulties in measurement, no precise figure is available. Hilz (*The International Toxic Waste Trade*, 21), however, has estimated that up to 56 percent of internationally traded wastes make their way to non-OECD countries. This figure is based on OECD country exports of hazardous wastes minus OECD country imports of hazardous wastes.

23. See for example Jim Vallette and Heather Spalding, eds., *The International Trade in Wastes: A Greenpeace Inventory* (Washington, DC: Greenpeace, 1990); Paul Heller, ed., *Database of Known Hazardous Waste Exports from OECD to non-OECD Countries, 1989–March 1994* (Washington, DC: Greenpeace, 1994); and Jennifer Clapp "The Toxic Waste Trade with Less-Industrialized Countries: Economic Linkages and Political Alliances," *Third World Quarterly* 15, no. 4 (1994): 505–18.

24. Katharina Kummer, "The International Regulation of Transboundary Traffic in Hazardous Wastes: The 1989 Basel Convention," *International and Comparative Law Quarterly* 41, no. 3 (July 1992): 532–33.

25. Francois Roleants du Vivier, Interview in *The Courier*, no. 113 (Jan.–Feb. 1989), 5.

26. See, for example, Third World Network, *Toxic Terror* (Penang: Third World Network, 1989).

27. Jennifer Kitt, "Waste Exports to the Developing World: A Global Response," *Georgetown International Environmental Law Review* 7, no. 2 (1995): 493–94.

28. Greenpeace's campaign included the publication of the newsletter, *Waste Trade Update*, which began in 1988.

29. See Willy Kempel, "Transboundary Movements of Hazardous Wastes," in *International Environmental Negotiation*, G. Sjostedt, ed. (Newbury Park: Sage, 1993), 51.

30. Karen Litfin, *Ozone Discourses: Science and Politics in Global Environmental Cooperation* (Columbia: New York, 1994), 58–59.

31. Edward Parson, "Protecting the Ozone Layer," in *Institutions for the Earth*, P. Haas, R. Keohane, and M. Levy, eds. (Cambridge, MA: MIT, 1993), 29.

32. Ian Rowlands, *The Politics of Global Atmospheric Change* (Manchester: Manchester University Press, 1995), 104.

33. Parson, "Protecting the Ozone Layer," 29.

34. Peter Haas, "Banning Chlorofluorocarbons: Epistemic Community Efforts to Protect Stratospheric Ozone," *International Organization* 46, no. 1 (Winter 1992): 197.

35. Haas, "Banning Chlorofluorocarbons," 197.

36. Litfin, *Ozone Discourses*, 61; and Rowlands, *The Politics of Global Atmospheric Change*, 106.

37. Richard Elliot Benedick, *Ozone Diplomacy* (Cambridge, MA: Harvard University Press, 1991), 10–11.

38. Benedick, *Ozone Diplomacy*, 10–13.

39. Litfin, *Ozone Discourses*, 64.

40. Haas, "Banning Chlorofluorocarbons," 200.

41. Parson, "Protecting the Ozone Layer," 36–37.

42. David Leonard Downie, "Road Map or False Trail? Evaluating the 'Precedence' of the Ozone Regime as a Model and Strategy for Global Climate Change," *International Environmental Affairs* 7, no. 4 (1995): 331.

43. For an analysis of the Vienna Convention, see Benedick, *Ozone Diplomacy*, 44–45.

44. Parson, "Protecting the Ozone Layer," 36; and Litfin, *Ozone Discourses*, 70.

45. Rowlands, *The Politics of Global Atmospheric Change*, 56–57.

46. Marian Miller, *The Third World in Global Environmental Politics* (Boulder: Lynne Rienner, 1995), 90.

47. See *The Basel Convention on the Control of Transboundary Movements of Hazardous Wastes and their Disposal* (Geneva: UNEP, 1989). For a legal analysis, see Kummer, "The International Regulation of Transboundry Traffic in Hazardous Wastes"; and Kitt, "Waste Exports to the Developing World."

48. Kitt, "Waste Exports to the Developing World," 497.

49. Basel Convention Secretariat Internet Homepage.

50. Wynne, "The Toxic Waste Trade," 123; and Miller, *The Third World in Global Environmental Politics*, 96.

51. For an analysis of these weaknesses, see Wynne "The Toxic Waste Trade"; and Kummer, "The International Regulation of Transboundry Traffic in Hazardous Wastes."

52. Moctar Kebe, "Waste Disposal in Africa," *Marine Policy* 14, no. 3 (1990): 252.

53. Interview with Jim Puckett, Greenpeace International Toxic Trade Campaign, October 1993; and Miller, *The Third World in Global Environmental Politics*, 91.

54. On the evolution of the various conventions and national laws, see Clapp, "Africa, NGOs and the International Toxic Waste Trade," 513–14; and Miller, *The Third World in Global Environmental Politics*, 92.

55. On the negotiating positions of these groups of countries, see Benedick, *Ozone Diplomacy*, 68–69.

56. Benedick, *Ozone Diplomacy*, 91; see also Duncan Brack, *International Trade and the Montreal Protocol* (London: Earthscan, 1996), 67–69.

57. Miller, *The Third World in Global Environmental Politics*, 73.

58. Litfin, *Ozone Discourses*, 150–51.

59. Downie, "Road Map or False Trail?" 331.

60. See the *Montreal Protocol on Substances that Deplete the Ozone Layer* (Geneva: UNEP, 1987).

61. On the trade provisions in the 1987 agreement see Parson, "Protecting the Ozone Layer," 44–45.

62. Katya Jestin, "International Efforts to Abate the Depletion of the Ozone Layer," *Georgetown International Environmental Law Review* 7, no. 3 (1995): 834.

63. Press Release, "The Task of Protecting the Ozone Layer is Far From Over," UNEP Ozone Secretariat Internet Homepage.

64. Donald Goldberg, "The Montreal Protocol," in *The Use of Trade Measures in Select Multilateral Environmental Agreements*, R. Housman, D. Goldberg, B. Van Dyke, and D. Zaelke, eds. (Geneva: UNEP, 1995), 63.

65. Heller, *Database of Known Hazardous Waste Exports*.

66. *West Africa*, no. 3917 (12–18 October 1992), 1735.

67. "Toxic Waste Adds to Somalia's Woes," *New Scientist* 135, no. 1839 (19 September 1992): 5; and "UNEP Official Urges African Nations to Approve Basel Accord on Waste Shipments," *International Environment Reporter*, 7 October 1992, 654.

68. *Waste and Environment Today* 5, no. 6 (1992): 16; and *Waste and Environment Today* 5, no. 7 (1992): 18.

69. "U.S. Toxic Waste Sold as Fertilizer in Bangladesh," *Toxic Trade Update* 6, no. 1 (1993): 13.

70. Jim Puckett, "Disposing of the Waste Trade: Closing the Recycling Loophole," *The Ecologist* 24, no. 2 (1994): 55.

71. Puckett, "Disposing of the Waste Trade," 55.

72. Jim Vallette, "Basel 'Dumping' Convention Still Legalizes Toxic Terrorism," *Toxic Trade Update* 6, no. 1 (1993): 2.

73. Heller, *Database of Known Hazardous Waste Exports*, 1–2.

74. See Heller, *Database of Known Hazardous Waste Exports*, 1–2; Puckett, "Disposing of the Waste Trade"; and the following Greenpeace reports: *Plastics Waste to Indonesia*, April 1994; *Pacific Waste Invasion*, November 1992; *Wasted Lives*, 1994; and *Lead Astray*, 1994.

75. Puckett, "Disposing of the Waste Trade," 54–55.

76. See Clapp, "Africa, NGOs and the International Toxic Waste Trade," 512–15.

77. See "U.S. Business Group Withdraws Support for Basel Treaty After Ban on Waste Trade," *International Environment Reporter* 17, no. 11 (1 June 1994), 463.

78. "Countries Developing List of Materials That Would Fall Under Proposed Trade Ban," *International Environment Reporter* 18, no. 15 (26 July 1995), 563.

79. "Ban on Waste Exports Outside OECD Pushed Through Basel Treaty Meeting," *International Environment Reporter* 18, no. 20 (4 October 1995), 753; and *Decisions and Reports Adopted by the Third Meeting of the Conference of Parties* (Geneva: Basel Convention Secretariat, 1995).

80. Interview with Pierre Portas, Basel Convention Secretariat, July 1996, Geneva.

81. These implications of the ban for sovereignty are summarized in Kitt, "Waste Exports to the Developing World," 506–7.

82. See Paul Hagen and Robert Housman, "The Basel Convention," in *The Use of Trade Measures in Select Multilateral Environmental Agreements*, R. Housman, D. Goldberg, B. Van Dyke, and D. Zaelke, eds. (Geneva: UNEP, 1995); David Wirth, "International Trade in Wastes: Trade Implications of the Recent Amendment to the Basel Convention Banning North-South Trade in Hazardous Wastes," draft paper, January 1996; and John Bullock, "The Basel Convention and Trade," draft paper, January 1996.

83. David Hanson, "International Hazardous Wastes Treaty Worries U.S. Industry," *Chemical and Engineering News* 74, no. 9 (26 February 1996), 22–23; Rod Hunter, "Good Intentions, Foolish Policy," *Chemistry and Industry*, no. 2 (15 January 1996), 68; and Bullock, "The Basel Convention and Trade."

84. Michael Roberts, "Montreal Protocol Speeds Phaseout of HCFCs and Methyl Bromide," *Chemical Week* 157, no. 23 (13 December 1995), 20.

85. "Holed Up," *The Economist*, 9 December 1995, 63.

86. Ozone Secretariat Internet Homepage.

87. Ronald Begley, Allison Lucas, and Michael Roberts, "Producers Set for CFC Phaseout," *Chemical Week* 155, no. 19 (16 November 1994), 40.

88. Brack, *International Trade and the Montreal Protocol*, 105.

89. Begley, Lucas, and Roberts, "Producers Set for CFC Phaseout," 40.

90. Edward Parson and Owen Greene, "The Complex Chemistry of the International Ozone Agreements," *Environment* 7, no. 2 (1995): 36.

91. Christine Chin, "Customs, EPA Crackdown on CFC Crooks," *Chemical Engineering* 103, no. 4 (April 1996): 43.

92. "EPA, Customs Service Cracking Down on Smuggling of CFCs, Hazardous Waste," *International Environment Reporter* 19, no. 6 (20 March 1996), 221–22.

93. Matthew Wald, "Group Sees Ozone Danger in Illicit Chemical Trade," *New York Times*, 17 September 1995, 30.

94. "Illegal Imports of CFCs Increase as Production Ban Nears, U.S. Officials Say," *International Environment Reporter* 17, no. 22 (2 November 1994), 884.

95. Ian Young and Michael Roberts, "Rise in Illegal CFCs Dogs HFC Producers," *Chemical Week* 157, no. 20 (22 November 1995), 18.

96. "Holed Up," 63.

97. Young and Roberts, "Rise in Illegal CFCs Dogs HFC Producers," 18.

98. "Holed Up," 63.

99. See W. Wayt Gibbs, "The Treaty that Worked—Almost," *Scientific American* 273, no. 3 (September 1995), 18; Michael Roberts "Europe's CFC

ban not fully enforced," *Chemical Week* 156, no. 3 (25 January 1995), 20; and "More Shipments of CFCs Said Entering Global Market as Phaseout Deadline Nears," *International Environment Reporter* 17, no. 12 (15 June 1994), 542.

100. Jim Vallette, *Deadly Complacency, U.S. CFC Production, The Black Market, and Ozone Depletion*, Ozone Action Report (September 1995), 5.

101. Parson and Greene, "The Complex Chemistry of International Ozone Agreements," 38.

102. Brack, *International Trade and the Montreal Protocol*, 111.

103. Parson and Greene, "The Complex Chemistry of International Ozone Agreements," 38.

104. Vallette, *Deadly Complacency*, 16–17.

105. Brack, *International Trade and the Montreal Protocol*, 106. Vallette (*Deadly Complacency*, 4) claims that the CIA and Interpol are also involved in this operation.

106. Chin, "Customs, EPA Crackdown," 43; and Vallette, *Deadly Complacency*, 4.

107. Wald, "Group Sees Ozone Danger in Illicit Chemical Trade," 30.

108. Chin, "Customs, EPA Crackdown," 43; and Brack, *International Trade and the Montreal Protocol*, 107.

109. Brack, *International Trade and the Montreal Protocol*, 108–9.

110. "Curb on Illegal Imports of CFCs Sought by EPA in Proposal for Petition Process," *International Environment Reporter* 18, no. 10 (17 May 1995), 377–78.

111. "EPA, Customs Service Cracking Down on Smuggling of CFCs, Hazardous Waste," *International Environment Reporter* 19, no. 6 (20 March 1996), 221–22.

112. Brack, *International Trade and the Montreal Protocol*, 112.

113. Parson and Greene, "The Complex Chemistry of International Ozone Agreements," 38.

114. Michael Roberts, "Europe's CFC Ban Not Fully Enforced," *Chemical Week* 156, no. 3 (25 January 1995), 20.

115. Terry Pedwell, "Import of Ozone Depleting CFCs probed," *Chronicle Herald*, 9 December 1994, A14; and Brack, *International Trade and the Montreal Protocol*, 109.

116. "The Vienna Meeting," *Environmental Policy and Law* 26, no. 2/3 (1996): 68.

117. UNEP (UNEP/OzL.Pro.8/12), *Eighth Meeting of the Parties to the Montreal Protocol on Substances that Deplete the Ozone Layer*, San José, 25–27 November 1996, 28–29.

5

When Policies Collide: Market Reform, Market Prohibition, and the Narcotization of the Mexican Economy

Peter Andreas

Although rarely acknowledged in International Monetary Fund (IMF) and World Bank reports, the production, processing, and transportation of illicit drugs (particularly cocaine, heroin, and marijuana) is one of the few market activities in which many parts of the developing world enjoy a significant comparative advantage in the international economy.[1] Indeed, in a highly competitive global marketplace dominated by multinational corporations from the industrialized world, sophisticated criminal organizations specializing in drug trafficking stand out as the developing world's most successful (even if least celebrated) multinationals.[2] Even though the products they sell are illegal, these trafficking organizations are in many ways the quintessential expression of the kind of private sector entrepreneurialism celebrated and encouraged by the neoliberal economic orthodoxy that guides IMF and World Bank policy prescriptions.[3]

But while neoliberal economics promotes market liberalization in developing countries, a global drug prohibition regime (institutionalized internationally through the UN system) promotes market prohibition.[4] A wide range of psychoactive substances, most notably cocaine, heroin, and marijuana, are outlawed in almost every country. This is a relatively new development in human history. As Ethan Nadelmann observes, "prior to the twentieth century, no global patterns were discernible in the norms and legal sanctions governing the trade and use of any of these substances."[5] Today, however, criminal justice agencies around the world "are deeply involved in investigating and prosecuting drug law violations; and even the rhetoric of the 'war on drugs' has been globalized."[6]

How such a global prohibition regime emerged is beyond the scope of the analysis here and has been discussed elsewhere.[7] It is important to emphasize, however, that while the United States has been the key promoter of drug prohibition since early in the century, prohibition norms are now thoroughly embedded at the international level through a set of United Nations organizations and international treaties. As Nadelmann notes, "the vast majority of states count themselves as members of the global drug prohibition regime." Virtually every country has ratified the 1961 Single Convention on Narcotics, and a majority of countries have signed the 1971 Convention on Psychotropic Substances.[8] More recent has been the 1988 adoption of the UN Convention Against Illicit Traffic in Narcotic Drugs and Psychotropic Substances.[9] The 1988 convention obligates signatory nations to criminalize the production, sale, transport, and cultivation of narcotic and psychotropic substances (including the profits from drug-related activity). Thus, even as U.S. antidrug activism and diplomatic arm-twisting remains decisive, the prohibitionist drug control framework is broadly legitimated internationally.[10]

The effort to tighten state controls over the flow of illicit drugs contrasts sharply with the current global trend to relax state controls over the flow of goods, services, and capital. The reversal of statist economic policies has been particularly pronounced in the developing world. Thomas Biersteker has called this the "triumph" of neoclassical economics: "the convergence of economic thinking and policy on a global scale."[11] As in drug market prohibition, the United States is a key promoter of free-market reforms. Yet the source of compliance does not emanate solely from Washington. For example, in the case of Latin America, Jorge Castaneda points out that if countries in the region became economically nationalistic, "the consequences would be expressed in terms of dried-up credit and investment flows and tense relations with the World Bank and the International Monetary Fund (IMF), rather than in difficulties with the U.S. State Department."[12]

Through these processes of market liberalization and criminalization, the regulatory apparatus of the state in many drug-exporting countries is being torn down and built up simultaneously. While market liberalization rolls the state back, drug market criminalization rolls the state forward in the form of an enhanced policing apparatus. Indeed, drug control remains one of the most notable cases in which the state is expected to remain highly interventionist in the market.

Promoting free-market reforms and enforcing drug market prohibitions are based on opposite logics: in the case of drug prohibition, suppressing the market is the goal and the coercive power of the state is the primary tool of intervention. Failure to curb the market is interpreted as evidence that controls should be tightened even further. In the case of free-market reforms, on the other hand, the unleashing of the market is the goal and excessive state intervention is perceived as the primary impediment. Poor economic performance is blamed on too much state control, and the solution is assumed to be a further loosening of economic regulations. In short, while the prohibition model pushes for a maximalist state, the free-market model pushes for a minimalist state.

However, this can be a highly problematic and contradictory combination in many drug-exporting countries. In practice, free-market reforms can end up facilitating and encouraging the drug trade, making it more difficult to enforce drug market prohibitions. Free-market reforms can unintentionally increase the incentives to enter the drug trade, facilitate the laundering of the profits from the drug trade, and make it more difficult for law enforcement to control the drug trade. Nevertheless, many drug-exporting countries face powerful pressures to embrace both free-market reforms and drug market prohibitions. While deception is a common practice, open defiance and defection are not viable options for most. Defection from the free-market orthodoxy risks punishment in the form of loan cutoffs from multilateral funding organizations, which in turn would help spark an outflow of foreign and domestic capital. Heavily reliant on international creditors, most debt-strapped developing countries have committed themselves to following strict IMF guidelines. The IMF "conditionality bargain" means that modest levels of external financial assistance are provided in exchange for adopting market-based economic reforms.[13]

The economic policy choices of debtor countries in the developing world, Barbara Stallings argues, have been powerfully shaped by a combination of factors: changes in the external environment (the drying up of new financing and the sharp decline in the terms of trade), increased international linkages (transnational social and political networks and coalitions that link international and domestic actors), and the growing leverage (financial, ideological, and political) of foreign creditors such as the IMF and the World Bank.[14] Together, these changes inhibit outright defection from the neoliberal economic agenda.

Open defection from the drug prohibition regime would also have severe consequences: it would place the defecting country in the category of a pariah "narcostate," generate material repercussions in the form of economic sanctions and aid cutoffs, and damage the country's moral standing in the international community. Even if their control efforts have a limited impact on the drug trade, leaders across the globe repeatedly pledge their commitment to the battle against drugs. Regardless of whether they are "true believers" or simply trying to pacify international critics, for drug-exporting countries to openly defect by officially advocating drug legalization would be unthinkable, not only because it would draw the wrath of the United States but also because their advocation would be universally condemned and would openly violate their pledge to uphold UN-based antidrug treaties.

Focusing on the recent Mexican experience, I argue that an unintended side effect of Mexico's market-based reforms—deregulation, privatization, and trade liberalization—has been to facilitate and encourage not only legal economic activity but also illegal economic activity, particularly drug production, trafficking, and money laundering. The drug trade appears to be an integral part (and a leading beneficiary) of Mexico's economic restructuring and integration with the United States.[15] This awkward predicament, however, is largely ignored in both scholarly and policy debates, and is understudied by the international organizations that monitor and encourage Mexico's implementation of market reforms and drug market controls.

The Mexican case is chosen for a variety of reasons. Few countries match Mexico's aggressive reversal of statist policies and commitment to free-market reforms. Similarly, few countries match Mexico's importance in the drug trade. As much as 70 percent of the cocaine bound for the U.S. market enters through Mexico, and Mexico supplies about 20–30 percent of the heroin consumed in the United States and up to 80 percent of the imported marijuana.[16] And few developing countries match the level of resources Mexico has devoted to drug control.

The Underside of Free-Market Reform in Mexico

Between the early 1980s and the early 1990s, Mexico underwent an economic metamorphosis, becoming a textbook case of neoliberal economic reform.[17] As David Gould puts it, "Mexico has transformed itself from an extremely closed economy with a huge government sector to a relatively open economy with a much smaller government sector."[18] Multilateral institutions have been instrumental in the economic adjustment process from the start. As the World Bank observes in a report on Latin American economic reform, "a good illustration of the World Bank's influence and persuasive powers is the Mexican reform." For example, in the case of trade, the report says, "the World Bank approved a Trade Policy Loan for Mexico, which built the base for that country's sweeping trade liberalization."[19] Similarly, "the IMF has been associated closely with the process of adjustment carried out in Mexico over the last decade."[20]

The economic statism that characterized past Mexican policies has been reversed since the debt crisis first hit the country in 1982.[21] For example, most state-owned enterprises have been privatized or eliminated, government spending has been reduced by cutting public sector wages and employment, and many financial obligations and services have been transferred to local governments. At the same time, the economy has been opened through reforms to attract foreign investment and further incorporate Mexico into the world economy.[22] Trade has been liberalized (Mexico became a member of GATT in 1986); capital markets have been deregulated, sparking an inflow of foreign capital in the early 1990s. Moreover, a constitutional reform of land distribution and the *ejido* system was pushed through by the end of 1991, transforming the agricultural sector. And finally, the crowning achievement of Mexico's economic reforms has been the North American Free Trade Agreement (NAFTA), which took effect in January 1994. The multilateral funding organizations, such as the IMF, have enthusiastically applauded Mexico's transformation.[23]

In his last state of the union speech on November 1, 1994, President Carlos Salinas declared that "Mexico has changed intensely . . . the goals of these changes were the establishment of a new relationship between the state and society, and to place Mexico in an advantageous position in the new international reality."[24] Although not mentioned by Salinas, part of Mexico's "advantageous position in the new international reality" has been its rising position in the illegal drug trade. According to Eduardo Valle, who resigned as personal advisor to the Mexican attorney general in May of 1994, Mexico's leading traffickers have now become "driving forces, pillars even, of our economic growth."[25] While obviously impossible to calculate with any precision, official estimates suggest that the illegal trade is a sizeable economic force. Mexico has long played a role in the drug trade, but the level of involvement has expanded considerably in the last decade. The U.S. Drug Enforcement Administration (DEA) calculates that Mexico earns more than $7 billion a year from the drug trade.[26] Mexico's prosecutor general's office calculates that drug traffickers operating in Mexico accumulated revenues of about $30 billion in 1994.[27] If either estimate is even remotely accurate, then the illicit drug trade is a leading (if not the leading) generator of foreign exchange for Mexico. Some financial analysts even warn that a sudden drying up of drug money from the Mexican banking system would have severe economic consequences.[28]

A largely overlooked side effect of Mexico's economic restructuring has been to open up the economy not only to licit economic activity but also to increased illicit activity. In other words, many of the reforms designed to encourage licit business have apparently also encouraged illicit business. This is particularly true in the case of drugs. Mexico's expanding role in the drug trade, most notably the transshipment of cocaine, parallels the opening of the Mexican economy and the deepening of U.S.-Mexican economic integration. The drug export sector, it seems, is a leading (albeit unintended) beneficiary of these economic changes.

For example, privatization, which is designed to attract foreign investors, has also attracted narcoinvestors. Agricultural reforms designed to make peasant farmers more responsive to market forces have unintentionally encouraged the cultivation of illicit drug crops. The lifting of restrictions on trucking has not only eased the transport of legal goods but illegal goods as well. Trade liberalization has not only increased the volume of legitimate cross-border trade, but also provided an ideal cover for hiding illegitimate trade.

Privatization, Financial Liberalization, and Foreign Investment

An important goal of Mexico's economic reforms has been to attract foreign capital. Privatization, financial liberalization, and the easing of restrictions on foreign investment have been key mechanisms to accomplish this. These policies were particularly successful during the Salinas years, when foreign capital flooded into Mexico.

However, the influx of capital appears to have included not only legitimate investors but also narcoinvestors looking to launder their profits and integrate themselves into legitimate sectors of the economy. As Peter Smith explains, "President Salinas was consummating a reconfiguration of the power structure in Mexico, and one of the elements of that power structure was international billionaires. People who qualify for membership in that group include the leaders of drug cartels."[29] Mexico's enthusiastic embrace of private sector entrepreneurialism has apparently encouraged not only licit but also illicit enrichment. Jose Luis Perez Canchola, the vice president of the Mexican Academy of Human Rights, observes that "there are honestly earned fortunes in Mexico." However, "in this past (Salinas) administration, multimillionaires appeared under rocks, like mushrooms—people for whom it was impossible to make so much money so fast by legal means."[30]

While Mexico's privatization process has been highly praised by multilateral funders, largely overlooked is the fact that privatization has provided a magnet for illicit investment.[31] According to the Federal Bureau of Investigation (FBI), many of the state-owned companies privatized under the Salinas administration were bought up by drug traffickers.[32] The State Department has also noted that purchasing privatized businesses has been a way for drug traffickers to launder and invest their revenues from drug sales.[33] One foreign investment analyst explains the process this way: "the vast amount of money generated by the drug trade must be legitimized or laundered and the recent privatization process has provided the perfect mechanism to handle the billions of dollars in profits that flow from illegal narcotics. A practice used by the drug trade during the Salinas government has been to buy the equity and debt issued to finance the sale of former state-run enterprises, particularly the commercial banks and large commercial enterprises."[34]

The purchasing of state-owned enterprises—by either licit or illicit investors—provides a large and immediate influx of desperately needed dollars for the cash-hungry government. Given Mexico's balance of payments problems and heavy debt servicing obligations to international creditors, Mexico has an incentive to tolerate funds from any source (and this is especially true after the December 1994 collapse of the peso).

Other economic policy changes have also facilitated money laundering and narcoinvestment. According to *The Economist Intelligence Unit*, the "liberalisation of the Mexican financial services sector and capital markets in recent years has provided opportunities for money-laundering and the investment of the illicit gains from the drugs trade."[35] The State Department notes that "Mexico's banking and financial sector lacks adequate controls on money laundering and has become one of the most important money laundering centers in the Western Hemisphere." The system "remains highly vulnerable to drug-related financial transactions. Foreign and domestic currency movements are unmonitored."[36] As drug profits filter into the local economy and are invested in legitimate industry, the line between the licit and illicit private sector blurs. Colombian and Mexican traffickers have reportedly purchased construction and cement companies, factories, aviation companies, and other businesses throughout Mexico.[37]

Agricultural Reform

Part of Mexico's economic restructuring has been to roll back the role of the state in the countryside. Since the late 1980s, Mexico has been reducing electricity, fertilizer, water, and credit subsidies to peasant farmers. Price supports for crops have also been cut. Moreover, restrictions on the sale of communal farm lands—about 70 percent of Mexico's cropland and one-half of its irrigated land—have been lifted. While the government initiated a fifteen-year direct income subsidy program in late 1993 for producers of corn and other basic crops, this has primarily served as a limited form of welfare rather than providing the kind of public investment (affordable credit, crop insurance, and infrastructural improvements such as irrigation and drainage) necessary to modernize Mexican agriculture and make small-scale farmers more productive and competitive. Meanwhile, the agricultural sector has been opened up to foreign competition, resulting in a large influx of agricultural goods from the United States.

The premise behind the reforms is that the agricultural sector will become more efficient and productive through reduced government supports and greater exposure to market forces.[38] In practice, however, the market force many peasant farmers are responding to is the drug trade. As U.S. agricultural exports to Mexico have increased and government support programs have been scaled back, many peasant growers have abandoned licit farming and turned to illicit farming.

This response is understandable. The logic of neoclassical economics, after all, suggests that peasant farmers should produce those crops that give them the greatest comparative advantage in the market—which, in some regions of Mexico, happen to be marijuana and opium poppy. One group of researchers reports that "social disruption and economic pressure from free-market reforms have intensified in rural areas, fueling the tendency to grow illicit crops as a household survival strategy."[39] Drug production has expanded in Mexico's more remote rural regions. The State Department notes that "adverse agricultural and economic conditions have forced farmers in nontraditional areas to turn to cultivating illicit crops."[40] Mexican opium production, the State Department reports, almost doubled between 1986 and 1995. There are already roughly 200,000 people earning a living from growing illicit drugs, and the Mexican attorney general's office calculates that the figure may be as high as 300,000.[41]

The links between Mexico's agricultural reforms and the expansion of drug crop cultivation have received little attention. However, an October 1992 internal DEA report in Mexico (obtained through the Freedom of Information Act by the National Security Archive) provides a detailed analysis of the situation in the Mexican countryside.[42] An important goal of the Mexican agricultural reforms of January 1992 was to "make the agricultural sector financially self-sufficient and more independent of government controls," notes the report. "As farm incomes fall, as has been the case for the past five years," farmers will be left with various options, including to "cultivate illicit cash crops such as marijuana and opium poppy." The report observes that "for the past several years, farmers in Michoacan and Guerrero have complained that the government has not adequately subsidized their corn crops, forcing them to turn to small, illicit cultivations in order to feed their families."

For many subsistence farmers, "these illicit crops often mean the difference between starvation and survival."

The DEA report predicts that "increased illicit drug production will probably be a direct result of the discontinuation of subsistence crop subsidies." The only viable solution, it concludes, runs directly counter to the current emphasis on scaling back government support in the countryside: "a long-term program of crop substitution credits, road construction, improved education facilities and assistance in purchasing new agricultural equipment may be the only recourse open to the GOM [Government of Mexico] in the Southwest. Such assistance would also require increased government intervention, the antithesis of Salinas's intent to modernize the agricultural arena by decreasing government participation, and encouraging private enterprise and investment."

The Liberalization of Trade and Transportation

Mexico has long been what one observer calls "the perfect smuggling platform."[43] However, the nature and extent of Mexican smuggling operations have been transformed in the last decade by the country's emergence as the key transshipment point for Colombian cocaine into the U.S. market. A strategic alliance has developed between Colombian and Mexican trafficking organizations. In this transnational joint venture, the Colombians process and ship the cocaine to Mexico, and the Mexicans specialize in smuggling it into the United States. Perhaps as little as 20 percent of Colombian cocaine was transshipped through Mexico in the mid-1980s, but increased to as much as 70 percent by the mid-1990s.[44]

There are a variety of reasons for this upsurge in cocaine smuggling through Mexico. The most obvious is that Colombian traffickers have turned to the Mexican route in response to U.S. law enforcement pressure on trafficking routes through the Caribbean and South Florida. However, another important (and far less recognized) reason is Mexico's economic opening and growing integration with the United States. Hiding drug shipments within the rising volume of trade between Colombia and Mexico and between Mexico and the United States (doubling between 1986 and 1993) has become an increasingly favored smuggling method.[45] The intermixing of licit and illicit commerce— especially at a time when the overall volume of trade is rising—makes "weeding out" the illicit from the licit extremely difficult. Moreover, the relaxation of transport regulations (particularly on trucking) that has accompanied trade liberalization has not only facilitated the movement of legal trade but illegal trade as well. Thus, even as traditional drug smuggling methods and routes have become riskier due to law enforcement, access to legitimate commercial transportation methods and routes has become easier due to economic liberalization.

The incentive to use legitimate commercial traffic as a cover for drug trafficking appears to be increasing under NAFTA. Imports from Mexico have doubled from about $40 billion in 1993, the year before NAFTA took effect, to an expected $81 billion in 1997. Phil Jordan, the former director of the DEA's El Paso Intelligence Center, calls NAFTA a "godsend" to drug trafficking, "the best thing that happened to product distribution since Nike signed up Michael Jordan."[46] An internal report written by an intelligence officer at the U.S. embassy in Mexico City claims that cocaine traffickers have established factories, warehouses, and trucking companies as fronts in anticipation of the boom in cross-border commerce expected under NAFTA.[47] Drug traffickers, concluded one press report, "seem to have embraced a vision of North American integration not unlike that with which NAFTA . . . was sold to skeptics in Washington."[48]

Significant increases in the volume of land traffic across the Southwest border provides an ideal cover for smuggling. Approximately 3.5 million trucks and rail cars entered the United States from Mexico in 1996. On any given day, 220,000 vehicles flow across the border into the United States from Mexico. Loaquin Legarreta, spokesperson for the DEA's Intelligence Center in El Paso, estimates that most cocaine enters through regular ports of entry along the border in commercial trucks and passenger vehicles.[49] In order to facilitate commerce and avoid long delays at the border, U.S. Customs agents can realistically only inspect a small percentage of the vehicles entering from Mexico. The more intensive and intrusive the inspection process, the longer the wait at the border. There is a growing tension between facilitation (of legal commerce) and enforcement (of drug controls). "Obviously, we're in an area of international trade," explains Rex Applegate, port director of the San Diego district. "We're not in a situation where we can just stop traffic for the sake of narcotics risk . . . we examined 3 percent of all the laden trucks that crossed."[50]

Trucking into the United States is increasing rapidly. For example, the number of laden trucks increased 51 percent and the number of empty trucks increased 38 percent in 1994 alone. Trucks, of course, can carry illegal goods as easily as legal goods. One truck that was stopped near San Diego was smuggling eight tons of cocaine stuffed into cans of jalapeno peppers. U.S. officials believe that the shipment belonged to the owner of one of Mexico's largest trucking companies.

The Mexican trucking industry was deregulated in 1989, meaning that licensed trucks can travel without inspection throughout Mexico. And under NAFTA guidelines, Mexican truckers will eventually be able to travel anywhere in the United States and Canada. According to the October 1992 internal DEA report discussed earlier, the lifting of trucking restrictions will "prove to be a definite boon to both the legitimate food industry, and to drug smugglers who conceal their illegal shipments in trucks transporting fruits and vegetables from Mexico to U.S. markets." Moreover, "the projected overhaul of the Mexican road system will expedite the exportation of both legitimate and illegitimate crops."[51] On the U.S. side of the border, meanwhile, plans are under way to improve the Southwest road network so that it can handle more than a doubling of today's traffic level.

Drug Market Prohibition in Mexico

As the drug trade has expanded during the economic reform process, Mexico has been under growing pressure to at least maintain the appearance of containing the illicit business. This has resulted in a significant expansion of the state's drug control apparatus. Mexico has devoted ever-increasing resources to drug enforcement, tripling its drug control budget and personnel since 1989. This growth is particularly striking given that it has occurred during a time of deep cuts in overall government spending. Drug control now dominates the federal criminal justice system, reflected in the fact that the majority of Mexico's federal budget for the administration of justice is devoted to the antidrug effort. The "Mexican attorney general's office," argues Marcia Celia Toro, "has basically become an antidrug law enforcement agency."[52]

Drug trafficking was declared to be a national security threat by Mexican President Miguel de la Madrid Hurtado in early 1988. And this was reinforced by Salinas, and more recently by President Ernesto Zedillo. Salinas announced that "the fight against drugs is a high priority in my government for three fundamental reasons: because it constitutes an assault on the health of Mexico's citizens, because it promises to affect Mexico's national security, and finally, because the community of nations must stand together on this issue."[53] Zedillo has gone further, declaring that drug trafficking is the country's number one security threat. Given that the language of national security is rare in Mexican political discourse, these pronouncements mark a major departure from the past.

Classifying drugs as a national security matter provided a rationale for expanding the national security apparatus under Salinas, while further reinforcing the military's antidrug role.[54] For example, Salinas created a national security council, developed a new national intelligence agency, set up a unit within the attorney general's office for drug control, and developed new interdiction units of the federal judicial police and a new army staff section that focused on drug enforcement.[55]

The Mexican military, especially the army, has long been involved in antidrug operations, but the level and form of involvement has reached new levels in recent years. According to some estimates, about one-third of the military's budget was devoted to drug control by the late 1980s. During the same period, some 25,000 Mexican soldiers were involved in drug control operations—compared to only 5,000 in the 1970s.[56] Under Zedillo, the military's antidrug mission has expanded even further. "In the past, there was always a reluctance to allow the military to play a stronger role," says one U.S. official. "But with the Zedillo administration, that mind-set has dissolved."[57]

The expansion of Mexico's drug control campaign is legitimated by the Mexican state as part of its pledge to support the global antidrug battle. As stated in Mexico's *National Drug Control Program 1995–2000*, "based upon the international agreements subscribed by Mexico, our government intends to readily react to the drug phenomenon." The report points to government initiatives to revamp and expand its drug enforcement capacity, and concludes that Mexico's efforts "coincide with the efforts made by the international community, and which are embodied in the *United Nations' Decade Against Unlawful Drug Consumption*, programmed by the United Nations' General Assembly to culminate in the year 2000 with the motto: 'a world response to a global challenge.' "[58]

Conclusion

While the triumph of neoclassical economics promotes market liberalization, a global drug prohibition regime promotes market criminalization. These sharply contrasting models of state-market relations are institutionalized internationally (through the IMF, World Bank, the UN system), and are backed by the leading industrialized countries, particularly the United States. Drug-exporting countries such as Mexico face considerable pressures to implement both liberal market reforms and punitive drug market controls. One result, as the Mexican case demonstrates, is a simultaneous tearing down and building up of the state regulatory apparatus: the creation of a minimalist state in regulating the legal economy, and a maximalist state in regulating the illegal drug economy. Thus, even as there is a general trend toward downsizing the state, the policing dimension of the state is revamped and redeployed.

However, as the Mexican experience reviewed here suggests (and as summarized in table 5.1), implementing market reforms can uninten-

Table 5.1: Impact of Mexico's Market Reforms on the Drug Trade

Market Reforms	Impact
Trade liberalization	Increased trade flows (Colombia–Mexico–U.S.) provide cover for increased drug smuggling
Privatization	Increased opportunity for money laundering; narcoinvestment
Deregulation of trucking	Increased use of trucking for drug shipments within Mexico and into U.S. market
Foreign debt payments	Increased incentive to tolerate influx of drug revenues
Lower public sector salaries	Increased incentive to accept bribes
Financial liberalization	Increased opportunity for money laundering; narcosector and capital markets investment
Agricultural reform	Increased drug cultivation as a household survival strategy; possible increase in narcoinvestment in the countryside

tionally contradict and undermine the goal of drug market prohibitions. In other words, part of the "collateral damage" of free-market reform is to help free up the illegal drug trade: lifting restrictions on foreign investment has attracted narcoinvestment; efforts to make the agricultural sector more responsive to market forces have made peasant farmers more responsive to drug market forces; financial deregulation has facilitated not only licit but also illicit financial flows; eliminating restrictions on trucking has eased the transport of both licit and illicit goods; and the growing volume of trade stimulated by the lifting of trade barriers has provided a convenient cover for illicit trade. In short, this is the "underside" of market liberalization and U.S.-Mexico economic integration.

Interestingly, while most of the evidence for this comes from official sources, rarely do government agencies or international organizations systematically explore how economic reform policies shape the illegal drug economy. This is partly due to the fact that evaluations of market reforms are largely divorced and insulated from evaluations of drug market prohibitions. Market reforms are viewed as a problem of economic policy, while market prohibitions are viewed as a problem of law enforcement policy. Rarely do the debates in these two policy arenas overlap. Thus, for example, while UN antidrug agencies tend to focus on how to curb drug trafficking and generate greater global cooperation in the effort, the IMF and the World Bank remain preoccupied with debt service records, export earnings, inflation levels, the pace of privatization and trade liberalization, and so on.[59] This is reinforced in the policy evaluation process at the national level, where market reforms and market prohibitions are also separated into distinct policy spheres. Thus, official economic reports rarely mention the drug export sector, let alone probe its ties to the formal economy. The end result is that the tensions and contradictions between market reform and drug market prohibition are rarely discussed or even mentioned.[60]

Indeed, despite the occasional remarks by government officials to the contrary, the largely unquestioned policy assumption seems to be that carrying out free-market reforms facilitates the enforcement of drug market prohibition. As the 1994 *U.S. National Drug Control Strategy* report states, the growth of "free market economies presents new international narcotics control opportunities." According to the report, "market-oriented governments are much easier to work with and more willing to cooperate with the international community in a common effort against the illicit drug industry."[61] While there is certainly some truth in this claim, the Mexico experience suggests that the growth of free-market economies can also facilitate the growth of illegal drug economies. Of course, this is not meant to suggest that market reforms are somehow the underlying cause of the drug trade. Obviously, the drug export sector in Mexico and elsewhere in the developing world predates the adoption of neoliberal economic policies. Yet the preliminary evidence does suggest that the illicit trade has in some ways been an unintended (and largely overlooked) beneficiary of such economic policies.

Notes

1. Research for this paper was supported by a fellowship from the Foreign Policy Studies Program at the Brookings Institution and a Social Science Research Council–MacArthur Foundation Fellowship on Peace and Security in a Changing World. The author also acknowledges the support of the Institute for the Study of World Politics.

2. Shelley writes that "drug trafficking is one of the primary vehicles of transferring wealth, albeit illicitly, from the industrialized to the third world." See Louise Shelley, "The Internationalization of Crime: The Changing Rela-

tionship Between Crime and Development," in *Essays on Crime and Development*, Ugljesa Zvekic, ed. (Rome: United Nations Interregional Crime and Justice Research Institute, 1990), 119–34.

3. See, for example, World Bank, *Latin America and the Caribbean: A Decade After the Debt Crisis* (Washington, DC: World Bank, 1993); and World Bank, *Global Economic Prospects and the Developing Countries* (Washington, DC: World Bank, 1995).

4. See Ethan Nadelmann, "Global Prohibition Regimes: The Evolution of Norms in International Society," *International Organization* 44, no. 4 (Autumn 1990): 479–526.

5. Nadelmann, "Global Prohibition Regimes."

6. Nadelmann, "Global Prohibition Regimes."

7. Nadelmann, "Global Prohibition Regimes."

8. Nadelmann, "Global Prohibition Regimes," 503.

9. See David Stewart, "Internationalizing the War on Drugs: The UN Convention Against Illicit Traffic in Narcotic Drugs and Psychotropic Substances," *Denver Journal of International Law and Policy* 18, no. 3 (1990): 387–404. See also Jack Donnelly, "The United Nations and the Global Drug Control Regime," in *Drug Policy in the Americas*, Peter H. Smith, ed. (Boulder: Westview Press, 1992), 282–304.

10. The UN treaties, it should be noted, are also used by the United States to legitimize its own policy initiatives. For example, the State Department makes an annual determination of whether drug source countries have fully cooperated with the United States and complied with the goals and objectives of the 1988 UN treaty. U.S. economic and military aid, votes in multilateral lending institutions, and trade preferences are linked to such cooperation and compliance. The United States has, essentially, appointed itself as the judge of whether drug source countries are complying with the UN treaties.

11. Thomas Biersteker, "The 'Triumph' of Neoclassical Economics in the Developing World," in *Governance Without Government: Order and Change in World Politics*, James Rosenau and Otto Czempiel, eds. (Cambridge: Cambridge University Press, 1992), 105.

12. Jorge Castaneda, "Latin America and the End of the Cold War: An Essay in Frustration," in *Latin America in a New World Order*, Abraham Lowenthal and Albert Fishlow, eds. (Westview Press, 1994), 30.

13. Miles Kahler, "External Influence, Conditionality, and the Politics of Adjustment," in *The Politics of Economic Adjustment*, Stephan Haggard and Robert Kauffman, eds. (Princeton: Princeton University Press, 1992).

14. Barbara Stallings, "International Influence on Economic Policy: Debt, Stabilization, and Structural Reform," in *The Politics of Economic Adjustment*, Stephan Haggard and Robert Kauffman, eds. (Princeton: Princeton University Press, 1992).

15. Of course, this is not to suggest that Mexico's economic opening is the underlying cause of the drug trade. Obviously, the drug trade predates Mexico's economic reforms. Rather, the argument here is that these reforms have in some ways unintentionally facilitated and encouraged the drug trade.

16. In addition, the DEA reports that Mexican traffickers have virtually taken over the growing U.S. market for methamphetamines.

17. See Nora Lustig, *Mexico: The Remaking of An Economy* (Washington, DC: Brookings Institution, 1992).

18. David Gould, "Mexico's Tectonic Shift," *Challenge*, March-April 1995, 26.

19. World Bank, *Latin America and the Caribbean: A Decade After the Debt Crisis* (Washington, DC: World Bank, 1993), 30.

20. Claudio Loser and Eliot Kalter, eds., "Mexico: The Strategy to Achieve Sustained Economic Growth," *Occasional Paper*, no. 99 (Washington, DC: International Monetary Fund, September 1992), 2.

21. See, for example, Gerardo Otero, ed., *Neoliberalism Revisited: Economic Restructuring and Mexico's Political Future* (Boulder: Westview Press, 1996).

22. Francisco Valdes-Ugalde, "The Changing Relationship Between the State and the Economy in Mexico," *Challenge*, May-June 1995, 32.

23. See, for example, Loser and Kalter, "Mexico."

24. Quoted in Soledad Loaeza, "Contexts of Mexican Policy," *Challenge*, March-April 1995, 22.

25. Eduardo Valle, in *Mexican Insights*, Washington Office on Latin America, July 1995, 45.

26. Cited in Tim Golden, "Mexican Connection Grows as Cocaine Supplier to U.S.," *New York Times*, 30 July 1995, A1.

27. Foreign Broadcast Information Service, 5 October 1995, 81.

28. Tim Coone, "Special Report: Money Laundering in Mexico," *Latin Trade*, September 1997.

29. Quoted in Sebastian Rotella, "Mexico's Cartels Sow Seeds of Corruption, Destruction," *Los Angeles Times*, 16 June 1995, 1.

30. Rotella, "Mexico's Cartels Sow Seeds of Corruption."

31. See, for example, World Bank, *Latin America and the Caribbean*; and Loser and Kalter, "Mexico."

32. Cited in Golden, "Mexican Connection Grows as Cocaine Supplier to U.S.," A1.

33. Cited in Tom Barry with Harry Browne and Beth Sims, *Crossing the Line: Immigrants, Economic Integration, and Drug Enforcement on the U.S.-Mexican Border* (Albuquerque: Resource Center Press, 1994), 71.

34. Chris Whalen, *The Mexico Report*, 3, no. 20, 7 October 1994.

35. "Political Outlook: Party Stability," *Economist Intelligence Unit Country Forecast*, 30 May 1995.

36. U.S. Department of State, *International Narcotics Control Strategy Report* (Washington, DC: U.S. Government Printing Office, March 1996).

37. *Narcotics Enforcement and Prevention Digest*, 20 July 1995, 9.

38. For a critical evaluation, see John Gledhill, *Neoliberalism, Transnationalization and Rural Poverty: A Case Study of Michoacan, Mexico* (Boulder: Westview Press, 1995).

39. Barry, *Crossing the Line*, 59.

40. U.S. Department of State, Bureau of International Narcotics Matters, *In-*

ternational Narcotics Control Strategy Report (Washington, DC: U.S. Government Printing Office, March 1991), 162.

41. Maria Celia Toro, *Mexico's War on Drugs* (Boulder: Lynne Rienner, 1995), 53.

42. Drug Enforcement Administration, *The New Agricultural Reform Program and Illicit Cultivations in Mexico*, 14 October 1992.

43. Quoted in Peter Reuter and David Ronfeldt, *Quest for Integrity: the Mexican-U.S. Drug Issue in the 1980s*, RAND, 1991, 10.

44. Kevin Jack Riley, *Snowjob? The War Against International Cocaine Trafficking* (New Brunswick: Transaction Publishers, 1996), 229–30.

45. See H. Richard Friman, "Just Passing Through: Transit States and the Dynamics of Illicit Transshipment," *Transnational Organized Crime* 1, no. 1 (Spring 1995): 65–83.

46. Quoted in *Christian Science Monitor*, 29 February 1996, 10.

47. Tim Weiner with Tim Golden, "Free Trade Treaty May Widen Traffic in Drugs, U.S. Says," *New York Times*, 24 May 1993, 1A.

48. Cited in Golden, "Mexican Connection Grows as Cocaine Supplier to U.S.," A1.

49. H.G. Reza, "Border Inspections Eased and Drug Seizures Plunge," *Los Angeles Times*, 12 February 1995.

50. Reza, "Border Inspections Eased and Drug Seizures Plunge."

51. Drug Enforcement Administration, *The New Agricultural Reform Program*.

52. Toro, *Mexico's War on Drugs,* 58.

53. Quoted in Reuter and Ronfeldt, *Quest for Integrity*, 23.

54. Reuter and Ronfeldt, *Quest for Integrity*.

55. Reuter and Ronfeldt, *Quest for Integrity*.

56. Maria Celia Toro, "Drug Trafficking from an National Security Perspective," in *Mexico: In Search of Security*, Bruce M. Bagley and Sergio Aguayo, eds. (Miami: North-South Center, 1993), 326.

57. Quoted in Tim Golden, "Mexico to Try New Weapon in Drug Fight: The Military," *International Herald Tribune*, 25 May 1995.

58. Government of Mexico, *National Drug Control Program 1995–2000*, October 1995, excerpted in *Trends in Organized Crime*, 1, no. 4 (Summer 1996): 26–27.

59. See, for example, Loser and Kalter, "Mexico."

60. Some UN analysts have begun to explore the links between the drug trade and broader economic changes. See, for example, "Drugs and Development," discussion paper prepared for the world summit on social development, UN International Drug Control Programme, June 1994; "A Routine Activity Approach to Trends in International Drug Trafficking," discussion paper, United Nations International Drug Control Programme, August 1995; and Douglas Keh, "Drug Money in a Changing World: Economic Reform and Criminal Finance," UNDCP technical series, no. 4, United Nations Drug Control Programme, 1996.

61. Office of National Drug Control Policy, *U.S. National Drug Control Strategy* (Washington, DC: GPO, 1994), 49.

6

The Limits of Coercive Diplomacy: U.S. Drug Policy and Colombian State Stability, 1978–1997

William O. Walker III

On February 28, 1997, the Clinton administration announced that it would not certify the government of Colombia as fully cooperating with the United States on drug control. The United States had "decertified" Colombia for the second straight year. Moreover, in July 1996 the Department of State had canceled the passport of Colombian President Ernesto Samper Pizano for allegedly accepting money during his 1994 presidential campaign from drug traffickers based in Cali. U.S. authorities had found suspect his June 1996 exoneration by the Colombian congress. Because of the decertification, loans from international banks could have been cut off and U.S. markets for Colombian exports such as coffee and cut flowers could have been subjected to restrictive tariffs. The White House chose not to apply sanctions at that time.[1]

The history of U.S.-Colombian drug diplomacy since the late 1970s offers a promising vantage point from which to explore linkages between domestic politics and international relations. To date, though, most scholars have shied away from studying the many dimensions of the illicit global economy. For more than two decades, the United States has dealt with the drug issue as a significant security-related matter. Given the multibillion-dollar profits annually produced by the illegal drug trade, it is demonstrably an important issue for producing and trafficking nations as well.

Building upon the body of literature concerning two-level games and state capacity, especially the pathbreaking work of Robert D. Putnam, it is possible to suggest how this aspect of the illicit global economy might find its proper place in the study of international relations.² Insights borrowed from the theoretical realms of either structural realism or liberal internationalism would at first seem to constitute appropriate frameworks for analysis. The dictum of Robert O. Keohane that "systemic theory is important because we must understand the context of action before we can understand the action itself" speaks directly to an issue like drug control, which is primarily dealt with on the international and state-to-state levels.³ Liberal internationalism also comes to the fore analytically because of the long history of global drug control agreements. The existing drug control regime has on balance been more the product of cooperative than coercive international diplomacy.

Both of these approaches possess conceptual limitations, however. Structural realism tends to posit states as unitary actors—a way of seeing that overlooks the complexity of decision making and state-society tensions. It evaluates the actions of states like Colombia on the world stage without sufficient regard for the historical context. Liberal internationalism tends to assume a commonality of interest among actors, which can slight historical context and minimize the domestic and international constraints on state capacity. Even in modified form, these approaches clearly privilege a systemic perspective on diplomacy and domestic politics.⁴ They do not, therefore, support analyses that require greater conceptual subtlety. Although realism and internationalism no longer evince their prior propensity to sharply distinguish between security considerations and economic issues as worthwhile venues for intellectual inquiry, they nevertheless remain unsatisfactory bases for a comprehensive understanding of the illicit global drug economy.⁵

The virtue of a two-level analysis lies in its insistence upon the centrality of state capacity at both the domestic and international levels. Statesmen, writes Andrew Moravcsik, "seek to manipulate domestic and international politics simultaneously. Diplomatic strategies and tactics are constrained both by what other states will accept and by what domestic constituencies will ratify."⁶ Though two-level analysis seems capable of considering the illicit global economy as an independent variable under most conditions, its applicability to coercive bargaining situations like that often existing between the United States and Colombia over drugs remains insufficiently tested.

What is put forward in this chapter is a structured, focused comparison of bilateral drug diplomacy.⁷ The period in question, 1978 to 1997, can be divided into three sections: 1978–1988, 1988–1994, and 1994–1997. Readily observable are the different objectives of the two negotiators, the governments of the United States and Colombia. Since the late 1970s, the principal goal of Washington has been to curtail the produc-

tion, manufacture, and trafficking of drugs—including marijuana, cocaine, and heroin—for reasons of security. For Bogotá, the fundamental
objective has been to prevent the illegal drug business from giving rise
to challenges to the integrity of the Colombian state. Authorities have
only indirectly sought to confront the illicit business per se. The illicit
global economy thus brought about responses that differed in Washington and Bogotá and in the process contributed to a heightening of tensions in the asymmetrical relationship between the two capitals.

By 1988 Colombia, though obviously the less powerful state, used
the moral advantage it gained from being on the front line of the U.S.
drug war to nearly control the negotiating process and effectively gain
U.S. acquiescence to its preferred course of action. Until then, U.S.
officials had dominated negotiations over what drug control policies
their counterparts in Bogotá should adopt. Following Samper's controversial election in 1994, the United States successfully reclaimed its
accustomed superior position and maintained it through the 1997 certification decision.

To understand these developments, it is necessary to look at state
capacity in the diplomatic process—which encompasses both the negotiation and ratification of agreements.[8] State capacity for the United
States remained inviolable throughout the period in question. The
United States faced no threat to the integrity of its territory, it could
call upon immense financial resources to carry out agreements, and it
easily met any challenges from Congress regarding specifics about the
agreements themselves or the cost of implementing them. Within the
executive branch prior to 1988, virtual unanimity concerning goals if
not tactics limited somewhat the flexibility of negotiators. Colombia
could derive no advantage from this situation because there was never
any thought that U.S. policy objectives were an inappropriate response
to the security threat posed by drugs. Authorities in Washington therefore did not have to concern themselves with building a "win-set," or
broadly based constituency, in order to make antidrug agreements effective.[9]

Colombian state capacity was less institutionalized. Chiefs of government were continually engaged in fashioning win-sets that reflected
their own preferences and addressed the interests of domestic groups
both in and out of government, and responded to U.S. interests as well.
As a result, the size of Colombia's win-set could change at any time.
Under the Putnam model, Colombia, as a weak state with scant freedom
from countervailing pressures on its negotiators, should have enjoyed a
stronger bargaining position vis-à-vis the United States in negotiations.
The historical record does not support that assumption, though.

Why Colombia rarely possessed the advantage in negotiations indicates the difficulty of applying the logic of two-level games when direct or subtle coercion by the stronger partner is an integral part of the diplomatic process. Such a situation can present a less powerful state with few alternatives other than defection, either voluntarily or involuntarily because of real or potential threats to state capacity, from drug control agreements acceptable to the stronger power. Closely related to the idea of defection is that of deception, or misrepresentation of what an agreement means in practice. On occasion, Colombia has resorted to deception and has faced the prospect of retaliation from the United States.[10] For officials in Bogotá, defection or deception appeared to be reasonable courses of action as resistance grew to the adoption of U.S.-style drug controls.

The Historical Setting

A look at drug diplomacy in the context of modern Colombian history provides the empirical basis for understanding how drugs became an issue of considerable magnitude when so defined by the United States in the 1970s. The role of drugs in the political economy of Colombia began shortly after the Second World War. Colombian officials admitted that in some regions of the country "the cultivation of coca . . . represents the basis of economic life of the family."[11] By 1960, the Federal Bureau of Narcotics, a predecessor of the Drug Enforcement Administration (DEA), was becoming concerned about Colombia's role as a supplier of cocaine for a growing market in the United States.[12]

At that time, La Violencia and its aftermath, not drugs, dominated Colombian politics. La Violencia refers to the period after the assassination on April 9, 1948, of Liberal Party leader Jorge Eliécer Gaitán, which sparked a decade of bloody fighting in Colombia between Liberals and their Conservative opponents.[13] By the mid-1950s, some 200,000 people had died in the chaos that had engulfed the country.

The first wave of La Violencia reached a conclusion in 1958 with the formation of the Frente Nacional, or National Front, under which the two major parties would alternate the presidency. A second round of violence ensued as oligarchic and clientalist politics as usual prevailed on the national scene. Organized peasants, some of whom became leftist guerrillas during years of fighting against the traditional parties, founded the Fuerzas Armadas Revolucionarias de Colombia (FARC) in 1964.

At the same time, other political-military organizations, including the Ejercito de Liberación Nacional (ELN) and the Ejercito Popular de Liberación (EPL), took shape. They denounced the conservative goals that characterized the reform programs of the National Front. They also contended that the state had traditionally treated peasants, urban and rural workers, and small landholders brutally and with contempt. Historian David Bushnell underscores this perspective, noting that, even with indicators of economic transformation to a modern capitalist economy emerging under the National Front, "there was not much change in overall patterns of inequality."[14]

Liberal and Conservative leaders welcomed the appearance of the Alliance for Progress in these troubled times. U.S. economic assistance to further the cause of social reform, combined with antiguerrilla military aid, was intended to make Colombia a model of peaceful revolution—one of the Alliance's initial goals for all of Latin America. Things did not work out as planned. The United States may have hoped for more comprehensive reforms, yet was pleased that Alliance programs helped return a semblance of order and stability to Colombia.[15]

U.S. policymakers held increasingly high expectations about what their counterparts in Bogotá could accomplish on matters of interest to Washington. Drug control was one such issue. Why these hopes were dashed by the late 1970s reveals much about the unstable nature of Colombia's political system and the difficulty of generating extensive support for antidrug agreements.

Rebel groups did not trust the established oligarchy to keep its promises to foster socioeconomic change and political reform. The limits of Conservative and Liberal politics were reflected as well in the actions of right-wing paramilitary forces, with their roots in the 1930s, who played a small role during La Violencia and the years of the National Front. Along with rural police in the late 1960s and early 1970s, they took up the cause of those large landholders who opposed reform. When the drug traffickers of a slightly later day needed to employ paramilitary forces for their own purposes, they had a tradition upon which to draw.[16]

That problems of governance and the resultant weakening of state authority could affect U.S. interests became evident in February 1976 when Henry Kissinger—as President Gerald R. Ford's secretary of state—journeyed to Bogotá to discuss drug control and other issues.[17] The essential failure of agrarian reform during the presidency of liberal Alfonse López Michelsen had driven 30,000 disgruntled agricultural workers into the fields of landowners who produced marijuana. The specter of class conflict that the political oligarchy feared thereby subsided, but in its place there appeared "a vertical block of classes controlled by regional mafias."[18] Thus, there emerged a potential challenge to state authority.

Guerrilla movements also received a new lease on life in the mid-

1970s. Reprisals by the military had decimated the ELN and the EPL in the late 1960s, but the fate of land reform won new recruits for them. Also, an urban-based guerrilla organization, the M-19, emerged in the mid-1970s in Bogotá, Cali, and Medellín and, in its denunciation of clientalist politics, "presented a much more immediate threat to the stability of the political system than the rural guerrillas."[19] The established order would respond to these challenges by intermittently declaring states of siege as a means of coping with leftist threats. Landowners in the Cauca and Magdalena Medio regions, many of whom were involved in nascent cocaine enterprises, formed private armies to protect their lands from guerrilla forces.[20] The possibility of societal disintegration made it virtually impossible for the state to build support for foreign-based policies like strict drug control.

As the first post–National Front president when he took office in 1974, the once liberal López Michelsen endeavored to implement a policy of neoliberal economic planning. He failed. Tax collections were lower than anticipated because of a program of tax amnesty. Consequently, government expenditures on social programs remained below what López had budgeted. Meanwhile, the credit market was booming and elevated coffee prices brought an influx of foreign exchange.

These developments led to a rate of inflation of nearly 30 percent, which the burgeoning production of marijuana and a resurgent trade in cocaine surely exacerbated. The foreign exchange surplus and extensive drug money allowed Colombia to reduce its foreign obligations but not to achieve its social objectives.[21] Neither in government nor in the private sector did there emerge the incentive to place stringent controls on the drug business, even had it been possible to do so. In fact, the Bank of the Republic countenanced the influx of drug-related revenues through a *ventanilla siniestra*, or unofficial window, which accepted illegal foreign exchange.[22]

This latter development implicitly questioned the promises by López to Kissinger concerning Colombia's ability and also its willingness to take action against drugs. Already, Colombian traffickers were delivering as much as 90 percent of the cocaine reaching the United States. Nevertheless, a report to the U.S. House of Representatives Committee on International Relations after a fact-finding trip to Colombia by several congressmen noted that although corruption was pervasive in his country, López was "totally committed" to expanding and improving antidrug enforcement efforts and was evidently prepared, as he put it, to "go to war" against drugs.[23]

In Putnam's terms, involuntary defection from drug control agreements, brought on by conditions beyond the control of the state, led Colombian officials to practice deception on a consistent basis. Had

López overestimated his ability to form a domestic consensus around the issue of drug control? More likely, he deliberately misled the United States about his capacity to do so. Indeed, he resisted following the U.S. lead on drug control for some time. Many Colombians believed that drug trafficking was a problem fundamentally created by consumer demand in the United States.[24] It therefore was not Colombia's to solve.

The 1976 House report constituted, however, an attempt to persuade Colombia, notwithstanding its reluctance, to take an active role in antidrug activities. Cocaine from Colombia had a street value in the United States of $500 million. Despite the kind words for López, the report observed that "Colombia is a major concern to the U.S. narcotic enforcement effort." It was unclear whether this kind of indirect pressure would induce López to implement antidrug agreements with the United States despite the political costs at home.

Eighteen months later, the new House Select Committee on Narcotics Abuse and Control described how the traffickers, or *narcotráficantes,* and their operations were pervading Colombian society. The committee drew attention to growing U.S. concern about the extent of high-level corruption.[25] The administration of President Jimmy Carter, confident that it could address such matters through diplomatic channels, began portraying the drug business as a threat to Colombia's national security, a position that Colombian officials did not share.[26] Drugs were about to come to the fore in U.S.-Colombian relations and affect that relationship as never before. How a state whose capacity to govern effectively was in doubt would respond to challenges to its authority remained uncertain.

Following Washington's Lead on Drug Control

Julio César Turbay Ayala had more on his mind than drugs and the United States upon becoming president of Colombia in August 1978. The second liberal in a row to hold the office, he kept the Conservatives as a loyal opposition by extending 40 percent of federal patronage to them. Unfortunately for Turbay, he had to cope not only with a rise in guerrilla violence, which he met with rapid, repressive means, but also with public hostility because he failed to present detailed plans for economic, and presumably social, development.[27]

When Turbay did finally experiment with government-sponsored economic development, the public debt rose to U.S. $9.4 billion—a figure that was nearly 225 percent higher than when he took office—by 1982, the final year of his term. Making matters worse still, revenues from taxation declined further and coffee prices also decreased. Meanwhile, the Bank of the Republic left open its vaults to accept illegal foreign exchange; money derived from the trade in marijuana and, increasingly, cocaine nearly equaled revenue from the sale of coffee.[28]

Turbay's conservatism underscored his inability to respond effectively to pressing public problems, which served in turn to hamper his relations with Washington over drugs. Left to his own devices he would have persisted in his National Front-style of rule by trying to soften the impact of a deteriorating economy and by permitting the military to contain leftist threats as it saw fit. In his ideal hierarchy of public policy issues, drugs would not have been in the top rank.

Yet because the Carter administration was prodding him to adopt a tough stance against drugs, he was compelled to address the issue—adding to the burdens of office an additional dilemma. Turbay's response to U.S. entreaties, a pledge to undertake crop eradication, which at the time appeared to be an aggressive step, in fact symbolized how Colombian leaders have handled Washington and the drug issue since the 1970s.

What Colombian chiefs of government did was typical of the "Janus-faced" executive, who seeks policymaking strategies that produce complementarity in domestic objectives and international goals.[29] In short, Turbay and his successors have consistently promised significant results where the control of drugs was concerned in an effort to create greater freedom of action to deal with domestic challenges to state capacity. Selectively, they have kept those promises while searching for what might be called a Colombian road to drug control. Their understanding about what it took to maintain the integrity of state authority led Colombia's presidents to adopt strategies of defection and deception over drugs. Whatever their personal preferences, they believed that they had limited freedom to implement agreements because of domestic constraints, particularly those portending violence against the state.[30]

Revelations in April 1978 on the CBS television program "60 Minutes" indicated that López's ministers of labor, Abrahám Varón Valencia, and defense, Oscar Montoya, were connected with the drug trade. (Rumors subsequently linked Turbay himself with marijuana traffickers.) The Carter White House, which was then reconsidering the wisdom of marijuana decriminalization because of a scandal involving Dr. Peter G. Bourne, the president's special assistant for health issues, sought to placate its critics by increasing the pressure on Turbay to get tough on drugs.[31]

Mexico, as a result of talks with Washington, had recently begun spraying a potent defoliant, paraquat, on its marijuana crop. Colombia was urged to spray along its northwest coast and in the eastern regions where marijuana grew in abundance.[32] The prospect of losing the lucrative North American market induced growers to enter the political arena. They recommended that the state adopt a policy of legalization of production rather than crop destruction.

As this drama played out, it became evident how difficult it was for officials to maintain a constituency supportive of an enforceable anti-drug agreement with the United States. Not to allow legal drug production would threaten jobs in areas where Bogotá's authority was already weak; unemployed peasants were likely recruits for guerrilla forces. Also, without the illicit sale of marijuana, the Bank of the Republic would lose revenue. As a result, it remained difficult to mobilize and maintain a reliable win-set for drug control in Colombia.

Possibly—and the evidence is not conclusive—with such a situation in mind, the Asociación Nacional de Instituciones Financieras (ANIF), headed by economist Ernesto Samper Pizano, proposed that the government consider legalizing marijuana. At a conference held in March 1979 to discuss the controversial idea, participants from the United States, including Ambassador Diego Ascensio, summarily rejected the idea. Samper's reasoning was greatly distorted in the heat of the moment and its aftermath. He contended that forcible repression of the marijuana industry would mean nothing but further trouble for the government.[33]

Not to repress the marijuana trade, though, meant trouble with Washington, which Turbay did not want. Thus, he accepted a substantial increase in counternarcotics aid and sent the army into the marijuana fields to begin crop eradication. (The use of defoliants was prohibited.) The outcome was predictable: U.S. officials praised Turbay's cooperation; state-sponsored violence broke out against growers in the Colombian countryside; and the state's capacity to govern deteriorated.

The campaign against marijuana also meant greater emphasis on cocaine in Colombia's illegal economy. The shift to cocaine brought to public awareness the likes of Pablo Escobar Gaviria and the Ochoas of Antioquia and the Rodríguez Orejuela clan of Cali. For several years Colombian and U.S. officials had known about their connection with the expanded cocaine trade. South Florida and the Queens section of New York, to take two examples, were already witnessing the ability of the narcotráficantes to rain violence upon innocent people.[34] The resultant fear of drugs linked the interests of state and society in the United States, thereby confirming decisions by the White House to take a hard-line approach in negotiations with Bogotá.

With few options at the conference table and with limited support at home, Turbay bowed to Washington's coercive diplomacy. By the end of 1979 he had signed six accords to combat drug trafficking and adopted a policy of extradition. Turbay had consented, in effect, to embark upon a supply-side war against drugs. In so doing he was gambling that he could export, if not actually prevent, the violence that would result from a program of crop eradication by the armed forces.[35]

Tacitly admitting that Turbay had failed to preserve state integrity by following Washington's lead on drugs, his successor, Belisario Betancur Cuartas of the Conservative Party, elected not to implement the drug accords, notably the extradition treaty, concluded with the United States. U.S. Ambassador Lewis A. Tambs insisted without success that Colombia initiate the extradition process. Betancur was unwilling, though, to commence extraditing Colombian narcotráficantes because he was hoping to open a dialogue with guerrilla forces and to address economic problems inherited from Turbay.[36] These preferences largely explain his defection from the 1979 agreements.

Betancur's risk-taking did not have a salutary impact at home. By the mid-1980s homicide was the leading cause of death in his country; the M-19 raised the level of urban guerrilla violence, and the FARC extended its reach into the coca-growing areas of southern Colombia. Meanwhile, private security forces were being established to protect the operations of the drug barons. In Antioquia, the Ochoa family combined its drug-related businesses with those of Pablo Escobar and José Gonzalo Rodríguez Gacha to form the Medellín cartel.[37]

Betancur's defection quickly brought retaliation and the prospect of even less flexibility on Washington's part at the bargaining table. The U.S. Congress rejected the idea that there should be a Colombian road to drug control and in November 1983 adopted the controversial process known as certification. By law, the delivery of foreign aid would be linked to acceptable counternarcotics activity—as defined by the Department of State. The House Select Committee charged that authorities in Bogotá lacked the political will to attack the drug industry. If the administration of President Ronald Reagan did not appreciate the self-insertion of Congress into the decision-making process, it did not mind having an additional weapon at its disposal in negotiations with Colombia over drugs.[38]

As pressure mounted against him, Betancur changed course and gave in to U.S. pressure. At home, the highly respected daily newspaper *El Espectador* had denounced the president's refusal to extradite the narcos.[39] At the same time, the Medellín cartel was promising a campaign of savage violence if the state failed to accord it the political legitimacy it could not attain through traditional processes. Then on March 10, 1984, Colombian forces destroyed a cocaine processing facility, Tranquilandia, located in Caquetá. Betancur also resumed extradition and approved the spraying of herbicides on marijuana.

The fruits of coercive diplomacy proved to be exceedingly bitter, however. In retribution for Tranquilandia, *sicarios*, or assassins, hired by the narcos killed Justice Minister Rodrigo Lara Bonilla. Betancur then declared a state of siege, thereby making the armed forces an integral part of a suddenly hot drug war in Colombia. By late 1986 sicarios had murdered the head of the narcotics unit of the National Police, Col. Jaime Ramirez Gómez, and the editor-in-chief of *El Espectador*, Guillermo Cano Isaza.[40]

For Betancur, as for all Colombian presidents since the 1970s, narcoterrorism threatened state authority far more than did narcotrafficking. This reality shaped his thinking about drugs in a way that challenged the supremacy of U.S. objectives. It motivated Betancur to assay a policy of deception in the eyes of U.S. officials and some of his erstwhile constituents. His administration began secret, though ultimately unproductive talks in Panama with key Medellín narcos in an effort to curb drug-related violence. He apparently wanted to bring both the cartel and guerrillas—via separate talks—into the national political arena. Liberal politicians including Sen. Ernesto Samper from Bogotá denounced the effort as quixotic, even though Samper was suspected of having received U.S. $3 million from the cocaine cartels to finance in part López Michelsen's unsuccessful run for the presidency in 1982.[41]

The attempted demarche with Medellín failed, as did appeals to the FARC and M-19. The rebels saw their numbers decimated by carefully orchestrated violence on the part of the armed forces and paramilitary groups in the pay of the narcos. By late 1985, one observer concluded, "Colombia fell headlong into undeclared war." Nothing more starkly represented the diminution of state authority and governing capacity than M-19's assault in November on the Palacio de Justicia at the behest of the Medellín cartel. The bloody retaking of the Palacio resulted in the death of half of Colombia's Supreme Court judges.[42]

Virgilio Barco's Autonomy

Liberal Party member and former ambassador to the United States Virgilio Barco Vargas took office as president of Colombia in August 1986. Barco, elected by a sizeable majority, hoped to implement wide-ranging programs of social and political reform with the goal of reducing the level of violence throughout his nation. Recent economic improvements and a decline in urban unemployment seemed to offer Barco the opportunity to put his plans into effect.[43] Time would not long be his ally, though, as developments in U.S. drug policy and terrorist actions by the Medellín cartel quickly overwhelmed his efforts.

Colombian journalist María Jimena Duzán writes that drug trafficking "was not [Barco's] first priority. It was, however, for the United States."[44] Four months before Barco assumed power, President Ronald Reagan had issued National Security Decision Directive No. 221, which declared drug trafficking a threat to U.S., and by implication Latin American, security. Three weeks prior to Barco's inauguration, the United States had militarized the drug war in the Andes by undertaking Operation Blast Furnace in a concerted effort to destroy cocaine processing facilities in Bolivia.[45] Within a year, Blast Furnace would metamorphose into a region-wide coca control program, Operation Snowcap.[46] Control at the source, one of the basic principles of the U.S.-led drug control effort, had taken on a new meaning. Intensification of the drug war ostensibly meant that Barco would soon have to act forcefully against his country's drug cartels.

The Colombian president's policy priorities were motivated more by a determined effort to curb cartel-induced and guerrilla-related violence than by a clear-cut decision to launch a direct attack on the drug business. In the second half of 1986, though, the Medellín cartel unleashed a wave of terror that was intended to intimidate the government into shelving compliance with the controversial 1979 extradition treaty. Caught up in the violence were members of the national judiciary, who presided over cases against cartel members, and also former guerrillas who had committed themselves to peaceful participation in the political process through the Unión Patriótica.[47]

On the one hand, the escalation of violence by the Medellín cartel galvanized Barco's determination to isolate Colombia's narcos. He responded by increasing the authority of the police to combat drugs. On the other hand, the lords of cocaine, self-described as the extraditables, had won an important victory in their effort to avoid punishment. On December 12, 1986, five days before the brutal killing of Guillermo Cano, the Supreme Court ruled invalid the law implementing the extradition treaty. Six months later, the court voided the treaty itself on procedural grounds. Thereafter, Barco employed his executive authority to threaten the cartel with reprisal for its actions.[48] His most public action undertaken in accord with Washington's wishes came in February 1987 when he ordered the extradition to the United States of Carlos Lehder, a member of the Medellín cartel.[49]

Barco's actions during his first two years in office pleased the United States. The International Narcotics Control Strategy Reports (INCSR) for 1986 and 1987, issued by the Department of State, paint a picture of quiescence in relations with Colombia over drugs. Colombia appeared to be accepting the rules of the regime: the 1986 INCSR recorded "dramatic progress" in Colombia's war on drugs through both the spraying of herbicides and the disruption of cocaine processing.[50]

The 1987 report observed that "Colombia continued its effective attack on narcotics production and trafficking" but cautioned that "judges, police officers, Congressmen, journalists, and private citizens have become victims of assassination attempts."[51]

The date when Barco decided to depart from the U.S. lead on drug policy is unclear. For a while after the assassination of Attorney General Carlos Mauro Hoyos in January 1988, Barco appeared willing to follow the example of his two immediate predecessors, Betancur and Turbay, and generally accept the U.S. lead on drug control. By August 1989, however, his independence became apparent in the wake of the murder of liberal presidential candidate Luis Carlos Galán.

The killing of Mauro Hoyos and the persistence of unabated violence (some 30,000 Colombians died in drug-related violence from 1984 to 1989) moved Barco toward fundamental reform of the Colombian political system. The Plan Nacional de Rehabilitación, with which he hoped to compensate for the lack of socioeconomic change since the demise of the National Front, could not succeed in an atmosphere paralyzed by fear.[52] The United States was demanding action against drug trafficking and production perhaps through joint military operations, as had occurred in Bolivia; influential Colombians wanted him to break up the paramilitary forces; and Barco's own military agreed to enter the war against drugs if it could set the terms for its participation.[53]

Barco wanted to seize the initiative for a strategy that would give him sufficient options so that he would not have to choose between all-out war, which would awaken memories of La Violencia, and negotiations. To negotiate with no preconditions amounted to surrender to either the cartels or insurgent forces like the various regional fronts of the FARC that had rejected the peace process.[54] The means Barco chose to accomplish these tasks were initially military in nature. He could not rely on the judicial system because it had been compromised by violence and corruption.[55]

Barco had no qualms about using force. Early in the 1980s, the Colombian National Police (CNP) had replaced the armed forces as the lead agency in charge of countering drug production and traffic. In 1987, the CNP further consolidated its authority by creating a Directorate of Anti-Narcotics, which included an airwing and a tactical operations branch. By mid-1988, as violence against the state continued, the military again became involved in antidrug operations, albeit in a subordinate role.[56]

The murder of Galán on August 18, 1989, demonstrated the boldness and recklessness of the Medellín cartel. Barco would have responded forcibly in any event, but favorable developments in the peace process with the M-19 gave him greater flexibility than he would otherwise have had.[57] The president declared total war on the cartel. He announced the resumption of extradition, thus circumventing the Supreme Court's ruling that the 1979 treaty was invalid. He ordered the confiscation of the assets of major traffickers. And he authorized the police to hold suspects incommunicado for up to seven days.[58]

Seeking to bolster Colombia's judicial system, Barco asked Washington to provide more than military aid in a $65 million assistance package.[59] The cartel responded by declaring its own all-out war against the government.[60] As the ensuing violence engulfed Colombia, it appeared as though the United States at last had a major, active battlefront in the war on drugs. José Gonzalo Rodríguez Gacha claimed that the siege of Colombia could last as long as three years, given the cartel's resources.[61]

Unlike Washington, Bogotá saw the war as a means to an end—healing the divisions in Colombian society—and would halt it quickly under the right conditions. Thus Barco did not rule out negotiations with the cartel; when he met with President George Bush in Washington at the end of September, he asked not for additional counternarcotics aid but for restoration of the International Coffee Agreement. The collapse of the accord in July threatened Colombia with an annual loss of revenue of U.S. $500 million to $1 billion.[62] In a meeting with congressional leaders, he urged them to do more to curb domestic demand for drugs; he also told the General Assembly of the United Nations that producer nations could not dismantle the cartels until governments in consumer states paid greater attention to money laundering and the trade in precursor chemicals.[63]

On the occasion of his trip to the United States, Barco began publicly to assert Colombia's right to be considered an equal partner in the drug war. Barco's acceptance of extradition indicated just how serious he was. Washington viewed extradition as a litmus test of Bogotá's will to pursue the Medellín cartel. Extradition remained for Barco principally a way to placate U.S. officials and simultaneously threaten the extraditables, while seeking a way to rebuild Colombia's judicial system.[64]

Barco knew that his challenge to the primacy of the United States could be dismissed if the war went badly. He therefore had to build the strongest possible win-set at home, while at the same time negotiating agreements with the United States to enhance state capacity.[65] In that sense, actually fighting the drug war became a secondary priority. Barco's plan for state reconstruction evidently led him to approve informal discussions between a *comisión de notables* and Medellín's extraditables.[66] This particular effort failed, but it served further notice to the United States that Colombia would endeavor to address the drug issue on its own terms.

Barco's movement toward policymaking autonomy in the drug war did not initially meet with favor in Washington. Officials in the Bush administration tried to short-circuit his efforts after Galán's murder. Director of the Office of National Drug Control Policy (ONDCP) William Bennett said that his government would be willing to send U.S. troops to Colombia. Barco resisted the presence of U.S. personnel beyond the few military trainers and DEA agents already in his country.[67] Massive aid, he believed, would retard the process of judicial reconstruction. Though he made it clear to the United States that judicial reform was a priority, the State Department's Agency for International Development (AID) did not begin funding a reform project until nearly one year after his successor, César Gaviria Trujillo, had taken office.[68]

What the Bush administration did do in the wake of Galán's assassination was to announce the creation of the Andean Drug Strategy, a multiyear $2.2 billion effort designed to wage war on drug production, trafficking, and corruption in Bolivia, Colombia, and Peru.[69] Critics pointed out that any extensive militarization of the drug war would likely result in greater illicit arms trafficking, the beneficiaries of which would be the cartels, their paramilitary forces, and those guerrillas who were disdaining the peace process.[70] Moreover, militarization would symbolize a desire by the administration to dictate the course of the drug war without due consultation. And, militarization on U.S. terms would indicate a lack of interest in the institution building that Colombia needed in order to guarantee political stability.[71] By 1990, the fate of state authority, and the very fate of U.S. drug policy in the region, may have depended upon Barco's ability to set his own policy priorities.[72] It seemed possible that coercive diplomacy might give way to an expanded win-set on both the national and international levels.

U.S. Learning and State Authority in Colombia

The human cost of the drug war had given Barco the upper hand in relations with the Bush administration. The sacrifices that Colombia was making as drug consumption persisted in the United States played an important role in Bush's decision to attend in February 1990 a drug summit in Cartagena, Colombia, together with the presidents of Bolivia and Peru.[73] Barco used the meeting to stress how important commercial growth and economic development were to managing the crisis in Colombia. Only prosperity would counter the appeal of the FARC and check the growing power of right-wing paramilitary forces.[74] Aiding Barco's effort to lessen U.S. influence over his country was the killing of José Gonzalo Rodríguez Gacha and his son in mid-December, six weeks before the start of the Cartagena summit. Significantly, U.S. intelligence played a supportive role in the operation by providing data to Colombian forces.[75]

At Cartagena, Bush and Secretary of State James A. Baker III agreed that consuming countries had to do more to curb demand for drugs.[76] Their acknowledgment of the importance of reciprocity was unique in the annals of U.S. drug diplomacy. Bush and Baker had implicitly recognized Barco's right to assert a Colombian road to drug control. It remained to be seen whether that recognition would become an enduring aspect of the U.S.-Colombian drug relationship.

President César Gaviria came to office in August 1990 determined to maintain relative freedom of action in the drug war. He specifically wanted to accelerate the process of democratization that Betancur and Barco had earlier initiated. To do so he agreed to rewrite the constitution to reflect a partial transfer of power from the capital to the rest of the country. He also sought to expand Colombia's foreign trade on a regional and hemispheric basis. In fact, as president-elect he told President Bush that economic aid would be more welcome from the United States than antinarcotics assistance. With such measures, traditional clientelism might lose its grip on national politics, local government might take root, and social reform might become a reality.[77]

U.S. officials were in no position to criticize the new administration, but they did wonder how the drug war would fare under Gaviria. Their concerns rose when Gaviria announced that he would not turn over to the United States any extraditables who agreed to submit to Colombian justice.[78] Like Barco, Gaviria was racing against time as he tried to bind his wounded nation together. By the end of 1990, the FARC had increased the level of violence just as elections for a new Constitutional Assembly were taking place. The Colombian army responded in kind, thereby raising the price of failure for the government.[79]

Some officials in the United States were less sensitive than they might have been to Colombia's plight. Melvyn Levitsky, head of the Bureau of International Narcotics Matters in the State Department, minimized the harm that the drug war could do to the prospects for democracy in the Andes. He praised militarization as "a sign of greater overall national commitment in dealing with the problem." Even the surrender of the Medellín cartel's Fabio and Jorge Luis Ochoa in late 1990 and early 1991 did not lessen pressure on Bogotá from some quarters in the United States. DEA chief Robert Bonner observed: "We will watch closely [their] prosecution by Colombian authorities."[80]

These discordant notes raised several important questions. What had U.S. officials learned from the Colombian experience with drugs? What was the composition of the U.S. win-set in narcodiplomacy with Colombia? In the early post–Cold War years, what was the place of drug control in the spectrum of foreign policy concerns? To the extent that members of the policymaking community in Washington viewed Bogotá's quest for autonomy as a serious challenge to the rules of the global drug regime, then it was hard to see that adaptive learning had taken place. A clear change in beliefs—as represented by a positive response to Colombia's delicate political situation—would indicate that learning had occurred. At the same time, if a hard-line approach to drug control characterized U.S. policymaking, then learning might indicate nothing more than the acquisition of knowledge.[81] It is therefore telling that, even after promising to address the issue of drug demand at home, Bush and Baker were not prepared to modify the traditional goal of control at the source.

Gaviria refused throughout his presidency to abandon the goals he set during his first months in office. He struggled against guerrilla- and narcoinduced terror, guided the writing of the new constitution, which was approved in July 1991, and sought larger, regional markets for Colombian products. The persistence of violence against the state and the disruption of essential services like electricity cost him dearly. By mid-1992, his previously elevated approval rating had dipped well below 50 percent. Support for his antidrug policy eroded as well.[82] This was particularly the case as narcotráficantes based in Cali began to replace their more visible counterparts in Medellín as the major suppliers of drugs.[83] U.S. Ambassador Thomas E. McNamara declared, and the crusading newspaper *El Espectador* agreed, that it had been "an error to prohibit extradition."[84]

The housing of the most feared extraditable, Pablo Escobar, in the comfortable Envigado prison after his surrender in June 1991 further showed how the impulse to engage in coercive diplomacy could reduce the likelihood of substantive change in U.S. policy. Bob Martinez, former governor of Florida and Bennett's successor as ONDCP chief, told the CBS television program "Face the Nation": "I think Colombia will be on trial with Pablo Escobar."[85] Martinez and others in Washington feared that a battle won in Colombia against narcoterrorism would prove to be a setback in the U.S. war on drugs.

Escobar's subsequent escape from Envigado in July 1992 led some U.S. officials to conclude that the Colombian road to drug control had really been a dead-end street. His violent death in December 1993 at the hands of security forces with the help of U.S. intelligence and the DEA helped to allay that fear.[86] It was at home, though, where Escobar's escape met with the most criticism.[87] Many Colombians were worried that leniency toward Escobar and other extraditables would undermine Gaviria's experiment with democratization. Deals with the cartel leaders might result in human rights abuses, give indirect support to the growth of the Cali cartel, or lead the FARC to conclude that it could continue its campaign of terror against the nation's oil reserves.[88] Executive autonomy depended, it seems, upon the extent of domestic support for the chief of government.

Why the lenient treatment of Escobar did not then impair relations with the United States owed little to Barco's or Gaviria's efforts to negotiate from a position of moral strength over drugs. Despite misgivings, U.S. authorities tolerated Colombia's independent course in the drug war, believing that flexibility in the short term would allow them to reassert the primacy of U.S. policy at some future date. Put differently, Washington's faith in coercive diplomacy proved hard to shake. Colombia could experiment with a variety of tactics in its struggle with drugs, but strategic decision making remained with the United States.

Between late 1989 and 1993, Colombia's effort to enhance state stability and the U.S. determination to wage war against drugs in South America had briefly coincided. Department of Defense and DEA training missions were assisting the CNP and the armed forces; information sharing was at an all-time high and the dollar value of military and other counternarcotics aid probably surpassed $500 million.[89] Additionally, an AID-funded program to restore judicial integrity began to show positive results.[90] At a drug summit held in February 1992 in San Antonio, Texas, the first general meeting since Cartagena, Bush could therefore speak in favorable terms about the course of the drug war in Colombia, noting that he had "learned" much about drugs and the Colombian economy.[91]

The Politics of Recrimination

Did the Bush administration bequeath to its successor a legacy of learning? The executive branch had treated the Barco and Gaviria governments more equitably than it had any of their predecessors. By 1993, U.S. drug policymakers, with the exception of some DEA personnel, were prepared to adapt their expectations about what was possible for Bogotá to accomplish to the realities of the Colombian scene.[92] Yet the learning that had occurred since Galán's death appeared to be more an example of individual learning through experience than an indication of organizational learning that could conceivably transform drug policy. Indeed, the Colombian case ultimately reinforces the proposition that organizational learning does not commonly occur. Learning, Jack S. Levy points out, does not necessarily involve substantive policy change or a more complex understanding of the world.[93] This conclusion seems particularly applicable to a situation like the one existing between the United States and Colombia. Differing views in the mid-1990s about individual state interests and, hence, about state authority itself impaired bilateral discussions about the proper course of drug control.

The inchoate nature of the Clinton administration's early drug policy destroyed the bonds that had developed with Colombia since 1989. Gaviria virtually had to divine the direction of U.S. policy after Clinton took office. If, as Arthur A. Stein contends, a commonality of interests determines the durability of regimes, then the miniregime that Bogotá and Washington had created—which could have served in turn to strengthen the global antidrug regime—was in jeopardy of collapsing.[94] Critical of the brief sentences that beleaguered judges were handing out to narcotráficantes, the Clinton White House ultimately expressed its displeasure by emphasizing control at the source more than its predecessor had done. The Bush administration, acknowledging the high cost of the drug war to Colombia, had increasingly since 1989 emphasized the interdiction of drugs in transit as its first line of attack against the Medellín and Cali cartels.[95]

As relations gradually deteriorated in 1993 and 1994, what might be termed the "Gaviria shocks" promised additional trouble. The United States suspended a 1991 evidence-sharing agreement after learning that Prosecutor General Gustavo de Grieff had secretly met with three leaders of the Cali cartel in order to negotiate a truce between Cali's narcos and the government.[96] De Grieff had also opined, as had U.S. Surgeon General Dr. Jocelyn Elders, that some form of drug legalization might constitute a feasible alternative to the costly failures that marked the war on drugs.[97] The strong negative response in Washington to these developments was predictable given the administration's lack of high-level attention to relations with the Gaviria government. Assistant Secretary of State for International Narcotics Matters Robert S. Gelbard, who had previously served as ambassador to Bolivia, where he had encouraged officials in La Paz to prosecute the drug war with vigor, asserted that de Grieff, and thus by implication Gaviria, was trying to "disrupt" existing antidrug operations.[98]

Disquiet in the United States over developments in Colombia reached even greater proportions with charges, leveled at the height of the 1994 presidential campaign by forces supporting conservative Andrés Pastrana Arango, that liberal candidate Ernesto Samper Pizano had accepted as much as U.S. $6 million from the Cali cartel.[99] By March 1996 when the Department of State refused to certify Colombia as cooperating fully in the war on drugs, revelations coming out of *Proceso 8000*—Colombia's own special investigation of the allegations—suggested complicity by Samper in an admitted effort by his former campaign manager and defense minister, Fernando Botero, to obtain "donations" from the cartel. Department of State officials explained that Samper's government had demonstrated a "lack of political will" and "lacked commitment to support the efforts of Colombian law enforcement entities and to strengthen the nation's institutions" in their fight against the corrosive impact of the cartel's activities. Even though most of the seven top-level Cali drug traffickers were in jail, they continued "to manage [their] criminal empire from prison."[100]

The first half of 1996 brought a chorus of calls by major Colombian newspapers, prominent citizens, and business leaders for Samper to vacate the presidency. He refused to do so. His subsequent exoneration by congressional investigators, who may have been tainted by drug money as well, hardened attitudes on all sides of the issue.[101] The Department of State threatened to impose economic sanctions on Colombia beyond those mandated by the March decision to decertify. Department spokesman Nicholas Burns warned that the decision would "not resolve the . . . crisis of confidence in Colombia." Yet "we will continue to cooperate with those elements of the Colombian Government that have proven to be reliable partners in the fight against narcotics."[102] In effect, the United States was trying to create a constituency in Colombia for its own policy preferences in the drug war.

Reaction in the United States showed little sympathy for Samper's troubles. Extradition again became a major political issue inside Colombia.[103] U.S. Ambassador Myles Frechette went out of his way to interject his voice, and thus the influence of the Clinton administration, into Colombia's internal affairs. He called for the United States to apply pressure that would result not just in the rapid resumption of extradition but in greater isolation for Samper within his country as well.[104]

That U.S. pressure was having an effect seemed evident when Samper proposed the adoption of further constitutional reforms to address the drug problem and because of the departure of several cabinet members from his government. Samper's address to the United Nations in September, in which he issued a call for social reform programs in producer nations and had the United States in mind when he declared that "intervention is not the way" to solve the drug problem, elicited minimal public response from the State Department.[105] Nor did it quiet his critics at home.

Meanwhile, a series of actions by fronts of the FARC and the EPL intended to disrupt national political and economic life intermittently overshadowed Samper's problems with Washington. First, the guerrillas endeavored to undermine state authority by encouraging massive protests against the government by coca growers in the departments of Putumayo, Guaviare, and Caquetá. Demonstrations such as these pointed to the inadequacy of the reform process under Samper and grabbed headlines in the national press in August and September. A hastily drafted proposal to trade eradication for economic development temporarily placated some of the *cocaleros* (coca growers).[106] Also, attacks by the FARC against the nation's largest oil pipeline reawakened fears in the business community that the continued presidency of Samper could destroy the nation's often precarious economic well-being.[107] With two years to go in his term of office, Samper's troubles on many fronts were far from over. Washington's 1997 decision not to certify guaranteed a rocky road in U.S.-Colombian relations through the 1998 presidential election.

Analysis and Conclusion

The impulse of U.S. authorities to engage in coercive drug diplomacy does not adequately explain their troubled relationship with Colombia since the late 1970s. Putnam's model of a two-level game properly examines the domestic origins of policy differences. In the crisislike atmosphere that often pervaded negotiations, the objectives of Washington and Bogotá frequently proved to be incompatible. The U.S. goal of control at the source clashed with the Colombian desire to curb narcoterrorism because of its direct threat to state stability.

Putnam's model would indicate that the relatively smaller size of the U.S. win-set favored the United States over Colombia in discussions, but made it hard to fashion mutually acceptable agreements.[108] Indeed, congressional pressures on the executive branch had the potential to limit the flexibility of presidential representatives. In contrast, the main problem for a clientalist state like Colombia was that its comparatively larger win-set was unreliable because of persistent challenges to state authority. Clientalist politics did provide, as Putnam would have it, some autonomy, notably for Barco and Gaviria. But that autonomy was from U.S. pressures, not from domestic-level constituents.

The practice of Colombian leaders either to engage in deception or to defect from agreements demonstrates that drug diplomacy possessed the attributes of a heterogeneous conflict, which complicated negotiations. A readiness to resort to forms of coercion limited the complications that U.S. officials had to consider. Colombians, however, could not count on the composition of their win-set, which varied greatly because of the changing domestic politics of the drug issue. Accordingly, the prospect for successful negotiations to bring about the control of drugs depended more on the extent of internal support for the preferences of Colombia's chief of government than on any other factor.

Building a durable win-set in Colombia was a task of immense difficulty. At any given time, the win-set included elements dedicated to the negation of state authority—guerrillas, drug traffickers, and small-scale drug producers. Only from late 1989 through approximately 1993 did U.S. officials try to work within such a situation. At other times, they urged Colombian leaders to crack down on the drug business in a way that tended to ignore the consequences for state authority.

Yet, as Patrick L. Clawson and Rensselaer W. Lee III note, drug-consuming nations like the United States may have a tangible interest in the success of negotiations with narcotráficantes such as those undertaken by the government of Colombia.[109] To denounce talks with traffickers is to deny the possibility that dialogue may prevent the further loss or compromise of Colombian governability. Hence, it is worth asking whether the alleged actions of Samper and his campaign officials have slowed the pace of the multifront assault on state authority, something that traditionalist clientalist politics have not yet been able to accomplish.[110] In the process, they might even have enhanced the chances for success of a reciprocal approach to drug control. On that basis alone, the study of the illicit global economy merits study by scholars of international affairs.

Notes

1. *New York Times*, 1 March 1997; and *Miami Herald*, 1 March 1997.

2. Robert D. Putnam, "Diplomacy and Domestic Politics: The Logic of Two-Level Games," *International Organization* 42, no. 3 (Summer 1988): 427–60.

3. Robert O. Keohane, "Theory of World Politics: Structural Realism and Beyond," in *Neorealism and Its Critics*, Robert O. Keohane, ed. (New York: Columbia University Press, 1986), 193.

4. Andrew Moravcsik, "Introduction," in *Double-Edged Diplomacy: International Bargaining and Domestic Politics*, Peter B. Evans, Harold K. Jacobson, and Robert D. Putnam, eds. (Berkeley and Los Angeles: University of California Press, 1993), 5–15.

5. On the convergence of realism and internationalism, see David A. Baldwin, ed., *Neorealism and Neoliberalism: The Contemporary Debate* (New York: Columbia University Press, 1993).

6. Baldwin, *Neorealism and Neoliberalism*, 15.

7. See Alexander L. George, "Case Studies and Theory Development: The Method of Structured, Focused Comparison," in *Diplomacy: New Approaches in History, Theory and Policy*, Paul Gordon Lauren, ed. (New York: The Free Press, 1979), 43–68.

8. Regarding state capacity, see Theda Skocpol, "Bringing the State Back In: Strategies of Analysis in Current Research," in *Bringing the State Back In*,

Peter B. Evans, Dietrich Rueschemeyer, and Theda Skocpol, eds. (New York: Cambridge University Press, 1985), 9–20; and H. Richard Friman, *NarcoDiplomacy: Exporting the U.S. War on Drugs* (Ithaca: Cornell University Press, 1996), 1–4.

9. Putnam ("Diplomacy and Domestic Politics," 437) describes a "winset" as those international-level agreements in which a majority of the constituents in a given state, or negotiating counterpart, would concur. The larger a domestic win-set, the more likely is an agreement at the global level; a small domestic win-set may create a bargaining advantage for one party at the international level but may not make an agreement easier to reach.

10. Regarding defection, see Putnam, "Diplomacy and Domestic Politics," 438–39; about deception, see Friman, *NarcoDiplomacy*, 2–3.

11. *United Nations Annual Reports of Governments: Colombia*, E/NR.1948, 10 July 1949, 8–10.

12. See, for example, U.S. Department of the Treasury, *Traffic in Opium and Other Dangerous Drugs for the Year Ended 31 December 1957* (Washington, DC: GPO, 1958), 22.

13. Strictly speaking, random violence had begun to plague Colombia in 1946 in the aftermath of a presidential election in which the Conservatives regained power for the first time since 1930. See David Bushnell, *The Making of Modern Colombia: A Nation in Spite of Itself* (Berkeley and Los Angeles: University of California Press, 1993), 181–211.

14. Bushnell, *The Making of Modern Colombia*, 223, 240–48; and Eduardo Pizarro, "Revolutionary Guerrilla Groups in Colombia," in *Violence in Colombia: The Contemporary Crisis in Historical Perspective*, Charles Bergquist, Ricardo Peñaranda, and Gonzalo Sánchez, eds. (Wilmington, DE: Scholarly Resources, 1992), 169–82.

15. Jenny Pearce, *Colombia: Inside the Labyrinth* (London: Latin American Bureau, 1990), 61–64; Stephen J. Randall, *Colombia and the United States: Hegemony and Interdependence* (Athens: University of Georgia Press, 1992), 220–40; and William O. Walker III, "Mixing the Sweet with the Sour: Kennedy, Johnson, and Latin America," in *The Diplomacy of the Crucial Decade: American Foreign Relations during the 1960s*, Diane B. Kunz, ed. (New York: Columbia University Press, 1994), 47, 49, 53, 55–57, 60, 67–69.

16. On ANUC, see especially Bruce Michael Bagley, "The State and the Peasantry in Contemporary Colombia," *Latin American Issues*, no. 6, Allegheny College, Meadville, PA, 1988. When ANUC collapsed in the mid-1970s, the various guerrilla organizations, particularly the FARC, increased in number and won greater rural backing. On paramilitary and counterreform activity, see Pearce, *Colombia*, 42; Fabio Castillo, *Los Jinetes de la Cocaína* (Bogotá: Editorial Documentos Periodísticos, 1987), 41–42; and León Zamosc, "Peasant Struggles of the 1970s in Colombia," in *Power and Popular Protest: Latin American Social Movements*, Susan Eckstein, ed. (Berkeley and Los Angeles: University of California Press, 1989), 112–19.

17. Randall, *Colombia and the United States*, 246.

18. Zamosc, "Peasant Struggles," 121. Perhaps another 50,000 persons were

involved in the marijuana economy at its height in the late 1970s. See Bruce Michael Bagley, "Colombia y la guerra contra las drogas," in *Economia y politica del narcotráfico*, Juan G. Tokatlian and Bruce M. Bagley, eds. (Bogotá: Ediciones Uniandes, 1990), 180.

19. Bagley, "The State and the Peasantry," 47–52, 51 (quotation). M-19 was more nationalist and populist than Marxist-Leninist in nature.

20. Alain Rouquié, *The Military and the State in Latin America*, trans. Paul E. Sigmund (Berkeley and Los Angeles: University of California Press, 1987), 213; and Bagley, "The State and the Peasantry," 47–48.

21. Pearce, *Colombia*, 104, 171. See especially Francisco E. Thoumi, *Political Economy and Illegal Drugs in Colombia* (Boulder: Lynne Rienner, 1995), 41–47.

22. Juan Gabriel Tokatlian, "Seguridad y drogas: su significado en las relaciones entre Colombia y estados unidos," in *Economia y politica del narcotráfico*, Juan G. Tokatlian and Bruce M. Bagley, eds. (Bogotá: Ediciones Uniandes, 1990), 217.

23. U.S. Congress, House of Representatives, *Report of a Study Mission to Mexico, Costa Rica, Panama, and Colombia* (6–8 January 1976), "The Shifting Pattern of Narcotics Trafficking: Latin America," 94 Cong., 2 sess., May 1976 (Washington, DC: GPO, 1976), 23–24.

24. Bagley, "Colombia y la guerra contra las drogas," 179–81, 187–89; Tokatlian, "Seguridad y drogas," 221–22; and Juan Gabriel Tokatlian, "La política exterior de Colombia hacia Estados Unidos, 1978–1990: El asunto de las drogas y su lugar en las relaciones entre Bogotá y Washington," in *Narcotrafico en Colombia: Dimensiones políticas, económicas, juridícas e internacionales*, Carlos Gustavo Arrieta, Luis Javier Orjuela, Eduardo Sarmiento Palacio, and Juan Gabriel Tokatlian, eds. (Bogotá: Tercer Mundo Editores), 293–94.

25. House of Representatives, "The Shifting Pattern," 23; and U.S. Congress, House of Representatives, *Report of the Select Committee on Narcotics Abuse and Control*, "South American Study Mission, August 9–23, 1977," 95 Cong., 1 sess., November 1977 (Washington, DC: GPO, 1977), 9–12.

26. Tokatlian, "La política exterior," 294–95.

27. One month after taking office, Turbay announced that he was invoking emergency powers under the Estatuto de Seguridad to crack down on domestic disorder. Mauricio Reina, *Las Relaciones entre Colombia y Estados Unidos (1978–1986)*, Documentales Ocasionales no. 15 (Bogotá: Centro de Estudios Internacionales de la Universidad de los Andes, Mayo-Junio 1990), 10.

28. Bushnell, *The Making of Modern Colombia*, 249–50, 253, 257; and Thoumi, *Political Economy and Illegal Drugs*, 47–52. On Turbay's response to guerrilla activities, see Pizarro, "Revolutionary Guerrilla Groups," 184–85, 189–90.

29. See generally Michael Mastanduno, David A. Lake, and G. John Ikenberry, "Toward a Realist Theory of State Action," *International Studies Quarterly* 33, no. 4 (December 1989): 457–74.

30. On preferences and coercive diplomacy, see Moravcsik, "Introduction," 30–31.

31. Thoumi, *Political Economy and Illegal Drugs*, 127–28; David F. Musto, *The American Disease: Origins of Narcotic Control*, expanded ed. (New York: Oxford University Press, 1987), 265–70; and Jill Jonnes, *Hep-Cats, Narcs, and Pipe Dreams: A History of America's Romance with Illegal Drugs* (New York: Scribner, 1996), 313–18.

32. Peter A. Lupsha, "Drug Trafficking: Mexico and Colombia in Comparative Perspective," *Journal of International Affairs* 35 (Spring-Summer 1981): 95–115; and Richard B. Craig, "Illicit Drug Traffic and U.S.-Latin American Relations," *Washington Quarterly* 8 (Fall 1985): 111–15.

33. U.S. Congress, House of Representatives, *A Report of the Select Committee on Narcotics Abuse and Control*, "Factfinding Mission to Colombia and Puerto Rico," 96 Cong., 1 sess. (Washington, DC: GPO, 1979), 1–10; and U.S. Congress, House of Representatives, *Hearings before the Select Committee on Narcotics Abuse and Control*, "Cocaine and Marihuana Trafficking in Southeastern United States," 95 Cong., 2 sess., 9–10 June 1978 (Washington, DC: GPO, 1978), 16; and Tokatlian, "La política exterior," 304–7.

34. Castillo, *Los Jinetes*, 41–76.

35. Reina, *Las Relaciones*, 41–42.

36. Reina, *Las Relaciones*, 42–46; Thoumi, *Political Economy and Illegal Drugs*, 212–13; and *El Espectador* (Bogotá), 15 September 1983.

37. For an overview of violence in the early 1980s, see Bushnell, *The Making of Modern Colombia*, 252–59; and María Jimena Duzán, *Crónicas que matan* (Bogotá: Tercer Mundo Editores, 1992), 73–78. In slightly different form, Duzán's book appeared in English as, *Death Beat: A Colombian Journalist's Life Inside the Cocaine Wars*, trans. and ed. Peter Eisner (New York: HarperCollins, 1994); see also Paul Eddy with Hugo Sabogal and Sara Walden, *The Cocaine Wars* (New York: W.W. Norton, 1988), 285–90.

38. U.S. Congress, House of Representatives, *Report of the Select Committee on Narcotics Abuse and Control*, "International Narcotic Control Study Missions to Latin America and Jamaica (6–21 August 1983); Hawaii, Hong Kong, Thailand, Burma, Pakistan, Turkey, and Italy (4–22 January 1984)," 98 Cong., 2 sess. (Washington, DC: GPO, 1984), 66–76, 100–2.

39. *El Espectador*, 15 September 1983.

40. *El Tiempo* (Bogotá), 1 May 1984 and 18 November 1986. See also Thoumi, *Political Economy and Illegal Drugs*, 213–18. At least ten persons accused of drug trafficking were extradited to the United States. See Reina, *Las Relaciones*, 45; Thoumi, *Political Economy and Illegal Drugs*, 214–15; U.S. Congress, House of Representatives, *Report of the Select Committee on Narcotics Abuse and Control*, "Latin American Study Missions Concerning International Narcotics Problems (3–19 August 1985)," 99 Cong., 2 sess. (Washington, DC: GPO, 1986), 9.

41. Betancur's involvement in the talks remains uncertain. Reina (*Las Relaciones*, 44–45) indicates that he rejected the deal out of hand. Others believe that the president was looking for a modus vivendi with the narcos. See Rensselaer W. Lee III, *The White Labyrinth: Cocaine and Political Power* (New Brunswick, NJ: Transaction, 1989), 130–32, 140–43.

42. Pearce, *Colombia*, 180; and Ana Carrigan, *The Palace of Justice: A Colombian Tragedy* (New York and London: Four Walls Eight Windows, 1993).

43. Thoumi, *Political Economy and Illegal Drugs*, 55–56.

44. Duzán, *Crónicas*, 71.

45. On Operation Blast Furnace, see Michael H. Abbott, "The Army and the Drug War: Politics or National Security," *Parameters* 18 (December 1988): 95–112; and Lt. Col. Sewall H. Menzell, U.S. Army, Ret., "Operation Blast Furnace," *Army* 39 (November 1989): 24–32.

46. On Operation Snowcap, see U.S. Congress, House of Representatives, *Thirteenth Report by the Committee on Government Operations*, "Stopping the Flood of Cocaine with Operation Snowcap: Is It Working," 101 Cong., 2 sess., 14 August 1990 (Washington, DC: GPO, 1990).

47. Duzán, *Crónicas*, 82–83; and Thoumi, *Political Economy and Illegal Drugs*, 217–18.

48. Tokatlian, "La política exterior," 335–38; and Thoumi, *Political Economy and Illegal Drugs*, 218–19.

49. Guy Gugliotta and Jeff Leen, *Kings of Cocaine: An Astonishing True Story of Murder, Money, and International Corruption* (New York: Simon and Schuster, 1990), 288–93.

50. U.S. Department of State, Bureau of International Narcotics Matters (INM), *International Narcotics Control Report Strategy Report 1987* (Washington, DC: GPO, 1986), 76–95.

51. U.S. Department of State, INM, *INCSR 1987*, 89, 92.

52. Gabriel Murillo Castaño, "Narcotráfico y Política en la Decada de los Ochenta: Entre la represión y el diálogo," in *Narcotráfico en Colombia*, Carlos Gustavo Arrieta, Luis Javier Orjuela, Eduardo Sarmiento Palacio, and Juan Gabriel Tokatlian, eds. (Bogotá: Tercer Mundo Editores), 212–13.

53. Tokatlian, "La política exterior," 338–42.

54. Murillo Castaño, "Narcotráfico y Política," 253–72.

55. United States General Accounting Office (GAO), Report to Congressional Requesters, *Foreign Assistance: Promising Approach to Judicial Reform in Colombia*, GAO/NSIAD-92-269, September 1992.

56. GAO, Report to the Congress, *Drug Control: U.S.-Supported Efforts in Colombia and Bolivia*, GAO/NSIAD-89-24, November 1988, 15–28; and U.S. Department of State, INM, *INCSR 1988* (Washington, DC: GPO, March 1989), 71.

57. Americas Watch, *The Killings in Colombia* (New York: Americas Watch, April 1989), 7–15. A brief truce with the FARC had broken down earlier in the year.

58. *El Tiempo*, 18 August 1989. Surprisingly, the Supreme Court upheld Barco's authority to extradite drug traffickers wanted in the United States.

59. *Washington Post*, 26, 28 August 1989.

60. *El Tiempo*, 25 August 1989.

61. "Por ahora no: Dialogo podria haber pero nunca con las personas que hoy lo buscar sangre," *Semana*, 19–25 September 1989, 28–33.

62. *Washington Post*, 29 September 1989.

63. *Washington Post*, 29 September 1989; *El Tiempo*, 30 September 1989.

64. *El Tiempo*, 24 September 1989.

65. Putnam, "Diplomacy and Domestic Politics," 437–38, 442.

66. Murillo Castaño, "Narcotráfico y Política," 271–72.

67. *Washington Post*, 21 August, 1, 4 September 1989.

68. GAO, Report to Congressional Requestors, *Foreign Assistance: Promising Approach to Judicial Reform in Colombia*, GAO/NSIAD-92–269, September 1992.

69. On the Andean strategy, see William O. Walker III, "The Bush Administration's Andean Drug Strategy in Historical Perspective," in *Drug Trafficking in the Americas*, Bruce M. Bagley and William O. Walker III, eds. (New Brunswick: Transaction Publishers and University of Miami North-South Center, 1994), 1–22.

70. Early in 1990, Colombia rejected as interference in its conduct of the war on drugs a plan to send an aircraft carrier group to waters off the Colombian coast in order to monitor drug traffic in the area. See *Washington Post*, 9 January 1990.

71. This assessment of institution building is echoed in GAO, Report to Congressional Requesters, *Drug War: Observation on Counternarcotics Aid to Colombia*, GAO/NSIAD-91–296.

72. William O. Walker III, "Drug Control and U.S. Hegemony," in *United States Policy in Latin America: A Decade of Crisis and Challenge*, John D. Martz, ed. (Lincoln: University of Nebraska Press, 1995), 313–15.

73. For a discussion of other possible factors shaping the U.S. position, see U.S. Congress, Senate, *Hearings before the Permanent Subcommittee on Investigations of the Committee on Governmental Affairs*, "U.S. Government Anti-Narcotics Activities in the Andean Region of South America," 101 Cong., 1 sess., 26, 27, 29 September 1989 (Washington, DC: GPO, 1989), 50–53.

74. Diego Cardona C., "El primer bienio de la administración Gaviria: algunas reflexiones sobre su política exterior," *Colombia Internacional* 19 (julio-septiembre de 1992): 7.

75. *El Tiempo*, 16, 17 December 1989; and Duzán, *Death Beat*, 176–83.

76. *New York Times*, 13 February 1990; and *Washington Post*, 16 February 1990.

77. Thoumi, *Political Economy and Illegal Drugs*, 7; and *Miami Herald*, 8 August 1990.

78. *El Tiempo*, 3, 8 August, 6 September 1990. Bringing narcotráficantes to justice meant acceptance of talks between the governments and its sworn enemies; many influential Colombians accepted the distasteful procedure as necessary, if only to decrease the level of violence against the state. Among those who supported negotiations was Bogotá's conservative mayor, Andrés Pastrana Arango, who would lose the 1994 election in a close race with Ernesto Samper Pizano. *Washington Post*, 24 April 1990.

79. Americas Watch, *Political Murder and Reform in Colombia: The Violence Continues* (New York: Human Rights Watch, April 1992), 60–61, 68–73.

80. U.S. Congress, House of Representatives, *Hearings before the Subcom-

170 *William O. Walker III*

mittee on Western Hemisphere Affairs of the Committee on Foreign Affairs, "The Andean Initiative," 101 Cong., 2 sess., 6 and 20 June 1990 (Washington, DC: GPO, 1990), 13, 94; and *New York Times*, 21 January 1991.

81. This discussion of learning derives from my reading of George W. Breslauer and Philip E. Tetlock, "Introduction," in *Learning in U.S. and Soviet Foreign Policy*, George W. Breslauer and Philip E. Tetlock, eds. (Boulder: Westview Press, 1991), 3–13; and Jack S. Levy, "Learning and Foreign Policy: Sweeping a Conceptual Minefield," *International Organization* 48, no. 2 (Spring 1994): 283, 287–94, 311–12.

82. *Washington Post*, 30 May 1992.

83. *Washington Post*, 9 July 1991; and *New York Times*, 14 July 1991.

84. *New York Times*, 4 June 1991; and *El Espectador*, 20 June 1991.

85. *Washington Post*, 24 June 1991.

86. *El Tiempo*, 23 July 1992 and 3 December 1993.

87. See, especially, *El Tiempo* and *El Espectador* for the last week of July and the first week of August 1992.

88. The general thrust of this argument about the effects of leniency on state legitimacy and the prospects for institution building builds on Thoumi, *Political Economy and Illegal Drugs*. On Colombia's guerrillas and state stability, see Lawrence Boudon, "Guerrillas and the State: The Role of the State in the Colombian Peace Process," *Journal of Latin American Studies* 28, no. 2 (May 1996): 279–97.

89. U.S. GAO, Report to the Chairman and Ranking Minority Member, Committee on Government Operations, House of Representatives, *The Drug War: Colombia Is Undertaking Antidrug Programs, but Impact Is Uncertain*, GAO/NSIAD-93-158, August 1993, 46–53.

90. GAO, *Promising Approach to Judicial Reform*, 2.

91. U.S. Department of State Dispatch, 2 March 1992, 145. Learning, as seen in toleration of Gaviria's independence, did not extend throughout the Bush administration. At the time of the San Antonio summit, a lower-level official in the State Department's Bureau of International Narcotics Matters told me: "at least we still have Bolivia to kick around."

92. *New York Times*, 22 December 1992; and *El Tiempo*, 22 December 1992.

93. Levy, "Learning and Foreign Policy," 279–312.

94. Arthur A. Stein, *Why Nations Cooperate: Circumstance and Choice in International Relations* (Ithaca: Cornell University Press, 1990), 48.

95. U.S. Department of State, INM, *INCSR 1993* (Washington, DC: GPO, April 1994), 104; *New York Times*, 17 September 1993; and *Washington Post*, 12 January 1994. This modus operandi had the added virtue of creating a significant role for the Department of Defense in the drug war.

96. *Washington Post*, 8 March 1994; and *El Espectador*, 8 March 1994.

97. *Washington Post*, 6 April 1994. On Elders, see *Washington Post*, 8 December 1993.

98. *Washington Post*, 21 April 1994.

99. *El Tiempo*, 21 June 1994; and *New York Times*, 23 June 1994.

100. U.S. Department of State, INM, *INCSR 1995* (Washington, DC: GPO,

March 1996), xxv. José Santacruz Lodoño, who together with the Rodríguez Orejuela brothers, Gilberto and Miguel, dominated the Cali cartel, died in a clash with police on 5 March 1996 (*El Tiempo*, 6 March 1996). A useful introduction to the charges of corruption in Samper's administration is Patrick L. Clawson and Rensselaer W. Lee III, *The Andean Cocaine Industry* (New York: St. Martin's Press, 1996), 119–22, 170–75.

101. *El Espectador*, 13 June 1996.

102. U.S. Department of State Daily Press Briefing, 13 June 1996.

103. See, for example, *El Tiempo*, 29 June 1996.

104. *Washington Post*, 30 June 1996.

105. *El Tiempo*, 24 September 1996.

106. See, for example, *El Tiempo*, 11, 13 August 1996.

107. *Miami Herald*, 8 August 1996; and *Washington Post*, 7 September 1996.

108. Putnam, "Diplomacy and Domestic Politics," 448.

109. Clawson and Lee, *The Andean Cocaine Industry*, 122–27.

110. On the evidence against Samper, see "El caso contra Ernesto Samper," *Semana*, 28 May—4 June 1996.

Obstructing Markets: Organized Crime Networks and Drug Control in Japan

H. Richard Friman

Transnational organized crime has emerged as an economic and a security issue for a wide array of countries in the 1990s.[1] Reports of government crackdowns against Colombian cocaine traffickers vie with warnings of expanded activities by Chinese Triads, Sicilian and Italian Mafia, Japanese Yakuza, and myriad other criminal organizations. For writers such as Claire Sterling, the trend is toward a transnational Pax Mafiosa composed of allied organized crime groups dividing up the global economy.[2] Others challenge such claims as overstated, noting cooperation among criminal groups as more of a limited strategic response to the resources and opportunities made available through globalization that can lead to more extensive partnerships.[3] Though differing in degree, both arguments posit globalization-induced cooperation among transnational organized crime groups as a challenge to state enforcement efforts. However, both arguments often downplay impediments to such cooperation and, in turn, risk overstating the impact of transnational crime on state power.

This chapter explores ways in which domestic crime networks can work as societal barriers to the market access sought by transnational organized crime groups. The exploration of market access by transnational organizations is common in analyses of the licit economy. Scholarship on multinational corporations, for example, reveals the host country's regulatory barriers and domestic competition as two factors inhibiting access to new markets.[4] The host government's "political jurisdiction to bar entry" creates the primary hurdle, leading multina-

173

tional corporations to turn to bargaining with the government to gain access. International relations theorists differ on the bargaining leverage states and multinationals bring to the negotiating table and, in turn, the degree of access multinationals are able to obtain. For dependency scholars the leverage multinationals hold and the access they gain are extensive; for statist scholars, strong states have the ability to deny access.[5]

Transnational criminal organizations (TCOs) are missing from this scholarly debate and raise questions for its relevance in understanding the illicit global economy. The interaction between TCOs and state control efforts differs from that of multinationals in the licit economy.[6] As Phil Williams writes, TCOs "obtain access not through consent but through circumvention" of state controls at the border.[7] Once having obtained a foothold, TCOs may turn to bargaining with state officials to enhance access but often with leverage facilitated by an overreliance on tools of violence and financial corruption. Though important, the impact of this difference between multinational corporations and TCOs should not be overstated. Simply evading formal prohibitions and enforcement measures does not resolve the second factor inhibiting market access—the problem of domestic competition. In the licit and illicit global economies alike, transnational organizations seek to bypass domestic competitors to gain access to potentially lucrative markets or, short of doing so, attempt to cooperate with domestic competitors through arrangements such as joint ventures. They are not always successful.

This chapter explores societal barriers to the access of TCOs engaged in drug trafficking, the core industry of the illicit global economy.[8] Despite globalization arguments noting the pervasiveness of illicit drugs, access into advanced industrial countries by TCOs engaged in drug trafficking remains uneven. The starkest example of this variation appears in the cocaine trade. Patrick Clawson and Rensselaer Lee argue that Colombian trafficking organizations have sought to obtain direct access to potentially lucrative foreign markets with volume shipments of drugs. Where such market potential exists but secure networks for market entry and/or repatriation of profits do not, however, traffickers have successfully turned to strategic cooperation with local crime groups. The authors reveal, for example, that extensive cooperation with Italian crime groups facilitated Colombian access into Western and Central European markets, overcoming problems with limited local contacts and the conspicuous presence of Colombians entering the region.[9]

Though Colombian traffickers have saturated the United States market and expanded access into Europe, they remain largely closed out of the potentially lucrative Japanese market. Lacking secure networks for market access, Colombian traffickers have sought cooperation with Japanese crime groups (the Yakuza) but with limited success. Drug seizure data offer a rough illustration of differences in market penetration.[10] From 1989 to 1994, for example, annual U.S. seizures of cocaine ranged from 99,407 to 137,556 kilograms. European seizure rates for this same period varied from 7,109 kilograms in 1989 to 29,890 kilograms in 1994. In contrast, Japanese seizures of cocaine reached 14 kilograms in 1989 and peaked at 69 kilograms in 1990. Seizures of cocaine from 1989 to 1994 averaged only 30 kilograms per year.[11] Even assuming that the efforts of Japanese authorities represent a worst case scenario of seizure rates at less than 5 percent of actual trade levels, Colombian access to the Japanese market still appears insignificant when compared to that of Europe and the United States.

Scholars have offered little insight into this variation in market access by transnational criminal organizations. Clawson and Lee, for example, only note in passing that societal barriers to strategic cooperation can exist. After briefly listing factors such as turf wars, cheating, "different national roots, organizational cultures, recruiting practices, and notions of what constitutes honor in a business relationship," they conclude that such barriers will have limited impact on future Colombian expansion into Europe as strategic cooperation evolves into more "sustained cooperation or a full partnership" with their Sicilian counterparts.[12] However, Japan reveals neither a full partnership on questions of market access nor a level of strategic cooperation that appears to be laying the groundwork for such a partnership.

Globalization arguments that posit a retreat of the state in the face of transnational actors also do not easily capture the limited access by Colombian trafficking organizations into Japan. At first glance, the Japanese case appears as if the state has not retreated. The secondary literature as well as interviews reveal prominent arguments between enforcement practitioners and scholars pointing to low levels of cocaine offenses as evidence of the effectiveness of Japanese law enforcement, broader norms linking society and the state in the preservation of social order, and even an historical Japanese aversion to narcotic drugs (cocaine being designated as such by international control treaties despite its stimulant properties).[13] Yet, all these arguments are problematic. The recurrent difficulties of Japanese law enforcement officials in curtailing extensive methamphetamine trafficking, the ebb and flow of accommodations between the state and Japanese organized crime, and the demand potential generated by the Japanese penchant for stimulant drugs and extensive wealth raise questions for efforts to attribute limited market access to state control efforts.

If not successful state controls, what explains the pattern of limited market access? Scholars do acknowledge the potential for variation in globalization's impact but tend to discount the role of domestic societal groups as sources of such variation. Those societal actors linked to transnational economic forces seek to reenforce the globalization process. Those societal actors disadvantaged by the forces of globalization attempt to resist but, short of the emergence of pervasive hypernationalist or religious fundamentalist movements, experience little success in doing so.[14]

International political economy scholarship on Japan also offers little insight. Analysts have explored questions of market access in trade and finance in great detail, addressing the impact of state and societal actors alike. State agencies including the Ministries of International Trade and Industry, Finance, and Post and Telecommunications have utilized formal and informal barriers to impede market access.[15] Policy networks linking state agencies with widespread trade and industry associations reenforce market impediments,[16] as do Japan's industrial conglomerates (*keiretsu*) and distribution networks.[17] Though exploring the licit economy, this literature has ignored the dynamics faced by foreign criminal organizations seeking to penetrate Japan's market for illicit goods.

This chapter contends that a focus on social networks—specifically, the formal and informal relational ties among criminals—helps to explain patterns of market access in the illicit global economy. Japanese organized crime during the late 1940s established extensive drug distribution networks. Formal and informal relational ties among actors in these networks continue to inhibit market access to foreign competitors, despite two potential sources of change. First, since the late 1980s Japanese immigration patterns have eased the ability of TCOs to evade state controls at the border and to sidestep Yakuza-controlled distribution networks. Second, steps by the Japanese government against organized crime have signaled a change in the nature of state accommodation toward the Yakuza and increased the willingness of the Yakuza to explore selective ties with foreigners. Shifts in market access by TCOs to date, however, remain limited.

Networks and Market Access

Transnational criminal organizations face social networks linking societal actors, and often societal to state actors, in host countries. At their most basic level, social networks consist of relations among participants in a given social system. More nuanced definitions of social networks tend to vary by subfield of social science, conceptualizing networks in terms of specified types of relational ties (such as association memberships, kinship, or business transactions) and the scale of the social system under analysis (including family units, corporations, interest groups, or nations).[18] Exploring crime groups as social networks reveals the impact of formal and informal relational ties on attempts by outsiders to gain market access.

Social networks pose greater challenges for cooperation in the illicit economy than in the licit due to their relative importance in offsetting risk in illegal transactions. In legal transactions, for example, businesses have recourse to binding contracts and the enforcement apparatus of the state. But in illegal transactions, participants face the risk of arrest rather than protection by state authorities. Conviction can lead to the potential disruption of business, loss of property, and incarceration. In addition to threats from the state, participants in the illicit economy face challenges from competitors. The agreements that participants in illegal transactions enter into are neither legally binding nor, short of official corruption, enforceable by the state. This condition poses risks of losses due to cheating, uncertainty due to threats, and the potential for violent conflict. Pino Arlacchi argues that these risks make trust and secrecy "far more necessary among criminals than among businessmen." To obtain them, criminals often turn to social networks centered on "common membership of the same culture, the same ethnic or regional community, or indeed the same family."[19]

Informal relational ties among participants in a given social network do not necessarily preclude cooperation with outsiders. Arlachi notes that despite the emphasis on traditional values between members of Sicilian and Chinese crime groups, each has "made selective use of them, with the aim of facilitating economic exchanges."[20] The extent to which limited economic exchanges with others develop into more extensive strategic cooperation or full partnerships, however, is influenced by the nature of informal relational ties. Common memberships based on kinship, for example, accord exclusionary status rights to network participants that limit the opportunities for access by outsiders into the crime group's decision making more so than memberships based on ethnicity, regional origin, or culture.[21] Similarly, the prioritization of long-term social relationships among members of a crime group decreases the flexibility necessary for exploring cooperation with outsiders. In short, the narrower the scope of common membership of network participants and the greater the emphasis placed by participants on long-term social obligations, the more likely informal relational ties are to pose a barrier to extensive cooperation with outsiders.

Concerns with risk also can lead criminals to more formal relational ties based on hierarchical organization.[22] Such ties include a centralized core of decision makers, the presence of a formal chain of command,

and a specified division of labor within the crime group.[23] The extent to which criminals actually are organized in such a fashion, however, remains highly contested. Contending interpretations of crime groups abound as do broader arguments questioning the underlying logic of organization as a path for criminals to mitigate risk.[24] Reviewing this literature, Sheldon Zhang and Mark Gaylord note the tendency of schools of thought to cluster at "opposite ends of a continuum" of tight versus loose criminal organization. The authors' alternative, followed here, is to explore a reality where criminals are characterized by variation in their "degrees of organization."[25]

Formal relational ties stemming from hierarchical organization can influence the extent to which limited economic exchanges with outsiders develop into more extensive strategic cooperation or full partnerships. However, they do so more by accentuating the impact of the social network's informal relational ties than by posing any inherent impetus toward or against external cooperation. For instance, tighter organizational structures increase the capacity for control by core network members over the group's deliberations with outsiders. This capacity can facilitate or limit external cooperation. Political science research illustrates the former, revealing that tighter internal organization of business, labor, and government increases the prospects for corporatist accommodation between the three.[26] Vincenzo Ruggiero's work on the extensive division of labor in European drug markets illustrates the latter, revealing how organized local crime groups initially tend to relegate their transnational counterparts to the margins of local distribution networks as primary importers and couriers.[27]

Relational ties stemming from loose formal organization show a similar dichotomy. The absence of a centralized core of decision makers, a formal chain of command, and specified division of labor decrease the capacity for control by a criminal group over facilitating or impeding deliberations by its members with outsiders. In short, where informal relational ties pose a barrier to extensive cooperation with outsiders, the tighter the group's organizational structures the more likely formal relational ties are to accentuate this barrier. The remainder of this chapter reveals that organized crime in Japan's drug trade tends toward a relatively closed social network.[28]

Social Networks in Japan: The Licit Economy

"The concept of the network," Shumpei Kumon writes, has become "conspicuous in Japanese studies in recent years."[29] Scholars have used the concept to explore government-business relationships as well as relationships among and within Japanese firms.[30] Daniel Okimoto's work on government-business relations reveals Japan as a "network state." The country's extensive formal and informal relationships between government and business are built on a "framework of long-term, obligatory, and effective ties."[31] Ken-ichi Imai explores networks more broadly as "patterns of linkages between units—people or firms—deeply embedded in the social and cultural system." He traces Japan's corporate networks from the "interfirm relationships" in the prewar *zaibatsu* ("large-scale, family owned, conglomerates"), to postwar business groups, and the more recent and specialized network industrial organizations.[32]

Michael Gerlach analyzes Japan's "pervasive" intercorporate alliances, defined as "coherent groupings of affiliated companies." Alliance members are linked through networks of formal institutional arrangements (such as the *keiretsu*) as well as informal ties, the latter emphasizing long-term and overlapping social relationships.[33] Where Imai and Gerlach address linkages among corporations, Thomas Lifson turns to relationships within the firm. Lifson's exploration of administrative networks focuses on the informal relationships between managers that facilitate information and resource sharing "without invoking formal organizational procedures."[34]

Japan is clearly not the only country distinguished by networks of social relations. But Japanese social networks are different. First, networks in Japan appear more pervasive than those in the United States and Europe. Okimoto argues that Japan's networks are shaped by the country's historically determined state and societal structures. The state and business community are relatively centralized in Japan, with limited differentiation between them. This domestic structure, Okimoto writes, has created conditions more conducive to the formation of a dense "thicket of policy networks" linking state and societal actors than conditions in other advanced industrial countries.[35]

Second, comparisons of Japanese social networks with those of other network societies in Asia suggest variations of type rather than extent. Imai argues that Japanese networks appear to be more oriented toward institutions than individuals, the latter characteristic found more in other Asian countries. He writes that Japanese networks tend to be "linkages mediated through 'place' . . . the experiences that people share by working in the same place or attending the same school."[36] Joel Kotkin captures a similar distinction when comparing Japanese and Chinese social networks. Kotkin observes that social relations among Japanese abroad tend to emphasize relationships linked to institutional affiliations and ties to the home islands. Chinese networks of social relations, by contrast, tend toward more ties based on region ("accent and place of origin") and especially family groups. Rather than centered on the mainland, these networks are spread across an "archipelago of critical nodes" throughout the Pacific, the United States, and Europe.[37]

Japan's pattern of extensive social networks centered on long-term, informal relational ties and tight hierarchical organization has acted as a barrier to cooperation with outsiders in the licit economy. The literature on foreign companies impeded by such networks in their efforts to obtain access to Japan is extensive.[38] Despite the prominence of social networks, however, their impact on Japan's illicit economy remains underexplored. The dynamics of risk in the illicit economy and the importance of social networks in mitigating its effects suggest that the barriers facing transnational criminal organizations seeking market access in Japan are likely to be even greater than in the licit.

Social Networks in Japan: The Illicit Economy

The roots of modern Japanese organized crime lie in the 1700s with the emergence of two types of crime groups, the *tekiya* (street peddlers) and *bakuto* (gamblers). A third type of crime group, the *gurentai* (or hoodlums), emerged after World War II. Since the 1940s, the lines between these groups have become blurred as each has branched out into an array of illicit activities and become linked through the emergence of national crime syndicates. These rival syndicates lie at the center of social networks in Japan's illicit economy and shape the ability of transnational criminal organizations to obtain market access.

Informal relational ties in the Yakuza draw first on the common outcast status of gang members. *Tekiya* and *bakuto* groups in the 1700s attracted recruits from Japan's lower social strata including "the poor, the landless, and the delinquents and misfits."[39] This strata also contained members from the country's lowest social class, the *burakumin*, a loose designation comprising those who "worked with dead animals, such as leather workers, and in 'unclean' occupations such as undertaking."[40] The economic and social displacement in Japan after World War II created a broader pool of social outcasts tapped by *tekiya* and *bakuto* groups and the emerging *gurentai*. This pool included a displaced ethnic Korean population of roughly 700,000 and a smaller ethnic Chinese population, the remnants of over 2 million laborers brought to Japan during the early 1900s. *Burakumin* and permanent foreign resident Koreans, and to a lesser extent permanent foreign resident Chinese, continue to comprise a source for Yakuza membership, the exact percentages varying by crime group.[41]

Even more than common membership, informal relational ties in the Yakuza emphasize the *oyabun-kobun* (father-role/child-role) system that characterized social relations in feudal Japan. As David Kaplan and Alec Dubro write, "the oyabun provides advice, protection, and help, and in return receives the unswerving loyalty and service of his kobun whenever needed." The *tekiya* and *bakuto* groups of the 1700s adopted the social system of the times and added to it a series of reenforcing ritual initiations and practices (including finger-cutting and tattoos). Though the broader influence of the *oyabun-kobun* system has faded with Japan's modernization, the system of long-term social ties of obligation and loyalty within a given crime group remain influential for Japanese organized crime.[42]

Formal relational ties among members of Japanese crime groups emphasize hierarchical organization, with members tied to gangs claiming specific areas of territorial operation and control. Though this practice has roots in the familial ties and practices of *tekiya* and *bakuto* organizations of the 1700s, it has carried over into the large-scale syndicates of affiliated crime groups that distinguish postwar Japan.[43] By the early 1990s, Japanese organized crime consisted of an estimated 3,000 local organizations with over 86,700 members. Roughly 40 percent of the organizations and membership were affiliated with three leading crime syndicates, the Yamaguchi-gumi, Inagawa-kai, and Sumiyoshi-kai. The remaining crime groups were fragmented across a number of smaller associations.[44]

The Yamaguchi-gumi remains the largest of the three syndicates, outnumbering the affiliates and membership of the other two majors combined. The syndicate's affiliates include a range of *tekiya*, *bakuto*, and *gurentai* groups under the central organization of a core leadership. Headquartered in Kobe, the Yamaguchi-gumi conducts operations in forty-two major prefectures of Japan including areas of Tokyo, Osaka, Kyoto, and Hokkaido. Though organizational hierarchies shape the relations of Yamaguchi-gumi members with outsiders, internal controls within the syndicate have been far from complete. Since the erosion of family composition of the core membership in the 1980s, the syndicate has faced an ebb and flow of factional splits and disputes between affiliates over methods, operations, and relative influence within the organization.[45]

The Sumiyoshi-kai and Inagawa-kai are based in Tokyo and conduct operations in eighteen and twenty-four prefectures, respectively, including areas of Tokyo, Osaka, and Hokkaido. In contrast to the Yamaguchi-gumi, the Sumiyoshi-kai is more of a loose federation of crime groups with traditional "*bakuto* roots," distinguished by the greater autonomy of its individual affiliates. The Inagawa-kai shares the centralized orga-

nizational structure that distinguishes the Yamaguchi-gumi. But unlike
its larger counterpart, the syndicate is distinguished by tighter formal
ties among its affiliates, familial dominance of core network positions,
and prominence of *bakuto* groups in its membership.[46]

Drug Networks in Japan

Drug trafficking, especially in methamphetamine, has played a central
role in Yakuza finances since the late 1940s. Initially, crime groups
diverted material from Japan's wartime stockpiles being held by the
U.S. occupation authorities. As supplies fell, the Yakuza turned to clandestine drug production. By the mid-1950s, government crackdowns on
drug trafficking and the deportation of Koreans and Chinese engaged in
methamphetamine production had disrupted the trade. The lull was only
temporary. A second major wave of stimulant trafficking emerged in
the 1970s with the Yakuza looking abroad to Korea and later Taiwan
and Hong Kong for supplies to meet resurgent domestic demand. The
three major syndicates continue to stand at the forefront of these efforts.[47]

The groundwork for selective cooperation with foreign suppliers had
been laid years earlier. During the Kobe and Osaka gang wars of the
late 1940s, for example, the Yamaguchi-gumi expanded by defeating
and assimilating rather than destroying its opposition. Those incorpo-
rated into the syndicate by this method included members of Korean
gangs such as the Meiyu-kai. By the 1960s, the syndicate furthered its
Korean connections by building alliance ties with the Tosei-kai—
specifically through Kazuo Taoko of the Yamaguchi-gumi ritually becoming "blood brother" to Hisayuki Machii (Chong Gwon Yong) of
the Tosei-kai. Established in 1948, the Tosei-kai was a "largely Korean"
gang that dominated the Ginza area of Tokyo as well as the early Tokyo
methamphetamine trade. During the mid-1960s, Machii recast the
Tosei-kai under the auspices of a broader array of licit enterprises and
turned to more extensive involvement in Japanese politics, including
the normalization of relations between Japan and Korea. By the early
1970s, the Korean government had granted Machii control over the
primary ferry concession between the two countries. This pipeline of
commercial traffic and Machii's connections with Korean crime groups
facilitated the Yamaguchi-gumi's expansion into financing methamphetamine production abroad.[48]

The Korean government's crackdowns on the methamphetamine
trade during the 1980s led the Yakuza to shift attention to financing
offshore drug production in Taiwan and Hong Kong, and eventually

China. The Yamaguchi-gumi was a relative latecomer in this process, engaging in selective cooperation with Hong Kong's 14K organization in the late-1970s and forging ties with Taiwan's United Bamboo Gang in the mid-1980s.[49] Lacking the extensive Korean connection of the Yamaguchi-gumi, the Sumiyoshi-kai and Inagawa-kai had begun a more active expansion into Taiwan and Hong Kong earlier in the 1970s.[50] The Sumiyoshi-kai's inroads appeared more extensive than that of the Inagawa-kai. Kakuji Inagawa's syndicate had emerged out of the Yokohama gang wars of the 1940s, as Japanese gangs (including Inagawa's initially small gang the Kakusai-kai) challenged the dominance of ethnic Korean and Chinese groups over the lucrative, postwar black market. Rather than the inclusion of other ethnic East Asians living in Japan, a practice characteristic of the Yamaguchi-gumi and the Sumiyoshi-kai, Inagawa emphasized a narrower sense of common membership and waged war against them.[51] These patterns of informal relational ties would continue to shape relations between the Yakuza and Korean and Chinese crime groups.

From the standpoint of formal relational ties, Japanese drug markets reveal an extensive chain of command and division of labor among gang bosses, executive members, wholesalers, and street-level dealers. Once again, these controls have been more extensive for the Inagawa-kai and the Yamaguchi-gumi than for the looser Sumiyoshi-kai. Gang bosses in all three syndicates are largely removed from direct participation in the trade. The executive members obtain the drug supplies from foreign smugglers and control their distribution to intermediate wholesalers, who in turn provide the link to street-level dealers. The wholesalers are Yakuza members and the majority of the street-level dealers are either ordinary (third-tier) or associate members (affiliated with but not formal members of the organization). The designation of street level is also partially misleading since the bulk of stimulant transactions have traditionally been conducted in Yakuza-owned or affiliated enterprises (ranging from entertainment establishments to day laborer recruitment networks).[52] This division of labor is crudely illustrated by the arrest patterns of Yakuza for stimulant offenses. From 1985 to 1994, for example, Yakuza members accounted for less than 7 percent of total arrests for stimulant drug smuggling but more than 57 percent of total arrests for stimulant distribution.[53]

Yakuza social networks have posed barriers to extending cooperation with East Asian gangs in the Japanese methamphetamine trade beyond that of trafficking the drug to executive members. These social networks also help to explain the limited access by transnational criminal organizations seeking markets for Latin American cocaine. Informal and formal relational ties dissuade the leading Yakuza syndicates from turning to extensive cooperation with cocaine traffickers. Latin Americans rarely fall within the scope of the syndicates' common membership base. More important, long-term *oyabun-kobun* ties in the syndicates' distribution networks are oriented toward facilitating the methamphetamine trade. Shifting to cocaine, a rival stimulant, risks disrupting these ties.[54]

The methamphetamine trade is also a lucrative enterprise suggesting little economic incentive for the leading syndicates to establish the initial steps at strategic cooperation. Some officials in Japan's National Police Agency argue that profit calculations—interpreted as the estimated difference between wholesale cost and retail price of a given drug—heavily influence the Yakuza. In this context, officials note that methamphetamine has tended to offer the greatest price spread of illegal drugs sold in Japanese markets, often by a factor of 50,000.[55] However, crime groups operating outside of the majors and low-level groups maneuvering to rise within the syndicates tend to be closed out of these distribution networks. Lacking the long-term social ties oriented toward the methamphetamine trade, such groups are more likely to be receptive to suppliers of cocaine. But such groups also lack the distribution networks to move large volumes of the drug.

During the 1980s, Japanese authorities began to express concerns over possible linkages between the Yakuza and the Medellín and Cali cocaine cartels. Information concerning the extent of this connection has been sketchy at best. Early in the decade, Japanese authorities began to arrest increasing numbers of Latin Americans on cocaine charges. Those arrested were caught with usually 1–2 kilograms of cocaine in their possession—basically market samples. In contrast, by 1990 authorities were arresting Latin Americans with alleged ties to the Medellín cartel and seizing individual caches of 24–42 kilograms.[56] But as noted above, since 1990, cocaine seizures have remained low. This pattern remains even despite an increased geographical distribution of arrests suggesting a spreading trade.[57]

By late 1993, Japanese authorities began to arrest an increasing number of Latin Americans allegedly tied to the Cali cartel. However, the Cali affiliates arrested through the mid-1990s appeared to be in the process of establishing initial contact rather than building on any existing, large-scale distribution networks. The amounts of cocaine seized were also relatively small, in the range of 1–7 kilograms, and the Yakuza organizations sought out by the traffickers at the time of their arrest were not affiliated with the top three syndicates.[58] By 1994, reports of cocaine offloading operations at sea and a market shortfall in methamphetamine again led to concerns among Japanese authorities of increased Yakuza interest in cocaine.[59] However, the absence of an established Yakuza distribution network in cocaine after over a decade of purported negotiations and experimentation suggests the limited interest in extensive linkages with cocaine traffickers among the top syndicates.

Sources of Change

The ability of the Yakuza to act as a check on the expansion of transnational criminal organizations faces two potential challenges in the 1990s. First, immigration patterns are beginning to offer transnational criminal organizations a path to direct market access. Second, government crackdowns against organized crime have increased Yakuza interest in selective cooperation with new immigrants.

Immigration

During the rise of Japan's bubble economy in the 1980s, lax enforcement of prohibitions against unskilled migrant labor led to a slow increase in the country's immigrant population. This shift created an ethnicity pipeline increasingly accessible to transnational criminal organizations. By the early 1990s, the collapse of the bubble and new sidedoor provisions in Japanese immigration law accelerated these trends by displacing illegal immigrant labor into the drug trade.

Drug historians and globalization scholars point to "networks of immigrant communities" that can facilitate the illicit drug trade.[60] For example, immigration flows can create pipelines within which transnational criminal organizations can recruit couriers, travel, and establish market operations in the host country. New immigrants also can create markets by bringing drug habits into the host country. The illustration most cited by drug historians is the linkage among ethnic Chinese, the illicit operations of the Chinese Triads and Tongs, and the practice of opium smoking in the United States during the early 1900s.[61] The pipeline argument is often found in more recent scholarship on drug trafficking pointing to Colombian and other immigrant populations facilitating the cocaine trade in the United States and Western Europe.[62] Similar pipeline arguments linking foreigners to drug trafficking have recently emerged in Japan.[63]

Japan's first major wave of immigration took place in the early to mid-1900s and consisted of the voluntary and involuntary migration of Korean and Chinese laborers to the country.[64] After the war, Japanese immigration regulations relegated those Koreans and Chinese remaining in the country to permanent foreign resident status. Japan's second major wave of immigration emerged in the mid- to late 1980s. Drawn by a combination of supply-push and demand-pull factors, immigration of unskilled, male, predominantly Asian and Middle Eastern workers surged in the country. Though illegal under Japanese immigration regulations, these workers took advantage of bilateral visa exemption accords (for tourist travel) and lax enforcement at ports of entry and at places of employment. This wave of illegal foreign visitors overshadowed a more limited influx of female immigrants from Asia (entering as tourists or foreign language students) during the early to mid-1980s feeding the sex/entertainment trade.[65]

By the late 1980s, employment downturns stemming from the collapse of the bubble economy had severely affected immigrant workers across an array of economic sectors. Amendments to the Japanese Immigration Act in 1989 and the suspension of visa exemption accords (with Bangladesh and Pakistan in the late 1980s and Iran in the early 1990s) enhanced this displacement effect. The revised immigration law retained the prohibition on unskilled foreign labor but added criminal penalties for promoting illegal employment (such as employer sanctions of up to ¥2 million in fines and 3 years' imprisonment). In contrast to the new risks of relying on illegal Asian and Middle Eastern workers, however, Japanese employers could turn to side-door provisions also included in the amended immigration law. These provisions allowed for the unrestricted entry of descendants of ethnic Japanese regardless of skill level (*nikkeijin*, primarily from Latin America and Asia), and the entry of unskilled foreign workers as participants in company trainee programs.[66]

The extent to which ethnicity pipelines have actually facilitated direct market access by transnational criminal organizations remains limited.[67] For example, the relatively few instances of transplanted drug habits into Japan have consisted of traditional opium gifts exchanged among Iranian workers.[68] The Latin American immigration pipeline did include a small number of Colombian prostitutes and bar hostesses in the early 1980s who attempted to facilitate the cocaine trade but with little success. More recently, however, the pipeline has been distinguished by a larger number of Brazilian *nikkeijin* with little apparent participation in the illicit economy.

Japanese arrest data also suggests limited access by TCOs. From 1985 to 1994, for example, foreign visitors accounted for only 1.2 percent of total stimulant law offenses, 8.0 percent of cannabis law offenses, and 25.1 percent of narcotics and psychotropics law offenses.[69] The higher narcotics figure, reaching over 40 percent by the mid-1990s, has raised concerns but appears to reflect patterns of Japanese law enforcement more than actual crime trends.[70]

One exception to this pattern of limited direct access by TCOs, however, has stemmed from Chinese immigration. During the 1980s, immigration from Taiwan, Hong Kong, and the mainland increased through a combination of student visa programs, recruitment for the entertainment industry, *nikkeijin* and trainee allowances, and labor smuggling operations. Taiwanese and Hong Kong criminal organizations, such as the United Bamboo Gang and the 14K, took advantage of the pipeline and long-standing relationships with top Yakuza syndicates in methamphetamine trafficking to establish selective gambling and prostitution operations within these communities.[71] However, in drug operations, the Taiwanese and Hong Kong organizations continued to limit their role to serving as upstream sources for the Yakuza rather than establishing competing distribution networks.

By the early 1990s, improving economic conditions in Taiwan had led to a partial return of Taiwanese and, in turn, a relative increase in the proportion of mainlanders among Chinese in Japan.[72] The subsequent relationship between the Yakuza and mainland Chinese has been distinguished by confrontation rather than cooperation. Growing numbers of mainlanders in the Shinjuku and Ikebukuro areas of Tokyo resulted in a displacement of Japanese and Koreans, a proliferation of Chinese businesses, and turf wars between competing Chinese gangs over protection fees and vice operations. Divided largely along mainland provincial lines (e.g., Shanghai versus Fujian), these gangs did not appear to be direct affiliates of transnational criminal organizations, nor did they initially appear to be seeking to establish a presence in the Japanese drug trade. Ethnicity pipelines combined with the proliferation of illicit drug production on the Chinese mainland (including the production of opium and ephedra, and heroin and methamphetamine), suggested the potential for expansion into the Japanese market. Instead, gang efforts were primarily focused on establishing a base of local protection, gambling, and prostitution rackets.[73]

The expanded area of such operations explicitly challenged traditional bases controlled by the Tokyo Yakuza. However, in the face of the apparent proclivity of the Chinese gangs to use massive, violent retaliation with minimal provocation, the Yakuza engaged in what Japanese analysts portrayed as a strategic and partial withdrawal from the area.[74] By 1994, as the intra-Chinese turf wars erupted into overt gun and knife battles in the Shinjuku entertainment district of Kabukicho, the Japanese police finally cracked down against the mainland gangs. Advance warnings by the police, aimed at avoiding a direct confrontation, allowed for an exodus of gang leaders and members to other parts of Japan and especially back to China. Japanese gangs, by contrast,

were not the target of the crackdown, allowing for a subsequent recon-
solidation of Yakuza operations in the area.[75]

State Crackdowns

In 1992, the Japanese government introduced the Anti-Organized
Crime Law. For the first time, the law allowed authorities to crack down
against the activities of any group designated as an organized crime
syndicate. The provisions criminalized by the law revealed the limited
extent of legal constraints that had allowed the operation of the Yakuza
in the past. Authorities would now be empowered to take steps against
an array of traditional protection operations, blackmail (personal and
company), subcontracting, loan sharking, property evacuations, and Yakuza interventions in civil disputes. Authorities would also be allowed
to bar groups from their properties, restrict basic rights of assembly,
interfere with recruitment, and promote citizen resistance and monitoring programs.[76]

With few exceptions, police and broader government tolerance for
Yakuza activities has characterized post-1945 Japan. Kaplan and Dubro
argue that the roots of this relationship lie in social networks linking
the Yakuza, Japanese government, and ultranationalist organizations
during the 1920s. During this period, Yakuza members served as political allies and enforcers, breaking union strikes, attacking political opponents, and conducting operations in Japanese colonial holdings in East
Asia. By the 1930s, Yakuza members were formally drawn into the
military or arrested if they refused. After the war, the Japanese government as well as the U.S. occupation authorities turned to the Yakuza as
labor brokers, strike breakers, and in some cases as a de facto police
force.[77]

Since the 1950s, the Yakuza have remained integrated into the fabric
of Japanese politics and business as well as into the broader social con-
sciousness.[78] The Yakuza have served as a check on freelance crime as
well as a path to socioeconomic advancement for Japan's lower
classes.[79] Police and public tolerance for the Yakuza has historically
waned, however, whenever gang violence and explicit corruption
spilled over into the public arena. A shift in the formal police designation of Japanese organized crime from the popular term Yakuza to *boryokudan* (or violent ones) followed Yakuza excesses in the 1970s.[80] Instances of corruption facilitated the introduction of the Anti-Organized
Crime Law in 1992.

Despite an array of loopholes in the new law as well as the cautious
nature of Japanese authorities in enforcing new measures, the intrusive
nature of the law has had an impact on the Yakuza.[81] Membership by

1996 had fallen to an estimated 79,900 members (of which 33,900 were associate members), though the three majors remained as the prominent syndicates.[82] Disputes over revenues increased violent conflicts between "smaller affiliated gangs," leading to drive-by shootings and armed confrontations with the police.[83] The law also resulted in revenue losses for the Yakuza, prompting a shift to less overt operations in an effort to minimize risk.

One prominent example has been the increased willingness of the Yakuza to allow foreigners to conduct licit and illicit transactions, albeit for a percentage, in Yakuza-controlled territory. More important, Yakuza organizations have been more willing to rely on foreigners as sub-contracted intermediaries in street-level transactions (especially in the areas of drugs and prostitution).[84] The result has been a visible increase since 1992 in the number of foreigners, especially Iranians, engaged in the methamphetamine trade in Yakuza territories in Tokyo and Osaka. Similar patterns have emerged with Iranians, Israelis, and Nigerians engaged in cannabis sales in Japan and increased Yakuza tolerance/protection of drug transshipment operations through Japanese air and port facilities.[85] Aside from allowing transshipment, however, these instances of foreign access to Japanese drug markets have not included transnational criminal organizations.

Conclusion

Social networks influence patterns of cooperation in the illicit economy. Informal and formal relational ties among the members of local crime groups can impose barriers to cooperation with outsiders that impede the ability of transnational criminal organizations to obtain access to new markets. This chapter explores this argument by posing two working hypotheses. First, the narrower the scope of common membership of network participants and the greater the emphasis placed by participants on long-term social obligations, the more likely informal relational ties are to pose a barrier to extensive cooperation with outsiders. Second, where informal relational ties pose a barrier to extensive cooperation with outsiders, the tighter the group's organizational structures the more likely formal relational ties are to accentuate this barrier.

This chapter reveals that organized crime in Japan's drug trade tends toward a relatively closed social network. Though the Yakuza have engaged in limited cooperation with transnational criminal organizations, social network characteristics decrease the likelihood of more extensive cooperation—especially with Latin American trafficking organizations. This pattern continues to hold despite shifts in immigration that have the potential to open channels for direct market access, and despite increased pressure on social networks stemming from government crackdowns against the Yakuza.

In the midst of the 1992 hearings by the prefectural public safety commission in Tokyo over the status of the Sumiyoshi-kai, Shigeo Nishiguchi, the boss, argued against the pending formal designation of his syndicate as an organized crime group. "Nowadays," he stated, "foreigners are smuggling a large amount of narcotics [into Japan]. Foreign mafias cannot act willfully because we are here."[86] The self-serving nature of this statement aside, Nishiguchi raises a point that merits further exploration. Domestic societal actors can influence the ability of transnational organized crime to obtain market access in the illicit global economy.

Notes

1. I thank Rawi Abdelal, Roger Haydon, Peter Katzenstein, and participants in the Peace Studies Program at Cornell University for their comments on an earlier version of this chapter. I also thank the Social Science Research Council and the Japan–U.S. Friendship Commission (Fulbright Program) for their financial support of the larger project on which this chapter is based.

2. For example, see Claire Sterling, *Crime Without Frontiers* (London: Warner Books, 1995).

3. For example, see Phil Williams, "Transnational Criminal Organizations and International Security," *Survival* 36, no. 1 (Spring 1994): 96–113; Louise I. Shelley, "Transnational Organized Crime: An Imminent Threat to the Nation State?" *Journal of International Affairs* 48, no. 2 (Winter 1995): 463–89; and Patrick L. Clawson and Rensselaer W. Lee III, *The Andean Cocaine Industry* (New York: St. Martin's Press, 1996).

4. For example, see Robert Gilpin, *The Political Economy of International Relations* (Princeton: Princeton University Press, 1987), 231–62; and Cal Clark and Steve Chan, "MNCs and Developmentalism: Domestic Structure as an Explanation for East Asian Dynamism," in *Bringing Transnational Relations Back In: Non-State Actors, Domestic Structure and International Institutions*, Thomas Risse-Kappen, ed. (Cambridge: Cambridge University Press, 1995), 112–45.

5. For example, see Clark and Chan, "MNCs and Developmentalism," 114.

6. Drawing on Louise Shelley, who in turn draws on the work of Phil Williams, I define transnational criminal organizations as "organized crime groups that are based in one state" and conduct their operations in "one but usually several host countries." Shelley, "Transnational Organized Crime," 464.

7. Williams, "Transnational Criminal Organizations and International Security," 101.

8. Peter Reuter, "The Mismeasurement of Illegal Drug Markets: The Impli-

cations of its Irrelevance," in *Exploring the Underground Economy: Studies of Illegal and Unreported Activity*, Susan Pozo, ed. (Kalamazoo, MI: Upjohn Institute, 1996), 63; and Paul Stares, *Global Habit: The Drug Problem in a Borderless World* (Washington, DC: Brookings Institution, 1996).

9. Clawson and Lee, *The Andean Cocaine Industry*, 62–64.

10. Seizure rates remain an imperfect indicator of drug flows. For example, see Stares, *Global Habit*, 11; and Clawson and Lee, *The Andean Cocaine Industry*, 4–10.

11. Clawson and Lee, *The Andean Cocaine Industry*, 64; H. Richard Friman, *NarcoDiplomacy: Exporting the U.S. War on Drugs* (Ithaca: Cornell University Press, 1996), 75; National Police Agency, *Anti Drug Activities in Japan 1994* (Tokyo: Japan International Cooperation Agency, 1995), 80; and National Police Agency, *Anti Drug Activities in Japan 1995* (Tokyo: Japan International Cooperation Agency, 1996), 81.

12. Clawson and Lee, *The Andean Cocaine Industry*, 65–66. For a similar argument on narcotics trafficking in Europe, see Joseph Albini, *The American Mafia: Genesis of a Legend* (New York: Appleton-Century-Crofts, 1971), 293.

13. See discussion of these arguments in H. Richard Friman, "Awaiting the Tsunami? Japan and the International Drug Trade," *Pacific Review* 6, no. 1 (January 1993): 41–50.

14. For example, see James H. Mittelman, "The Dynamics of Globalization," and "How Does Globalization Really Work?" in *Globalization: Critical Reflections*, James H. Mittelman, ed. (Boulder: Lynne Rienner, 1997), 1–20, 229–42; Hans-Henrik Holm and Georg Sorensen, eds., *Whose World Order: Uneven Globalization and the End of the Cold War* (Boulder: Westview Press, 1995); and the literature review by H. Richard Friman and Peter Andreas in the first chapter of *The Illicit Global Economy and State Power*.

15. For example, see Chalmers Johnson, *MITI and the Japanese Miracle: The Growth of Industrial Policy, 1925–1975* (Stanford: Stanford University Press, 1982); and Frances McCall Rosenbluth, *Financial Politics in Contemporary Japan* (Ithaca: Cornell University Press, 1989).

16. The literature here is extensive. Examples include Peter J. Katzenstein, ed., *Between Power and Plenty: Foreign Economic Policies of Advanced Industrial States* (Madison: University of Wisconsin Press, 1978); Robert M. Uriu, *Troubled Industries: Confronting Economic Change in Japan* (Ithaca and London: Cornell University Press, 1996); and Brian Woodall, *Japan Under Construction: Corruption, Politics and Public Works* (Berkeley: University of California Press, 1996).

17. For example, see Hideto Ishida, "Anticompetitive Practices in the Distribution of Goods and Services in Japan," trans. John O. Haley, *Journal of Japanese Studies* 9, no. 2 (Summer 1983): 317–34; Michael R. Czinkota and Jon Woronoff, *Japan's Market: The Distribution System* (New York: Praeger, 1986); and Dennis J. Encarnation, *Rivals Beyond Trade: America Versus Japan in Global Competition* (Ithaca and London: Cornell University Press, 1992).

18. For example, see John Scott, *Social Network Analysis: A Handbook* (London: Sage Publications, 1991), 7–38; and Stanley Wasserman and Kather-

ine Faust, *Social Network Analysis: Methods and Applications* (Cambridge: Cambridge University Press, 1994), 4–27.

19. Pino Arlachi, *Mafia Business: The Mafia Ethic and the Spirit of Capitalism*, trans. Martin Ryle (London: Verso, 1986), 198. For a similar argument couched in terms of contract uncertainty and transaction costs, see Janet Tai Landa, *Trust, Ethnicity, and Identity: Beyond the New Institutional Economic of Ethnic Trading Networks, Contract Law, and Gift Exchange* (Ann Arbor: University of Michigan Press, 1994); and Annelise Anderson, "Organized Crime, Mafia, and Governments," in *The Economics of Organized Crime*, Gianluca Fiorentini and Sam Peltzman, eds. (Cambridge: Cambridge University Press, 1995), 33, 42–43.

20. Arlachi, *Mafia Business*, 219–20.

21. See Landa (*Trust, Ethnicity, and Identity*, 107, 113) for a discussion of "embedded" status rights.

22. Minimization of risk is not the only reason why groups may turn to organization. Other considerations can include price manipulation, scale economies, and efforts to reduce overhead. For example, see Thomas C. Schelling, "Economic Analysis and Organized Crime," in *Task Force Report*, The President's Commission on Law Enforcement and the Administration of Justice, 1976, 117–18.

23. For example, see Vincenzo Ruggiero, "Drug Economics: A Fordist Model of Criminal Capital?" *Capital and Class* 55 (Spring 1995): 133–40; Vincenzo Ruggiero, *Organized Crime and Corporate Crime in Europe* (Aldershot: Dartmouth Publishing Co., 1996), 28–30; and Gerald M. Easter, "Personal Networks and Postrevolutionary State Building," *World Politics* 48, no. 4 (July 1996): 557–60.

24. The literature here is extensive. For example, see Schelling, "Economic Analysis and Organized Crime," 114–26; Donald R. Cressey, *Theft of the Nation: The Structure and Operations of Organized Crime in America* (New York: Harper and Row, 1969); Joseph L. Albini, *The American Mafia: Genesis of a Legend* (New York: Appleton-Century-Crofts, 1971); Diego Gambetta, *The Sicilian Mafia: The Business of Private Protection* (Cambridge: Harvard University Press, 1993); Gianluca Fiorentini and Sam Peltzman, "Introduction," in *The Economics of Organized Crime*, Gianluca Fiorentini and Sam Peltzman eds. (Cambridge: Cambridge University Press, 1995), 1–30; and Ruggiero, *Organized Crime and Corporate Crime in Europe*.

25. Sheldon X. Zhang and Mark S. Gaylord, "Bound for the Golden Mountain: The Social Organization of Chinese Alien Smuggling," *Crime, Law & Social Change* 25 (1996): 3–4. For an argument calling for the exploration of both ends of the continuum, see Fiorentini and Peltzman, "Introduction," 6.

26. For example, see Peter J. Katzenstein, *Small States in World Markets: Industrial Policy in Europe* (Ithaca: Cornell University Press, 1985).

27. Ruggiero, *Organized Crime and Corporate Crime in Europe*, 115–16; and Ruggiero, "Drug Economics," 142–43.

28. Zhang and Gaylord's ("Bound for the Golden Mountain," 1–16) observation on variation in their study of Chinese alien smuggling suggests that char-

acteristics of social networks may not only vary by country but also by activity. Thus, the characteristics of Japanese drug networks are not necessarily those of other aspects of Yakuza networks in the illicit economy.

29. Shumpei Kumon, "Japan as a Network Society," in *The Political Economy of Japan: Cultural and Social Dynamics*, vol. 3, Shumpei Kumon and Henry Rosovsky, eds. (Stanford: Stanford University Press, 1992), 110. See also, Peter J. Katzenstein, *Cultural Norms and National Security: Police and Military in Postwar Japan* (Ithaca and London: Cornell University Press, 1996), 35–37.

30. Kumon, "Japan as a Network Society," 110–11.

31. Daniel I. Okimoto, *Between MITI and the Market: Japanese Industrial Policy for High Technology* (Stanford: Stanford University Press, 1989), 152–65, 226.

32. Ken-ichi Imai, "Japan's Corporate Networks," in *The Political Economy of Japan: Cultural and Social Dynamics*, vol. 3, Shumpei Kumon and Henry Rosovsky, eds. (Stanford: Stanford University Press, 1992), 198–230.

33. Michael L. Gerlach, *Alliance Capitalism: The Social Organization of Japanese Business* (Berkeley: University of California Press, 1992), xiii, 3–27.

34. Thomas B. Lifson, "The Managerial Integration of Japanese Business into America," in *The Political Economy of Japan: Cultural and Social Dynamics*, vol. 3, Shumpei Kumon and Henry Rosovsky, eds. (Stanford: Stanford University Press, 1992), 246–47, 253.

35. Okimoto, *Between MITI and the Market*, 152–53. This argument draws heavily on Peter J. Katzenstein, "Conclusion: Domestic Structures and Strategies of Foreign Economic Policy," in *Between Power and Plenty: Foreign Economic Policies of Advanced Industrial States*, Peter J. Katzenstein, ed. (Madison: University of Wisconsin Press, 1978), 295–336.

36. Imai, "Japan's Corporate Networks," 228.

37. Joel Kotkin, *Tribes: How Race, Religion, and Identity Determine Success in the New Global Economy* (New York: Random House, 1993), 166–67.

38. For example, see Gerlach, *Alliance Capitalism*; Ishida, "Anticompetitive Practices in the Distribution of Goods and Services in Japan," 317–34; and Czinkota and Woronoff, *Japan's Market*.

39. David E. Kaplan and Alec Dubro, *Yakuza: The Explosive Account of Japan's Criminal Underworld* (Reading, MA: Addison-Wesley, 1986), 18 (quote), 144.

40. Kaplan and Dubro, *Yakuza*, 22–23.

41. Given the sensitive nature of the subject, the numbers remain highly contested. For example, see discussion in Kaplan and Dubro, *Yakuza*, 193; Walter L. Ames, *Police and Community in Japan* (Berkeley: University of California Press, 1981), 112; and George A. Devos, *Social Cohesion and Alienation: Minorities in the United States and Japan* (Boulder: Westview Press, 1992), 117.

42. Kaplan and Dubro, *Yakuza*, 18–19, 25–26. On the fading importance of informal ties among younger gang members and within newer crime groups, see Kaplan and Dubro, *Yakuza*, 143.

43. Kaplan and Dubro, *Yakuza*, 20–25.

44. National Police Agency, *White Paper on Police 1994 (Excerpt)* (Tokyo: Police Association, 1995), 54.

45. National Police Agency, *White Paper on Police 1993 (Excerpt)* (Tokyo: Police Association, 1994), 17; Kaplan and Dubro, *Yakuza*, 129–38; and unpublished materials received by the author from the Japanese National Police Agency, 1995.

46. National Police Agency, *White Paper on Police 1993*, 17; Kaplan and Dubro, *Yakuza*, 138–48; and unpublished materials received by the author from the National Police Agency, 1995.

47. National Police Agency, *Anti Drug Activities in Japan, 1995*, 62–63; Department of State, Bureau for International Narcotics and Law Enforcement Affairs, *International Narcotics Control Strategy Report* (Washington, DC: GPO, March 1995), 256, 284; Bill Salvadove, "High Society," *Far Eastern Economic Review*, 12 September 1991, 20–21; and interviews with narcotics agents, prefectural police officials, and journalists (Japan, 1995).

48. For a more detailed discussion, including the role of Yushio Kodama in brokering the Yakuza alliances, see Kaplan and Dubro, *Yakuza*, 90–91, 191–200.

49. Kaplan and Dubro, *Yakuza*, 217; and David E. Kaplan, *Fires of the Dragon: Politics, Murder, and the Kuomintang* (New York: Athenaeum, 1992), 373–74.

50. Earlier roots of Yakuza cooperation with Chinese Triads lie in the Japanese occupation of China, Formosa, and Hong Kong during the 1930s and 1940s. Kaplan and Dubro, *Yakuza*, 214–15; and Ko-Lin Chin, "Triad Societies in Hong Kong," *Transnational Organized Crime* 1, no. 1 (Spring 1995): 47–64.

51. Kaplan and Dubro, *Yakuza*, 92–93, 147.

52. Masayuki Tamura, "The Yakuza and Amphetamine Abuse in Japan," in *Drugs, Law, and the State*, Harold H. Traver and Mark S. Gaylord, eds. (Hong Kong: Hong Kong University Press, 1992), 105.

53. The percentage of Yakuza in total arrests for distribution has been falling since the late 1980s for reasons discussed in greater detail below. National Police Agency, *Anti Drug Activities in Japan 1990* (Tokyo: Police Association, 1991), 75, 89; and National Police Agency, *Anti Drug Activities in Japan 1995*, 73.

54. In contrast, Yakuza members have worked with cannabis sources abroad, such as Filipino and Thai groups, building on earlier linkages from the sex tourism and prostitution trades. For example, see National Police Agency, *White Paper on Police 1992 (Excerpt)* (Tokyo: Police Association, 1993), 94; National Police Agency, *White Paper on Police 1993 (Excerpt)* (Tokyo: Police Association, 1994), 45; and interviews with the National Police Agency and prefectural police officials (Japan, 1995).

55. National Police Agency, *Anti Drug Activities in Japan 1995*, 22; and interview with National Police Agency official (Japan, 1995). For example, during the mid-1980s this spread reflected prices of ¥2,200 per kilogram at the wholesale level versus ¥100 million per kilogram at the retail level. National Police Agency, *Anti Drug Activities in Japan 1990*, 102.

56. For example, see *Mainichi Daily News*, 5 May 1983, 5, 25 September 1986, 24 February 1990; *Japan Times*, 18 May 1983, 22 February, 17 May, 18 September 1990; and *Daily Yomiuri*, 4 September 1986, 6 November 1990.

57. National Police Agency, *White Paper on Police 1993*, 97–99; *Mainichi Daily News*, 27 May, 15 July 1992; and *Japan Times*, 27 May 1992.

58. *Mainichi Daily News*, 8 August, 16 October 1992, 30 September 1993; *Japan Times*, 30 January 1993; and *Daily Yomiuri*, 20 August, 21 October, 1992.

59. National Police Agency, *White Paper on Police 1994*, 75–76; *Daily Yomiuri*, 2 March 1993; *Mainichi Daily News*, 11 May 1993; and interview with journalist (Japan, 1995).

60. Stares, *Global Habit*, 55.

61. For example, see Douglas Clark Kinder, "Shutting Out Evil: Nativism and Narcotics Control in the United States," in *Drug Control Policy: Essays in Historical and Comparative Perspective*, William O. Walker III, ed. (University Park, PA: The Pennsylvania State University Press, 1992), 117–42.

62. For example, see Clawson and Lee, *The Andean Cocaine Industry*, 63; and Stares, *Global Habit*, 35–39.

63. For example, see H. Richard Friman, "Gaijinhanzai: Immigrants and Drugs in Contemporary Japan," *Asian Survey* 36, no. 10 (October 1996): 964–77.

64. For example, see Michael Weiner, *Race and Migration in Imperial Japan* (New York and London: Routledge, 1994); Robert H. Mitchell, *The Korean Minority in Japan* (Berkeley and Los Angeles: University of California Press, 1967); and Changsoo Lee and George DeVos, *Koreans in Japan: Ethnic Conflict and Accommodation* (Berkeley and Los Angeles: University of California Press, 1981).

65. For example, see Keiko Yamanaka, "New Immigration Policy and Unskilled Foreign Workers in Japan," *Pacific Affairs* 66, no. 1 (Spring 1993): 72–90; Haruo Shimada, *Japan's 'Guest Workers': Issues and Public Policies* (Tokyo: University of Tokyo Press, 1994); and Yoko Selleck and Michael A. Weiner, "Migrant Workers: The Japanese Case in International Perspective," in *The Internationalization of Japan*, Glenn Hook and Michael K. Weiner, eds. (London and New York: Routledge, 1992), 205–28.

66. For example, see Shimada, *Japan's 'Guest Workers*,' 54–71; and Wayne Cornelius, "Japan: The Illusion of Immigration Control," in *Controlling Immigration: A Global Perspective*, Wayne Cornelius, Philip L. Martin, and James F. Hollifield, eds. (Stanford: Stanford University Press, 1994), 375–410.

67. For a discussion of access patterns in illicit activities aside from drugs, see K. Shiiki, "Kokusaiteki shokugyo hanzai gurupu ni taisuru sousajo no ryuijiko (Investigation of Crimes by International Professional Criminal Groups)," *Keisatsugaku Ronshu (Journal of Police Science)* 46, no. 7 (July 1993): 45–59.

68. *Daily Yomiuri*, 5 August 1992, 3 December 1993; *Mainichi Daily News*, 6, 11 August 1992; and interview with Maritime Safety Agency official (Japan, 1995).

69. Calculated from National Police Agency, *Hanzai Tokei (Criminal Statis-*

tics), 1993 (Tokyo: National Police Agency, 1994), 406–7, 420–21; National Police Agency, *Hanzai Tokei (Criminal Statistics), 1992* (Tokyo: National Police Agency, 1993), 406–7, 420–21; Drug Enforcement Division, National Police Agency, *Drug Situation in Japan, 1994,* 10 February 1995, 3, 34.

70. See Friman, "Gaijinhanzai," 975.

71. *Mainichi Daily News,* 5 April 1988; *Asahi Evening News,* 20 August 1988; George A. DeVos and Keiichi Mizushima, "Organization and Social Function of Japanese Gangs: Historical Development and Modern Parallels," in *Aspects of Social Changes in Modern Japan,* R.P. Dore, ed. (Princeton: Princeton University Press, 1967), 308; Kaplan and Dubro, *Yakuza,* 214, 219; and interviews with narcotics agents and journalists (Japan, 1995).

72. Jonathan Friedland, "Traffic Problem: Rising Tide of Chinese Illegal Immigrants Worries Japan," *Far Eastern Economic Review,* 4 August 1994, 20; Hirokatsu Gozuma, *Mafia no Sumumachi: Shinjuku, Kabukicho (Mafia Presence: Shinjuku, Kabukicho)* (Tokyo: Shukan Bunshu, 1995); and interview with National Police Agency official (Japan, 1995). For a discussion of continued operations by 14K affiliates in Japan, see *Asahi Shimbun,* 13 February 1997.

73. *Asahi Evening News,* 29 August 1994; *Mainichi Daily News,* 2 September 1994; *Japan Times,* 3 September, 18 October 1994; Iren Maciulis-Kuni, "Trouble in Little China," *Time,* 10 October 1994, 42; "Nihon no 'yamishakai' gaijin hanzai hakusho" (Japan's Illegal Societies Foreign Crime White Paper), *Marco Polo,* February 1995, 45–67; and interview with National Police Agency official (Japan, 1995).

74. Interviews with National Police Agency official and journalist (Japan, 1995); and "Nihon no 'yamishakai,' " 54, 64.

75. Interviews with National Police Agency official and journalist (Japan, 1995); "Nihon no 'yamishakai,' " 54, 64; and *Mainichi Daily News,* 19 February 1995.

76. National Police Agency, *White Paper on Police 1993,* 4–5; "New Gangster Law to Start Next March," *The Japan Law Journal,* October 1991, 2; "Police Hope New Strategies Locate Victims of Gangs," *The Japan Law Journal,* April 1992, 7; and "New Law Unlikely to Stop Companies Funding Gangsters," *The Japan Law Journal,* April 1992, 8.

77. Kaplan and Dubro, *Yakuza,* 32–51.

78. This pattern is not unique to Japan. For example, see Gambetta, *The Sicilian Mafia.*

79. For example, see DeVos and Mizushima, "Organization and Social Function of Japanese Gangs," 289–325; Kaplan and Dubro, *Yakuza;* DeVos, *Social Cohesion and Alienation,* 117, 142, 187; and Ames, *Police and Community in Japan,* 112.

80. Kaplan and Dubro, *Yakuza;* Karel Van Wolferen, *The Enigma of Japanese Power* (Tokyo: Charles E. Tuttle, 1993), 55, 133; Ames, *Police and Community in Japan,* 124, 127; and David H. Bayley, *Forces of Order: Policing Modern Japan* (Berkeley: University of California Press, 1991), 185.

81. National Police Agency, *Anti Drug Activities in Japan, 1994,* 36–37; National Police Agency, *White Paper on Police 1993,* 36–38; *Asahi Evening*

News, 2 February 1996; and interviews with foreign law enforcement and National Police Agency officials, and journalist (Japan, 1994, 1995).

82. *Daily Yomiuri*, 31 January 1997; and *Mainichi Daily News*, 31 January 1997.

83. *Daily Yomiuri*, 11 July, 25 September 1996; *Japan Times*, 7 March, 11 July, 16 September 1996; and *Mainichi Daily News*, 17 September 1996.

84. The law has also increased Yakuza participation in immigrant smuggling. For example, see *Daily Yomiuri*, 11 September 1993, 11 March, 11, 28, 30 May 1994; *Japan Times*, 5 April 1993, 15, 20 May, 21 June 1994, 7 February 1997; *Mainichi Daily News*, 5, 9, 16 April 1993, 3 February 1997; and *New York Times*, 13 March 1997.

85. National Police Agency, *Anti Drug Activities in Japan, 1995*, 96; Drug Enforcement Division, National Police Agency, *Drug Situation in Japan, 1994*, 35–39, materials received by author; and interviews with narcotics agents and prefectural police officials (Japan, 1995).

86. "Syndicates React to New Anti-Gang Law," *The Japanese Law Journal*, April 1992, 3.

Index

African, Caribbean, and Pacific (ACP) countries, 103
African crime groups, 43
Agency for International Development (AID), 157, 160
Alliance for Progress, 147
Alliance for Responsible Atmospheric Policy, 113
Alliance for Responsible CFC Policy, 100
Andean Drug Strategy, 157
Andreas, Peter, 16
Andreotti, Giulio, 34–35
ANIF (Asociación Nacional de Instituciones Financieras), 151
Anti-Drug Abuse Act (1988), 72
anti–money laundering regime, 65–70; deregulation and, 71–76
Anti-Organized Crime Law (Japan), 188–89
Applegate, Rex, 134
Arlacchi, Pino, 39, 177
Ascensio, Diego, 151
Asian crime groups, 35–36, 43. *See also* Japan; Yakuza; *individual crime groups*
Asian Development Bank, 107
Asociación Nacional de Instituciones Financieras (ANIF), 151
Australia, 79
authoritarianism; civil society and, 37–38; economy and, 28, 40–43; ideological control, 28, 38; non-state-based, 15, 31–33; state control and, 32–33; state relation to citizens, 27, 32, 37–39; traditional, 30–31
authority (state), 9

Bahamas, 55, 73
Baker, James A., III, 158, 159
bakuto, 180–81, 182
Bamako Convention, 103
Bangladesh, 107
Bank of Commerce and Credit International (BCCI), 12
Bank for International Settlements (BIS), 65, 67, 75, 76, 89n99
Bank of Nova Scotia, 73
Bank of the Republic (Colombia), 148, 150, 151
bank secrecy laws, 55, 56, 63–64, 65, 67, 68–69, 70
Barco Vargas, Virgilio, 153–57, 158
Basel Convention on the Transboundary Movement of Hazardous Wastes and Their Disposal, 92, 100, 101–3, 106–10, 116; Conferences of Parties (COP), 108, 109–10
Basle Accord (1988), 54, 61, 71–72, 74, 76
BCCI. See Bank of Commerce and Credit International
Bennett, William, 157
Betancur Cuartas, Belisario, 152–53, 158, 167n41
Biersteker, Thomas, 126

BIS (Bank for International Settlements), 65, 67
black markets, 5; in environmental hazards, 107–8, 111, 117
Bolivia, 36, 161
Bonner, Robert, 158
boryokudan, 189
Bossard, Andre, 5
Botero, Fernando, 162
Bourne, Peter G., 150
Bretton Woods conference (1944), 63, 64, 70, 77
Buendia, Manuel, 39
burakumin, 180
Bureau of International Narcotics Matters, 158, 161
Bureau of International Recycling, 110
Burns, Nicolas, 162
Bush, George, 156, 157, 158, 159, 160
Bushnell, David, 147

Cairo Guidelines on the Environmentally Sound Management of Hazardous Wastes (1987), 97, 101–2
Cali cartel, 12, 13, 33, 34, 143, 159–62, 184
Camorra, 35
Canada, 36, 114, 115
Canchola, Jose Luis Perez, 130
Cano Isaza, Guillermo, 153, 154
capital adequacy standards, 54, 61, 71–72, 74, 75
capital controls, 54, 56–57, 63–64, 82n16
capital flight, 54, 56–58, 63; liberal ideology and, 57–58; United States and, 61
Caribbean Basin Initiative, 73
Caribbean Financial Action Task Force, 69
Cartagena summit, 157–58
cartels, 40; Cali cartel, 12, 13, 33, 34, 143, 159–62, 184; Medellín cartel, 12, 13, 33–34, 36, 152–56, 158, 184

Carter, Jimmy, 149, 150
Castaneda, Jorge, 126
Cayman Islands, 55, 65, 73
Cerny, Phil, 71, 72, 73–74, 75
CFCs. *See* chlorofluorocarbons
Chamber of Commerce, 110
China: drug trafficking and, 182–83; social networks, 179–80; Triads, 35, 36, 185
Chinese immigrants, 35, 36, 185, 187
CHIPS, 72, 78–79
chlorofluorocarbons (CFCs), 92, 103–6, 116–17; black market in, 111, 117; border controls and, 114; as ozone-depleting substances, 98–100; production, 98, 112; recycled, 113, 114. *See also* environmental hazards; Montreal Protocol
Chong Gwon Yong, 182
citizens: passivity of, 46; state relation to, 27, 32, 37–39, 59
civil liberties, 47
civil society, 37–38, 92–93
Clapp, Jennifer, 15, 16
Clawson, Patrick L., 13, 164, 174
Clinton, Bill, 161
CNP (Colombian National Police), 155, 160
coalitions, cross-border, 14
cocaine, 149, 151, 175, 184–85. *See also* Colombia; drug trafficking
Cold War, end of, 2, 26
Colombia, 16; cocaine trade, 149, 151, 175, 184–85; constitution, 158, 159; deception and, 146, 148–49; decertification and, 143, 161–62, 163; economy, 42, 149–50; extradition treaty and, 151–52, 154, 156, 159, 162; guerrillas, 147–48, 152, 162–63; historical context, 146–49; Italy and, 174, 175; La Violencia, 146, 147; M-19, 148, 152, 153, 155–56; marijuana trade, 150–51; militarization and, 147, 157, 169n70; narcoterrorism and, 151–53; penal in-

stitutions, 45, 159; state authority, 13, 147, 150; Supreme Court, 153, 154, 156; violence in, 46. *See also* drug trafficking

Colombian National Police (CNP), 155, 160

COMECON, 40

communist states, 30, 40

complex interdependence, 3–4

control (state), 9–10

Copenhagen Meeting of the Parties, 105, 106

corporations, 173–74; environmental hazards and, 93, 94–95, 99–100, 102–3, 111, 115; Japanese, 179; state authority and, 93

corporatism, 40

corruption, 10, 26, 33–35; in Japan, 188

Cosa Nostra, 39, 42, 44

Council of Europe, 64

Cox, Robert, 11

criminalization, 9, 10, 16, 67

Customs Service, 7, 11, 114, 134

Czech Republic, 42

debtor countries, economic policy, 127–28

Decision VIII/20 on Illegal Imports and Exports on Controlled Substances, 115

Defense Department, 114, 160

De Grieff, Gustavo, 161

democracies, 36–37

deregulation, financial, 16, 71–76

Diaz-Alejandro, Carlos, 57

dictatorships, 30

Drage, John, 55

Drug Enforcement Administration (DEA), 129, 132–34, 146, 157, 160

drug trafficking: debtor countries and, 127–28; differing state interests and, 144–45, 149–50, 152–54, 158–59, 163–64; immigration and, 185–88; increase in, 6–7; marijuana trade, 150–51; market access

and, 174–76; market liberalization and, 126–27, 129–30, 136–38; methamphetamine, 175, 182–83; money laundering and, 66, 73, 86–87n57; opium trade, 9, 12; revenues, 129, 149; United Nations and, 14–15, 126, 136, 139n10; United States and, 60, 66, 73, 126, 139n10. *See also* cartels; Colombia; Mexico

Dubro, Alec, 181, 188

DuPont, 98, 99

Eastern Europe, 34, 41; capital flight and, 57; privatization and, 42; transnational crime and, 35, 36–37

Economist Intelligence Unit, The, 131

economy: authoritarianism and, 28, 40–43; businessmen and, 41; cartels and, 40; debtor countries and, 127–28; illicit, definitions, 5–7; investment, 41; privatization, 41–42; shadow economy, 40; strategic economic alliances, 42–43. *See also* financial regulation

Ejercito de Liberación Nacional (ELN), 146, 148

Ejercito Popular de Liberación (EPL), 146, 148, 162–63

El Espectador, 152, 153, 159

Elders, Jocelyn, 161

elections, 34

ELN (Ejercito de Liberación Nacional), 146, 148

environmental groups, 99, 101, 102, 103, 116

environmental hazards, 2, 15, 16; black market in, 107–8, 111, 117; defining, 94–95; epistemic communities and, 92–93, 116; free trade goals and, 101, 106–7, 116; industry players and, 93, 94–95, 99–100, 102–3, 111, 115; nongovernmental organizations and, 92–93, 94, 104, 106; North/South dynamics and, 93–94, 97, 103, 104, 106, 116; prohibition, 100–101;

recycling and, 108–11; structural position of states and, 93–94, 115. *See also* Basel Convention; chlorofluorocarbons; hazardous wastes; Montreal Protocol

Environmental Protection Agency (EPA), 114

epistemic communities, 16; environmental issues and, 92–93, 116

EPL (Ejercito Popular de Liberación), 146, 148, 162–63

Escobar Gaviria, Pablo, 36, 151, 152, 159–60

Europe: CFCs and, 113, 114–15; environmental hazards and, 102, 104; financial regulation and, 64, 66, 82n16, 85n47, 85–86n48; Russian organized crime and, 36; tax evasion and, 55–56

European Economic Community (EEC), 103

FARC. *See* Fuerzas Armadas Revolucionarias de Colombia

FATF (Financial Action Task Force), 14, 65–68, 72, 76, 78

Federal Bureau of Investigation (FBI), 130–31

Federal Bureau of Narcotics, 146

Fedwire, 72, 78–79

Financial Action Task Force (FATF), 14, 65–69, 72, 76, 78

financial regulation: anti–money laundering regime, 65–70; bank secrecy laws, 55, 56, 63–64, 65, 67, 68–69, 70; capital adequacy standards, 54, 61, 71–72, 74, 75; capital controls, 54, 56–57, 63–64, 82n16; contemporary state responses, 64–66; deregulation pressures, 71–76; domestic rules, 65, 67, 69–70, 80–81; effectiveness of, 76–79; external border controls and, 66, 69; globalization and, 54–57, 61–62, 68, 71–76; historical context, 62–64; information technology and, 55, 76–79, 81; interna-

tional cooperation and, 64–65, 69–70, 77, 81, 85–86n48, 88n85; liberal ideology and, 62–64, 69–70, 75, 80, 82n16; offshore financial centers and, 12, 55, 56, 59, 65, 69, 73, 74–75, 85n44; reregulation, 57, 62, 64–66, 74–75, 80, 83n25. *See also* capital flight; money laundering; tax evasion

Fiorentini, Gianluca, 10

Ford, Gerald R., 147

14K crime group, 187

Frechette, Myles, 162

free trade: environmental hazards and, 101, 106–7, 116; Mexican reforms, 128–30, 136–37

Frente Nacional, 146, 147

Friman, H. Richard, 16–17

Fuerzas Armadas Revolucionarias de Colombia (FARC), 146, 152, 153, 158, 160, 162–63

Gaitán, Eliécer, 146

Galán, Luis Carlos, 155, 157, 160

Gambetta, Diego, 10, 44

GATT (General Agreement on Tariffs and Trade), 104, 105, 106, 111, 129

Gaviria Trujillo, César, 157, 158–60, 161

Gaylord, Mark, 178

Gelbard, Robert S., 161

General Agreement on Tariffs and Trade (GATT), 104, 105, 106, 111, 129

General Motors, 98

Gerlach, Michael, 179

Germany, 77

Gill, Stephen, 6

globalization, 4; financial deregulation and, 54–57, 61–62, 68, 71–76; state authority and, 71–76, 80

Gould, David, 128

Greenpeace International, 101, 103, 109, 110

Group of Seven (G-7), 14, 65

Guinea-Bissau, 96, 118–19n19
gurentai, 180, 181

hazardous wastes, 92; costs of disposal, 95–96; disguise of, 107–8;
  export of, 95–98, 102; North to
  South trade, 94, 95–97, 106. *See
  also* chlorofluorocarbons; environmental hazards
Helleiner, Eric, 15, 16
Holm, Hans-Henrik, 4
Hong Kong, 182, 187
House of Representatives: Committee
  on International Relations, 148,
  149; Select Committee, 152
human rights violations, 31, 38
Hurtado, Miguel de la Madrid, 135

ideological control, 28, 38–39
Imai, Ken-ichi, 179
IMF. *See* International Monetary Fund
immigration, 11, 12; Japan and, 180,
  182, 185–88
Immigration Act (Japan), 186
Inagawa, Kakuji, 183
Inagawa-kai, 181–82, 183
INCSR (International Narcotics Con-
  trol Strategy Reports), 154–55
information technology, 55, 76–79,
  81
interdependence, 3–4
International Chamber of Commerce,
  110
International Coffee Agreement, 156
International Financial Conference
  (Brussels, 1920), 62–63
International Financial Conference
  (Genoa, 1922), 62
International Monetary Fund (IMF),
  2, 26–27, 85n42, 126–29
International Narcotics Control Strat-
  egy Reports (INCSR), 154–55
International Organization for Migra-
  tion, 7
International Organization of Securi-
  ties Commissions (IOSC), 65

international political economy (IPE),
  53
Interpol, money laundering and,
  65–66
intimidation, 33, 36, 38–39, 41
investment, 41
IOSC (International Organization of
  Securities Commissions), 65
Iranians, in Japan, 186, 189
Israel, 35
Italy: civil society, 37–38; Colombian
  drug trafficking and, 174, 175; export of hazardous wastes, 96; legal
  institutions, 44; privatization, 42;
  transnational crime groups and, 32,
  34–35; violence in, 46
Itami, Juzo, 39
ivory trade, 14

Japan, 16–17, 36; cocaine and,
  184–85; drug networks in,
  182–85; ethnicity pipelines, 185–
  86, 187; immigration and, 180,
  182, 185–88; law enforcement,
  188–89; legal institutions, 44; origins of crime groups, 180–81; social networks in, 178–80, 188,
  189–90. *See also* Yakuza; *individual crime groups*
Jimena Duzán, María, 153–54
Jordan, Phil, 134
judiciary, 40, 44

Kaplan, David, 181, 188
Kapstein, Ethan, 54, 71–72, 74, 75
keiretsu, 179
Keohane, Robert O., 3, 144
Kerry Amendment, 72–73
Keynes, John Maynard, 77, 78
Keynesian economics, 63
Kissinger, Henry, 147, 148
Korea, 182
Kotkin, Joel, 179
Kristanovskaya, Olga, 39
Kumon, Shumpei, 178

Lansky, Meyer, 55
Lara Bonilla, Rodrigo, 153

Latin America: corporatism and, 40;
  market prohibition and, 126; tax
  evasion and, 56. *See also* individual states
Law, David, 6
law enforcement, 16; authoritarianism
  and, 30–31; citizen passivity and,
  46; Japan and, 188–89; privatization of, 44–45
League of Nations, 62–63, 70, 84–
  85n37
Lee, Rensselaer W., III, 13, 164, 174
legal systems, 43–46
Legarreta, Loaquin, 134
Lehder, Carlos, 154
Lehder-Rivas, Carl, 34
Levitsky, Melvyn, 158
Levy, Jack S., 160
liberal ideology, 57–59, 144; capital
  controls and, 63–64, 82n16; deregulation and, 75; drug trafficking
  and, 126–27, 129–30, 136–38; financial regulation and, 62–64, 69–
  70, 75, 80, 82n16
Lifson, Thomas, 179
lobby groups, 93
Locke, John, 41
Lomé IV Convention, 103
London Meeting of the Parties, 105,
  106
López Michelson, Alfonse, 147, 148–
  49, 153
Love Canal, 95, 118n14

M-19 crime group, 148, 152, 153,
  155–56
Machii, Hisayuki, 182
Mafia, 32, 34–35
market access, 173–74; networks and,
  176–78; state controls and, 175–76
market liberalization, drug trafficking
  and, 126–27, 129–30, 136–38
market prohibition, 10, 16, 126–27,
  135–36
Martinez, Bob, 159
Mauro Hoyos, Carlos, 155
McNamara, Thomas E., 159

Medellín cartel, 12, 13, 33–34, 36,
  152–56, 158, 184; Japan and, 184
media, intimidation of, 33, 38–39
Meiyu-kai, 182
Mexico: agricultural reform, 131–33;
  drug trafficking and, 7, 150–51;
  economic statism and, 129; free-
  market reform in, 128–30,
  136–37; law enforcement, 44–45;
  market prohibition and, 126–27,
  135–36; policy evaluation and,
  137–38; trade and transportation
  reform, 133–35; transnational
  crime groups and, 32, 39
Meza, Garcia, 10
military: authoritarianism and, 30;
  Colombia and, 147, 157, 169n70;
  Mexico and, 135
Mittelman, James, 4
money laundering, 2, 12, 54; anti–
  money laundering regime, 65–70;
  charities and, 37; deregulation and,
  71–76; drug trafficking and, 66,
  73, 86–87n57; effect on financial
  stability, 59; financial institutions
  and, 59; law enforcement and, 45;
  liberal ideology and, 58–59; private interests and, 59–60; revenues, 25–30, 55; state responses,
  contemporary, 64–66; United
  States and, 14–15, 60–62, 66, 73,
  75–76, 84n28, 86–87n57
Montoya, Oscar, 150
Montreal Protocol, 92, 100, 101,
  103–6, 107, 111–12, 114–15
Moravcsik, Andrew, 144
Movimento Latino Nacional, 34
Multilateral Convention on Mutual
  Administrative Assistance in Tax
  Matters (1988), 64
Multilateral Fund, 105, 106
Murphy, Craig, 63

Naarden case, 7
Nadelmann, Ethan, 9, 91, 125–26
NAFTA (North American Free Trade
  Agreement), 129, 134–35

National Drug Control Program 1995–2000 (Mexico), 136
National Front (Frente Nacional), 146, 147
National Police Agency (Japan), 183
National Security Decision Directive No. 221, 154
Naylor, R. T., 5
'Ndrangheta, 42
Netherlands Antilles, 61, 114
NGOs. *See* nongovernmental organizations
Nigeria, 96
nikkeijin, 186
NIMBY syndrome, 94, 95
Nishiguchi, Shigeo, 190
nongovernmental organizations (NGOs), 92–93, 94, 104, 106
nonstate actors, 91, 92–93, 115
Noriega, Manuel, 10
North American Free Trade Agreement (NAFTA), 129, 134–35
Norway, 110
Nye, Joseph, 3

Ochoa family, 151, 152, 158
OECD (Organization for Economic Cooperation and Development), 57, 64, 97, 109–10
Office of National Drug Control Policy (ONDCP), 157
offshore financial centers, 12, 55, 56, 59, 65, 69, 73, 85n44; competitive reregulation and, 74–75
Okimoto, Daniel, 179
ONDCP (Office of National Drug Control Policy), 157
Operation Blast Furnace, 154
Operation Cool Breeze, 114
Operation Snowcap, 154
opium trade, 9, 12
Organization for Economic Cooperation and Development (OECD), 57, 64, 97, 109–10
Organization of African Unity, 96
oyabun-kobun system, 181
Ozone Action, 113

Pastrana Arango, Andrés, 161, 169n78
Pax Mafiosa, 42, 173
Paz, La, 161
Peltzman, Sam, 10
penal institutions, 45, 159
PIC (prior informed consent), 102, 103, 108
Plan Nacional de Rehabilitación, 155
policy evaluation, 137–38
polychlorinated biphenyls (PCBs), 96
Possamai, Mario, 72
Princen, Thomas, 14
prior informed consent (PIC), 102, 103, 108
privatization, 41–42; of law enforcement, 44–45; Mexico and, 130–31
Proceso 8000, 161
prohibition: capital controls and, 63–64; drug trafficking and, 125–26; environmental hazards and, 100–101; financial activity and, 53; foreign states and, 14–15; market prohibition, 10, 16, 126–27, 135–36; retreat of state and, 15–16
prostitution, 36, 38
Putnam, Robert D., 143, 148, 163, 165n9

Ramirez Gómez, Jaime, 153
Reagan, Ronald, 152, 154
Rebollo, Gutierrez, 44
recycling, 108–11, 113, 114
regional government, transnational crime groups and, 32
Reichsbank, 40
Retreat of the State, The (Strange), 69
Riina, Toto, 39
Rodríguez Gacha, José Gonzalo, 152, 156, 157
Rodríguez Orejuela clan, 151, 152
Ruggiero, Vincenzo, 178
Russia; capital flight and, 57; CFCs and, 112, 113, 114; émigrés, 36–37; intimidation and, 38–39, 41, 46; law enforcement, 45; penal

institutions, 45; transnational crime groups and, 32, 34, 35, 37–38. *See also* Eastern Europe

Salinas, Carlos, 129, 133, 135–36
Samper Pizano, Ernesto, 34, 138, 145, 151, 153, 161–63, 164
Schelling, Thomas, 5
scholarly debate, 3–4
scientists, 99, 101, 104, 116
Seveso, 95, 118n14
shadow economy, 40
Shelley, Louise, 12, 15
Sherman, Tom, 59
shipping industry, 11
Sicily, 44, 46
Single Convention on Narcotics (1961), 126
Smith, Peter, 130
Social Democratic party (Italy), 34
social networks, 176–80, 188–90
social welfare, 35–36, 37
Somalia, 107
Sorenson, George, 4
Soros, George, 14
Soviet Union, former. *See* Eastern Europe
Stallings, Barbara, 127
Stares, Paul, 6, 11
State Department, 131, 132, 139n10, 143, 152, 158, 161–62
states: authority of, 9–10, 13–14, 31–32, 43–44; challenges to power, 11–15; definition, 8; differing interests, 144–45; environmental issues and, 93–94, 115; financial regulation, responses to, 64–66; foreign states and, 14–15; globalization and, 54, 71–76, 80; historical perspective, 8–10; legal system, 43–46; nonstate violence and, 13, 147–48, 151–52, 156; organizational learning and, 160–61, 170n91; relation to citizens, 27, 32, 37–39, 59; retreat of, 3–4, 15–17, 31–32
Stein, Arthur A., 161

Sterling, Claire, 42, 173
Strange, Susan, 3, 8, 69, 71
Suarez, Roberto, 36
Sumiyoshi-kai, 181, 183, 190
SWIFT, 78–79
Switzerland, 55, 63, 65
systemic theory, 144

Taiwan, 34, 182, 183, 187; CFCs and, 114, 115
Tambs, Lewis A., 152
Tanzi, Vito, 56
Taoko, Kazuo, 182
tax evasion, 54, 55–56; CFCs and, 113, 114; League of Nations and, 63; liberal ideology and, 57–58; OECD and, 64; United States and, 56, 60–61
tekiya, 180–81
Thomson, Janice, 4, 8, 9
Tobin tax, 61–62
Tongs, 185
Toro, Marcia Celia, 135
Toronto Group, 104
Tosei-kai, 182
toxic waste. *See* environmental hazards; hazardous waste
Tranquilandia, 152–53
transnational crime groups, 5–6, 190n6; assumption of state responsibilities, 35–36; civil society and, 37–38; defined, 26; democracies and, 36–37; division of labor and, 178, 183; *vs.* domestic crime groups, 173–74; economy and, 40–43; human rights and, 31, 38; ideological control and, 38–39; infiltration of government, 33–35; international reach of, 45; intimidation and, 33, 36, 38–39, 41; investment and, 41; judiciary and, 40, 44; legal system and, 43–46; market access and, 173–78; social networks and, 176–78; social welfare and, 35–36, 37; state authority and, 10, 12–14; state weakness and, 31–32; types of, 7; unpun-

ished violence and, 46. *See also individual countries and groups*
transshipment, 11–12, 133–35
Treasury Department, 72, 73
Triads, 35, 36, 185
Turbay Ayala, Julio César, 149–52
two-level analysis, 143–44, 145, 163

Ukraine, 34, 41
umbrella companies, 97
UN Convention against Illicit Traffic in Narcotic Drugs and Psychotropic Substances (1988), 14–15, 65–66, 67, 126
UN Convention on Psychotropic Substances (1971), 126
underground economy, 5
UNEP (United Nations Environment Program), 93, 94, 97, 99
Unión Patriótica, 154
United Bamboo Gang, 183, 187
United Nations, 14–15; drug trafficking and, 7, 126, 136, 139n10, 156; environment and, 93, 94, 97, 99; financial regulation and, 64
United Nations Decade against Unlawful Drug Consumption, 136
United Nations Environment Program (UNEP), 93, 94, 97, 99
United States: Basel Convention and, 102, 108, 110; bribery in, 45; capital flight and, 61; CFCs and, 98, 112–15; deregulation pressures and, 72–74; electronic fund transfers and, 72, 78–79; export of hazardous wastes, 107, 118n14; extradition treaties and, 151–52, 154, 156, 159, 162; money laundering

and, 14–15, 60–62, 66, 73, 75–76, 80, 84n28, 86–87n57; Russian organized crime and, 36; tax evasion and, 56, 60–61. *See also* Colombia; drug trafficking; Mexico
UN Model Treaty, 85n47
U.S. National Drug Control Strategy, 138

Valencia, Abrahám Varón, 150
Valle, Eduardo, 129
Venezuela, 42
Vienna Convention for the Protection of the Ozone Layer, 99–100, 103
Vienna Convention (UN Convention against Illicit Traffic in Narcotic Drugs), 14–15, 65–66, 67
Violencia, La, 146, 147

Walker, William, III, 16
Wall Street Journal, 39
Williams, Phil, 174
win-sets, 145, 156, 158–59, 163–64, 165n9
World Bank, 126, 127, 128
World Customs Organization, 111
World Drug Report, 7
World Trade Organization (WTO), 111

Yakuza, 33, 35–36, 39, 44, 175, 176; law enforcement and, 188–89
Yamaguchi-gumi, 181, 182–83

zaibatsu, 179
Zamora, Stephen, 79
Zedillo, Ernesto, 135, 136
Zhang, Sheldon, 178

About the Contributors

Peter Andreas is Academy Scholar at the Weatherhead Center for International Affairs, Harvard University.

Jennifer Clapp is Assistant Professor in the Comparative Development and Environmental and Resource Studies Programs at Trent University.

H. Richard Friman is Associate Professor and Assistant Chair in the Department of Political Science at Marquette University.

Eric Helleiner is Associate Professor in the Department of Political Studies at Trent University.

Louise I. Shelley is Professor in the Department of Justice, Law, and Society and the School of International Service at American University.

William O. Walker III is Professor of History and International Relations at Florida International University.